INFORMATION LAW SERIES - 3
Challenges to the Creator Doctrine

International Board of Editors

INFORMATION LAW SERIES - 3

Challenges to the Creator Doctrine

Authorship, copyright ownership and the exploitation of creative works in the Netherlands, Germany and the United States

Jacqueline M.B. Seignette

1994
Kluwer Law and Taxation Publishers
Deventer • Boston

Kluwer Law and Taxation Publishers

P.O. Box 23
7400 GA Deventer / The Netherlands
Tel.: +31 5700 47261
Fax: + 31 5700 22244

675 Massachusetts Avenue
Cambridge MA 02139 / USA
Tel.: +1 617 354 0140
Fax: +1 617 354 8595

Cover design: Studio DUMBAR

ISBN 90 6544 876 4

Table of Contents

List of abbreviations

AA	Ars Aequi
ACA	Austrian Copyright Act of 1936
ALAI	Association Littéraire et Artistique Internationale
BAG	Bundesarbeitsgericht (federal high court for labour matters, Germany)
BC	Berne Convention of 1886 for the Protection of Literary and Artistic Works
BCA	British Copyright, Designs and Patents Act 1988
BDMA	Uniform Benelux Designs and Models Act of 1966
BGB	Bürgerliches Gesetzbuch (Civil Code, Germany)
BgBl	Bundesgesetzblatt (federal statutes, Germany)
BGH	Bundesgerichtshof (federal highest court, Germany)
BIE	Bijblad Industriële Eigendom
BVerfG	Bundesverfassungsgericht (federal constitutional court, Germany)
BW	Burgerlijk Wetboek (Netherlands Civil Code)
Cf.	compare
Cir.	United States Court of Appeals
CLR	Copyright Law Revision (legislative history U.S. Copyright Act of 1976)
C&R	Computer und Recht
D.	United States District Court
DCA	Dutch Copyright Act of 1912
EC	European Community
e.g.	*exempli gratia*, for example
EK	Eerste Kamer (the Dutch upper house)
F.	Federal (decisions U.S. Court of Appeals)
F.2d	Federal Second (decisions U.S. Court of Appeals)
FCA	French Copyright Act of 1957
F.Supp.	Federal Supplement (decisions U.S. District Court)
GCA	German Copyright Act of 1965
Ger.	Gerechtshof (court of appeals, Netherlands)
GRUR	Gewerblicher Rechtsschutz und Urheberrecht
HR	Hoge Raad der Nederlanden (highest court, Netherlands)
H.R.	U.S. House of Representatives Bill
H.R.Rep.	U.S. House of Representatives Report
i.e.	*id est*, which is to say

IER	Intellectuele Eigendom en Reclamerecht
JS	Jacqueline Seignette
KG	Kammergericht (court of appeals, Berlin); Kort Geding (decisions president district court, Netherlands)
Ktg.	Kantongerecht (court of petty jurisdiction, Netherlands)
LG	Landgericht (court of first instance, Germany)
NBW	Nieuw Burgerlijk Wetboek (New Netherlands Civil Code)
NJ	Nederlandse Jurisprudentie (decisions, Netherlands)
O.J. Eur.Comm.	Official Journal of the European Community
OLG	Oberlandesgericht (court of appeals, Germany)
Parl.Gesch.	Parlementaire Geschiedenis (parliamentary history of the Dutch Copyright Act of 1912)
pma	*post mortem auctoris*
Pres.Rb.	President Rechtbank (president district court, Netherlands)
Prg.	Praktijkgids (decisions petty court, Netherlands)
Pub.L.	Public Law
RG	Reichsgericht (supreme court, German Reich)
RGBl	Reichsgesetzblatt (statutes of the German Reich)
RvdW	Rechtspraak van de Week (decisions, Netherlands)
S.	Staatsblad van het Koninkrijk der Nederlanden (Netherlands statutes); U.S. Senate Bill
SCA	Swiss Copyright Act of 1992
S.Ct.	Supreme Court Reporter (decisions U.S. Supreme Court)
S.Rep.	United States Senate Report
Stat.	Statutes, U.S.
TK	Tweede Kamer (the Dutch lower house)
Trb.	Tractatenblad van het Koninkrijk der Nederlanden (treaties, Netherlands)
UCC	Universal Copyright Convention
UFITA	Archiv für Urheber-, Film-, Funk- und Theaterrecht
U.S.	United States; U.S. reports (decisions U.S. Supreme Court)
USCA	United States Copyright Act of 1976
U.S.Const.	United States Constitution
U.S.P.Q.2d	United States Patents Quarterly Second
v.	versus
W.	Weekblad van het Recht
WahrnG	Wahrnehmungsgesetz (German Act of 9 September 1965 on the administration of author's rights and related rights)
WIPO	World Intellectual Property Organization
WNR	Wet op de Naburige Rechten (Dutch Act of 18 March 1993 concerning rules for the protection of performing artists, producers of phonograms and broadcasting organizations)
ZUM	Zeitschrift für Urheber- und Medienrecht

Chapter 1

Introduction

1.1 Challenges to the creator doctrine

When we talk about copyright, we usually refer to the 'work' as the subject matter of protection and to the 'author' as creator of the work and as first owner of the copyright. Although some countries traditionally take the work as point of departure and others the author,[1] most modern copyright laws are indeed founded on the basic principle that copyright vests in the 'author' and that the 'author' is the natural person who created the work.

This principle, which will hereinafter be referred to as the *creator doctrine*, has found explicit and unconditional recognition in German law. Entitled to protection under the German Copyright Act of 1965[2] is the 'Urheber', defined as the creator of the work (§ 7 GCA). In American and Dutch copyright law, the creator doctrine is less explicit. Pursuant to the clause in the U.S. Constitution according to which Congress has power to secure 'to Authors the exclusive Right to their Writings',[3] the U.S. Copyright Act of 1976 provides that copyright initially vests in the 'author of the work' (§ 201(a) USCA).[4] According to the U.S. Supreme Court, the 'author' is, as a general rule, the party who actually creates the work, that is the person who translates an idea into a fixed, tangible medium of expression entitled to copyright protection.[5]

Under the terms of the Dutch Copyright Act of 1912,[6] the author's right is vested in the 'maker' of a work (§ 1 DCA). Although the Dutch term 'maker' does not necessarily refer to intellectual labour, it is clear from the legislative history and

---

1. *See* § 102(a) USCA: 'Copyright protection subsists, in accordance with this title, in original works of authorship...' § 1 GCA: 'The authors of literary, scientific and artistic works enjoy protection for their works in accordance with the provisions of this Act.' [translation JS] Section 1 of the Dutch Copyright Act seems to strike a compromise: 'An author's right is the exclusive right of the author of a literary, scientific or artistic work...' [translation JS] *See also* Strowel, at 19-20. *See also infra* 2.16.

2. Act of 9 September 1965 on Author's Right and Related Rights, BGBl. I 1273, as amended. *See infra* 2.13.

3. U.S. Const. art. I, § 8, cl. 8: 'The Congress shall have Power...to promote the Progress of Science and useful Arts by securing for limited Times to Authors and Inventors the exclusive Right to their respective Writings and Discoveries.' *See also infra* 2.14.

4. Copyright Law of the United States of America, Pub.L. 94-553, 19 October 1976, 90 Stat. 2541, as amended. *See infra* 2.14.

5. Community for Creative Non-Violence v. Reid, 109 S.Ct. 2166, at 2171 (1989). *See infra* 2.14; 7.2.

6. Act of 23 September 1912, S. 308, containing a new regulation of the author's right, as amended.

case law that, in general, 'maker' refers to the originator of an intellectual creation.[7]

The Berne Convention of 1886 for the Protection of Literary and Artistic Works secures protection to literary and artistic works throughout the Berne Union for the benefit of authors and their successors in title (Articles 1, 2(6) BC). Although not further defined in the Convention, 'author' will usually refer to the creator of the work.[8] This is where the uniformity stops, however, and where the problem of this study presents itself. Lacking an explicit, unconditional definition of the 'author' as the natural person who has created the work, and allowing member states to determine who is the first owner of the copyright in cinematographic works (Article 14bis (2)(a) BCA), the Berne Convention has been ratified by a number of countries that do not always consider the creator to be the first owner of the copyright. In these countries, the factual term 'creator' does not always coincide with the legal status of 'author', and the legal status of 'author' does not always imply initial copyright ownership.[9] Both the American and Dutch Copyright Acts award authorship and initial copyright ownership to the employer in the case of works prepared by an employee within the scope of his employment.[10] Under the British Copyright, Designs and Patents Act 1988, an employee is author of a work prepared in the course of his employment, but his employer is designated first owner of the copyright.[11]

The notion of 'author' becomes even more diffuse if account is taken of the fact that each national copyright law sets its own minimum standard of authorship. Differences may occur with respect to the results of more industrious and technical labour, such as compilations of facts, computer programs and sound recordings. While there may be general agreement that such products merit protection, one country may choose to protect them under its copyright regime, while another decides to introduce *sui generis* rights. Sound recordings, for example, are protected as works of authorship in American law and as the subject matter of neighbouring rights in Dutch and German law.[12]

Aside from this jumble of different 'author' concepts, there are many differences within and between the various copyright systems as to what a creator can do with his copyright if he is considered to be author and first copyright owner. In its purest form, the creator doctrine implies that any person wishing to exploit a work must

---

7.   *See* Memorandum to § 6 DCA, Parl.Gesch. 6.3 (1912). Memorandum to § 45a DCA, Parl.Gesch. 45.a.9 (1985). *See also* Judgment of June 1, 1990, HR, Netherlands, NJ 1991, 377, note Verkade (Kluwer v. Lamoth): the Copyright Act, as also appears from section 6, serves to protect the work as intellectual creation, which means that it is not merely decisive who has made the tangible object in which this creation is expressed. *See also infra* 2.15; 3.3.3.

8.   Ricketson, at 158. *See also infra* 3.4.

9.   *See* Grosheide, at 177. Grosheide distinguishes between 'connected systems' in which the originator of the work is the main beneficiary of protection and 'disconnected systems', in which the main beneficiary is not necessarily the originator of the work.

10.   § 201(b) USCA; § 7 DCA. *See infra* 2.14; 2.15; 6.3; 7.2; 7.4.

11.   § 9(1) BCA: In this Part 'author', in relation to a work, means the person who creates it. § 11(2) BCA: Where a literary, dramatic, musical or artistic work is made by an employee in the course of his employment, his employer is the first owner of any copyright in the work subject to any agreement to the contrary.

12.   § 102(a)(7) USCA; §§ 1, 5 WNR; § 85 GCA.

2

derive title from the creator, thus enabling the latter to set conditions for the use of his works by others. There are however many situations in which exploitation rights can be lawfully acquired without an express grant by the creator. In German copyright law, for example, an employee who has made a work in the fulfilment of his employment duties is generally presumed, in the absence of an express agreement, to have granted to the employer those rights of use which are necessary for his regular business.[13]

It appears that, however strong the commitment to the creator doctrine may be, every country to some extent is sensitive to the interests of those involved in the financing, production and exploitation of creative works. The various instruments applied to accomodate these entrepreneurial interests - expansion of the copyrightable subject matter, introduction of *sui generis* rights and statutory allocation of rights in works of authorship to employers, film producers, publishers, etc. - have caused great uproar within the international copyright community, conjuring up images of Trojan Horses,[14] growing cancers,[15] Lochness Monsters,[16] slippery slopes[17] and authors' rights without authors.[18]

This study will concentrate on the third instrument, i.e. on rules which allocate rights in works of authorship to someone other than the creator in order to allow this other person to exploit the work without having to expressly negotiate for such rights. The other instruments, expanding the list of copyrightable works and introducing *sui generis* rights, will be discussed only to the extent relevant for the allocation of rights in works of authorship. Rather than to discuss, therefore, whether the activities of producers and publishers merit protection 'in their own

---

13. *See* Judgment of February 22, 1974, BGH, Germany, 76 GRUR 480 (1974) ('Hummelrechte'); Judgment of February 6, 1985, BGH, Germany, 87 GRUR 529 (1985) ('Happening'). *See infra* 2.13; 6.2.

14. *See* Dietz, *Copyright Protection for Computer Programs: Trojan Horse or Stimulus for the Future Copyright System*, lecture given at Stanford Law School on 24 July 1986, cited in: Corbet, at 68, n. 7.

15. *See* Kerever, at 137, arguing that the expansion of the field of copyright for the purpose of protecting investments in industrial activities constitutes 'at best, a sign of adipose anemia, and, at worst, a growing cancer'.

16. *See* Corbet, at 82, with regard to the international phonographic industry's attempts to obtain recognition for copyright protection of sound recordings.

17. *See* Ricketson, *People or Machines*, at 35, using the term 'slippery slope' to illustrate that if the Berne Convention allows one exception to the concept of human authorship (referring to § 14bis(2)(a) BC), such an exception is likely to be used as an argument in favour of many more exceptions.

18. *See* Hirsch Ballin, at 84, referring to the protection of impersonal writings under the Dutch Copyright Act of 1912. Hirsch Ballin regards the protection of impersonal writings under the Copyright Act and the development of neighbouring rights for producers of phonograms as symptoms of the blurring distinction between creation (as expressed in the Dutch word 'maken') and the manufacturing of tangible copies (as expressed in the Dutch word 'vervaardigen'). *Id.* at 82-85. On impersonal writings, see also infra 2.15; 4.4. The phrase 'Author's right without authors' has also been used to criticize the producer-oriented approach of the EC Commission's 1988 Green Paper on Copyright and the Challenge of Technology (COM (88) 172). *See* Möller, at 65. *See also* 'Author's right without authors', title of the conference of the International Copyright Society INTERGU held in Brussels on 21-23 September 1989, reported in: 3 Informatierecht/AMI 148 (1989). *See also* Cohen Jehoram, *The Nature*, at 75: 'They [producers] argue that it would be much more efficient if in "author's rights", "author's" was replaced by the "information industry"; thus, they seek an author's right without authors.'

right', I will examine whether legislators and courts differentiate in the allocation of copyright ownership according to the amount of authorship involved,[19] and what the role of neighbouring rights for producers and publishers may be in situations in which their products incorporate works of authorship.[20]

Proceeding on the assumption that legislators and courts generally only allocate rights to a person other than the creator if this person has a certain relationship with the creator (employment relationship, publishing agreement, audiovisual production agreement, commission, etc.), I will focus on the allocation of rights between the creator and the natural or legal person who or which enters into a contractual relationship with the creator with the explicit or implied object of becoming entitled to use the work. For the purposes of this study, I will refer to this person as the *producer*. In the chain of title, the producer is the person closest to the creator.[21] If I adhere to this definition, the term 'producer' includes:

- persons who contract with a creator to acquire rights to an existing work;
- persons who contract with a creator to adapt a work;
- persons who contract with a creator to include a work in a compilation or collection;
- persons who commission the creation of a work;
- employers in respect of works made by employees in the scope of their employment.

Based on a comparative study of American, Dutch and German copyright law, I will examine the situations in which rights are statutorily allocated to producers in deviation from the general rule, the different methods applied in the various copyright laws to allocate rights to producers, and the admissibility of these different methods in view of the nature and purpose of copyright. As such, this study is also an exploration of the theoretical foundations and practical limitations of the creator doctrine.

Apart from the fact that comparative study can serve as an instrument for discovering alternative solutions to specific problems and for an improved understanding of the domestic law, it is also the basis for any constructive effort towards international harmonization. From either perspective, a comparative study of American, Dutch and German copyright law seems fruitful. With the German concept of the author's right as a creator's inalienable right with interrelated economic and moral aspects,[22] the American concept of copyright as a fully alienable right which, in certain cases, vests in the producer,[23] and the Dutch concept of the author's right

---

19. *See infra* 4.4.
20. *See infra* 6.4.
21. This definition of 'producer' does not in all cases coincide with 'producer of a film work' (Dutch: 'producent van een filmwerk') in § 45a DCA and 'film producer' (German: 'Filmhersteller') in § 89 GCA. *See infra* 7.6.
22. *See infra* 2.13.
23. *See infra* 2.14.

as the pragmatic compromise between the two,[24] the American, Dutch and German copyright laws provide an interesting cross-section of what legislation on copyright ownership at the end of the twentieth century may look like.

For the purpose of the comparative study, I will define 'creator' as the originator of what makes a work eligible for copyright protection under the applicable law. Aside from the historical analysis in Chapter 2, in which 'author' mainly refers to the writer of a literary work, I will use the word 'author' in the legal sense of the word only, i.e. the natural or legal person who is considered first owner of the copyright under the applicable law. The German term 'Urheber' and the Dutch term 'maker' will be translated as 'author'. In this study, 'copyright' may refer to copyright in the Anglo-American sense of the word as well as to the continental-European concept of 'author's right'.

Although collecting societies may arguably fall under the above-mentioned definition of 'producer', this study shall not deal with the specific issues related to the collective administration of rights and agreements between creators and collecting societies. As we will see in the following chapters, however, legislation on the allocation of rights between creators and individual producers acquires a whole new meaning in light of the expanding area of exploitation that is subject to collective administration.[25]

1.2 Structure of the study

In Chapter 2, I will describe the origins of the creator doctrine and its elaboration in the present copyright statutes of the three countries dealt with in this study. Starting from the era of printing privileges, I will examine the beneficiary of protection and analyze at what moment in time the focus of attention has shifted from the publisher to the author. This analysis will explain why the creator doctrine is considered less imperative in Anglo-American countries than in continental Europe.

If the copyright legislator decides to deviate from the general rule that copyright vests in the creator of the work, this apparently serves to avoid certain consequences of that rule. In Chapters 3 and 4, I will discuss these consequences of the creator doctrine and analyze in which situations the American, Dutch and German legislators have sought to avoid these consequences through statutory allocation of rights to producers.

Once the decision has been made to statutorily allocate certain rights to a producer, the next question is how this should be done. At this point, the different views on the nature and purposes of copyright lead to different choices. In Chapter 5, I will discuss the admissibility of attributing authorship and initial copyright ownership to producers. How does this method of allocating rights relate to the

---

24.   *See infra* 2.15.
25.   *See infra* 3.3.4; 3.3.6; 6.4.

protection of the creator's moral and economic interests? Is it possible to attribute economic rights to the producer and moral rights to the creator?

Chapter 6 deals with the practical consequences of the two most important methods for allocating rights to producers: statutory or judicial presumptions of transfers and attribution of authorship. To what extent do these methods solve the problems to which the creator doctrine may give rise (see Chapter 3)? In this Chapter, I will also discuss the role of neighbouring rights for producers in those situations in which their products incorporate works of authorship. To which extent can neighbouring rights solve the problems connected with the creator doctrine?

If the copyright law provides rules that allocate rights to producers in deviation from the general rule, it must be clear when such rules apply. Producers must know whether or not they have to negotiate for an express grant in order to secure title, and creators must know what their position is in negotiating remuneration and what they have to do in order to retain rights. From this perspective of predictability of copyright ownership, I will analyze how courts interpret the wordings of the provisions in the American, Dutch and German Copyright Acts that allocate rights to employers, commissioning parties and film producers. I will also examine the predictability of co-authorship and sole authorship of producers in case of works made on their commission (Chapter 7).

Chapter 8 contains a summary of this study's results and a brief outlook on the international developments in respect of the allocation of rights in works of authorship.

Definitions:

Creator: the originator of a work eligible for copyright protection under the applicable law.

Producer: the natural or legal person who enters into a contractual relationship with a creator of a work with the explicit or implied object of becoming entitled to use the work in a certain manner.

Author: the natural or legal person who is considered to be the initial owner of the copyright under the applicable law.

Creator doctrine: the principle that the creator is the author and first owner of the copyright in a work made by him.

Chapter 2

The historical development of the creator doctrine

2.1 Introduction

For a proper understanding of the creator doctrine in its Anglo-American and continental-European manifestations, it is necessary to return to the origins of copyright. Starting point for this historical survey[1] is the development of the book trade subsequent to the invention of the printing press. Without denying any sense of authorship that may have existed before the event of the printing press,[2] the recognition of the author as beneficiary of legal protection is the direct result of the need of the book trade to maintain exclusivity in printing and publishing.[3] The analysis therefore concentrates on the different instruments that have been applied during the centuries to secure exclusivity in printing and publishing, with a focus on their underlying policies and their beneficiaries. Arriving at the twentieth century, I will describe how the creator doctrine has been elaborated in the present copyright laws of Germany, the Netherlands and the United States.

---

1. The historical survey is predominantly based on secondary sources. On the history of copyright, see e.g. Bappert; Gerbrandy (1992), 15-32; Ginsburg, *A Tale of Two Copyrights*, 124-289; Grosheide, 43-119; Hirsch Ballin, 9-76; Patterson; Ransom; Ricketson, 3-125; Saunders, 35-185; Schricker/Vogel, 73-84; Spoor/Verkade, 14-19; Stewart, 3-27; Strömholm, I; Strowel, 82-129; Ulmer, 50-65.

2. Several authors have presented evidence to the effect that there was already a clear sense of authorship before the advent of the printing press. *See* Dock, at 126-158. Hirsch Ballin, *Urheberrecht am Scheideweg*, at 15, suggests that the invention of the printing press slowed down the development of author's rights: 'The fact that the emerging awareness of the concept of authorship coincided with the invention of a machine - the printing press -, is an utter tragedy ... The place of the creating human being was taken over by the owner of a machine: I] the printer-publisher, i.e. a third party who did not participate in the creation.' [translation JS] In other areas such as the theatre, however, access to the market was also controlled by privileged entrepreneurs, perhaps even more to the detriment of the author's moral and economic interests than in the field of printing. Playwrights were paid by the theatre they worked for, if they were paid at all. Theatres maintained their monopoly by keeping the play out of print. *See* De Beaufort (1909), at 15.

3. *But see* Grosheide, at 43, regarding the end of the eighteenth century as the prehistory of copyright, arguing that this was the first period that represented the social and paradigmatic state of affairs necessary for the recognition of copyright. *See also* Grosheide, *Paradigms*, at 205.

2.2 The development of the book trade

The process of printing books dates back to the invention of the printing press, generally attributed to Johann Gensfleisch von Gutenberg in 1450.[4] The new opportunity for large-scale reproduction of literary works[5] would turn books into an interesting commodity, but it also introduced the element of risk. The printing process required investments in equipment and supplies which could only be recouped if a larger number of copies were sold. The risks involved in the new art of printing were exacerbated by competitors who printed and sold books which had never been in print before, but also by competitors who reprinted books which were being succesfully sold by other printers. The reprints were often marketed at a lower price, thereby undercutting the profitability of the original prints.

In order to minimize the risks involved in printing, printers turned to the authorities, who appeared to be willing to meet the demands of this new industry. By the turn of the century, kings, emperors, land-owners and city-states started to guarantee printers territorial exclusivity by granting privileges, the most common instrument for creating rights in the feudal system.[6]

2.3 The nature of printing privileges

In the beginning, the authorities attracted craftsmen skilled in the new art of printing by granting them privileges which guaranteed a general printing monopoly within a certain territory for a certain time.[7] Most privileges, however, awarded the printer the right to print a particular literary work to the exclusion of others. Privileges were granted for religious works and the works of classical authors, but also for more down-to-earth items such as almanacs, atlases and calendars.[8]

The fact that privileges were granted for the works of classical authors indicates that printing privileges served to benefit the printer, not the author of the work being printed. The fact that privileges were granted to reprint works which had already been printed and published abroad, furthermore indicates that the granting of a privilege was not necessarily dependent on the printer making a creative contribution to the work printed. The collection by the printer of material, the design of typefaces and illustrations and the translation or adaptation of the text, could however be a motive for a printing privilege.[9]

---

4. Bappert, at 136.
5. Texts were reproduced manually before the invention of the printing press, but that process was much more labour-intensive than the printing process. *See* Larese, at 36, n. 51, referring to Ancient Rome, where slavery allowed labour-intensive manual reproduction.
6. Bappert, at 179, Grosheide, at 53.
7. Ulmer, at 51.
8. De Beaufort (1909), at 10.
9. Dock, at 172; Kerever, at 130.

While most privileges were granted for one particular work, printers were also granted privileges for all the works they had already printed or intended to print,[10] or for works that needed to be regularly updated, such as calendars and dictionaries.[11] The latter type of 'general privileges' served the purpose of what we would call derivative work rights nowadays. While a privilege to print one particular work could never extend to adaptations of that work, a general privilege could guarantee an exclusive right to print subsequent versions of that same calendar or dictionary.

Printing privileges were also granted for tax purposes and as a means of exercising censorship. The printing press had proved to be an effective means of communication for the state and the church, but it also posed a threat to these same interests. States, often representing the interests of a particular church, therefore sought to gain control over the products of the printing press.[12] In England and France, where printing privileges were most strongly motivated by the desire to exercise censorship, printing privileges were made dependent on membership of a printers' guild, which cooperated with the government in censoring the products of the press in return for the guild's guaranteed market monopoly.[13] This system not only turned out to be an effective means of controlling the press, but it also heavily monopolized the book market in these countries. This, in turn, gave rise to the development of an underground publishing industry which concentrated on censored works and on importing foreign reprints for which the printers' guild had a privilege.[14]

It appears from the above that printing privileges were granted for all kinds of reasons and for all kinds of works. This, in fact, reflects the nature of privileges: a public favour, granted on an *ad hoc* basis, by and at the complete discretion of a government authority.[15] This public, *ad hoc* nature is what distinguishes privileges from copyrights, as the latter can be claimed by any person who meets the more or less fixed criteria laid down in the copyright statute and elaborated in case law. Printing privileges resemble modern copyright in that they created an exclusive right to reproduce and distribute copies of a literary work within a certain territory, which in case of infringement could lead to fines, seizure of infringatory copies and to damages.[16]

Although the printing press turned literary works into commercial commodities, there was no clear perception at the time of a right in the intellectual creation which was printed and published.[17] The grantors regarded printing

---

10. Hilty, at 38.
11. *See* Feather, at 377, referring to a printing privilege granted by Mary I to Richard Tottel in 1553 for the printing of existing and future common law books.
12. For the instruments applied to control the printing press, see Nieuwenhuis, at 9-12.
13. Feather, at 377; Darnton, at 187. *See also infra* 2.7.
14. Darnton, at 183.
15. In this sense, the privileges based on statutory rules and guild regulations, such as the privileges granted to the Stationers' Company in 17th century England, must be regarded as an intermediate stage between privileges and statutory copyright protection. *See infra* 2.6.
16. *See also* Hösly, at 22; Stewart, at 16, 26.
17. Grosheide, at 53.

privileges as an instrument of censorship and trade regulation, policies which could be enforced most effectively by granting privileges to the person who intended to distribute the books.[18] Copyright, on the other hand, would come to be vested in the author of the literary work embodied in the print. In the next paragraphs we will see that this fundamental shift has been a gradual process, characterized by institutionalization of the protection against copying and the publisher's increased dependence on the author's cooperation. In this transitional period, there were several intermediate forms of protection, such as privileges granted to authors and statutory protection of publishers. Before I deal with this transitional period, however, I will briefly discuss the impact of the printing press on the social position of creators.[19]

2.4 The renaissance of the individual author

Whereas the works of the classical authors reflect a certain awareness of authorship, most religious works written in the early Middle Ages were perceived as a proclamation of God's word, rather than as the expression of the writer's personal thoughts.[20] In this non-individualistic age, writers and artists tended to remain anonymous behind the guilds and monasteries for which they performed their, often collaborative, creative labour.[21] In the Renaissance, authors slowly emerged from anonymity. As writing was not yet being exploited commercially at the time, this awareness was restricted to recognition of authorship. Authors generally did not mind their work being copied, as long as the copyists did not mutilate the work or put their own name to it.[22]

The printing press marked the rise of a new industry which created a demand for literary works. The increased supply of books considerably reduced illiteracy. Reading and writing were no longer restricted to the clergy. Renaissance and Humanism inspired many to think, philosophize, discuss and write. The printing press gave these writers an audience and social recognition, although many authors were forced to write and publish in secret as a result of censorship.

In spite of the recognition of this new class of authors, the increased demand for their works was not automatically reflected in high prices for manuscripts. Most writers could not or did not wish to live off the sale of their manu-

---

18. Dock, at 168; Nieuwenhuis, at 10.
19. On the social position of authors, see generally Grosheide, 100-119. On the recognition of authorship before the 18th century, see generally Strömholm, I, 46-114.
20. Hubmann, at 10; Schricker/Vogel, at 74.
21. *See* Dock, at 156, arguing that the anonymity was a result of the situation in which the monk wrote his works, as these works were usually a transcription of the doctrine adhered to by the community to which the monk belonged, elaborated in collaboration by its members. As such, the work was the result of a collective, indivisible effort, attributed to the community as a whole. Dock also mentions, however, that there have been writers of lay literature, such as Eike von Repgow, who are still known today and who did actually express the fear of distortion and false attribution. *Id.* at 154.
22. Examples by Hubmann, at 13.

scripts.[23] They either were supported by the nobility or earned their living with other professions.[24] As such, most authors concentrated on finding a generous *Maecenas*, rather than on getting a lucrative deal from a publisher. Publishers nevertheless became more and more dependent on authors for their protection, which as we will see in the next paragraphs, became manifest in the practice of granting privileges and, after the privilege system broke down, in the publishers' struggle for new forms of protection.

2.5 Authors' privileges

History records several cases in which a privilege was granted to the author of a literary work. In some of these cases the author printed his own works, or had his work printed by others at his own expense,[25] but there is also evidence of privileges granted to authors who did not arrange the printing and publishing themselves.[26] The nature of these author's privileges is disputed, in particular as to whether these privileges recognized an author's right of first publication.[27]

Some privileges were granted to authors by land-owners in return for the author's contribution to their cultural standing.[28] Instead of directly supporting the author with money, the land-owner induced the author to sell his manuscript and transfer the privilege to the printer of his choice, who then would have the exclusive right to print the work. This improved the author's negotiating position in respect of the printer, both with regard to the financial consideration and to the way in which the manuscript was to be printed.[29]

As the German book trade developed and became concentrated in Frankfurt and Leipzig in the 16th and 17th centuries, it became customary for the authorities to grant privileges to authors upon request.[30] Especially this practice has convinced Pohlmann that author's privileges were a confirmation of a non-statutory author's right upon creation.[31] In his view, the printer was only authorized to print and publish a work if the author had transferred the rights that

---

23. Dock, at 178, mentions that some authors considered it 'shameful to their sacred art' to discuss material preoccupations.

24. *See* Darnton, at 16, discussing the literary underground in 18th century France. The authors who did not manage to obtain a place in the 'monde', had to earn their own living. Many did this by writing and compiling works for which there was a demand, such as encyclopaedias and anthologies. Others engaged in gutter journalism about the perversities and corruption of the 'monde', published in so-called 'libelles'.

25. De Beaufort (1909), at 18.

26. Examples by de Beaufort (1909), at 19; Pohlmann, at 97.

27. Ulmer, at 53, refers to a case in which the Council of the City of Nurenberg, confronted with two conflicting editions of the same work, gave priority to the printer who had acquired a privilege from the author, over the printer who had a general privilege for his entire publishing list.

28. Hösly, at 16.

29. Hösly, at 17.

30. Pohlmann, at 64; Hubmann, at 12.

31. Pohlmann, at 65. Less explicit, Hubmann, at 12.

automatically arose from the fruits of his intellectual labour to him.[32] Bappert, on the other hand, argues that most privileges stipulated that the work should be put into print first, so that the protection did not commence until the work had been printed.[33] Some privileges, indeed, specifically required that the work be put in print. Other privileges, however, merely required the author's intention to disclose the work.[34] It should probably be concluded that privileges were still being granted for different reasons. Some privileges may have resembled an author's right upon creation, whereas others still constituted a publisher's monopoly to print. Author's privileges nevertheless reinforced the link between the exclusive right to print and the originator of the literary work, even though the grantors did not yet link the privilege to the intellectual creation embodied in the manuscript.

2.6 Towards a more institutionalized protection against copying

Apart from the practice of granting privileges to authors upon request, protection against copying became more institutionalized as a result of guild monopolies and the introduction of statutory protection. In the 15th and 16th centuries, the German states issued several ordinances granting a minimum protection against reprinting. This statutory protection was introduced in addition to privileges, which remained necessary for criminal enforcement.[35] The ordinances granted protection to the person who printed a work for the first time within the territory for which the ordinance was issued, and was based on the investments he had made in the printing process.[36]

Some of the ordinances required the printer to obtain the manuscript from the author or the author's consent to print the work.[37] This was in keeping with the practice, which had become general in publishing then, of including an announcement in the book that it had been printed with the author's consent. Here again, opinion is divided. Pohlmann has argued that the author's consent represented a transfer of his rights to the printer,[38] but others regard it as merely a justification, moral or otherwise, of the publisher's protection or as proof against copying, not as an author's right of first publication.[39]

In England and France, a more institutionalized form of protection developed as a result of the corporatistic structure of the book trade and the government's

---

32. Pohlmann, at 91.
33. Bappert, at 186.
34. Pohlmann, at 86, 88.
35. Ulmer, at 53, 57.
36. Bappert, at 217.
37. Ulmer, at 53, 58; Bappert, at 129, 160, 169.
38. Pohlmann, at 82, 83, gives the example of the Dutch publisher Moretus, who claimed an exclusive printing right, presenting a document in which the author Torinelli declared to have once again transferred the right to publish his adapted version of the 'Annales Sacri' to him.
39. Bappert, at 164, 170; Hilty, at 39; Hubmann, at 14.

efforts to control the printing press. In 1557, Queen Mary I granted the Stationers' Company of London the privilege of regulating the book trade. In return, the Stationers subjected their manuscripts to the censorship of the Privy Council or the Company itself.[40] In 1618, the French government forced the Parisian booksellers and printers to form a guild which in return for a printing monopoly would censor the books it published.[41] The censorship task of the Paris Community of Book Sellers and Printers was maintained by government decrees until immediately before the revolution of 1789.

The guilds' monopolies institutionalized the system of printing privileges. Every guild member could obtain a perpetual and exclusive right to print and publish works as long as they passed the censor and were recorded in a special register kept by the guild. These rights, in England often designated as 'Stationer's copyrights', were sold as if they were commodities and passed on to the printer's descendants upon his death.[42] However, contrary to what we might expect on the basis of the present meaning of the word 'copyright', a Stationer's copyright did not vest ownership in the literary work being published, but merely granted an exclusive right to publish it.[43] It did not include the right to alter the work, nor was it considered possible to acquire a new right to copy an adapted version. It was commonly agreed amongst the Stationers that it was better for sales if original editions did not need to compete with altered or even distorted versions.[44]

As in Germany, the protection of publishers thus evolved from an *ad hoc* printing privilege into a more institutionalized form of protection, albeit that the protection offered in France and England was based on a guild monopoly and was therefore available to guild members only. The guilds' monopolies were not to hold out for much longer, however, as new concepts of freedom were beginning to undermine the established practices of government censorship and trade monopolies. The system of privileges and, with it, the monopolies of the established book trade, started to crumble. By the end of the 18th century, printing privileges had been banned in almost every country in Europe. The increased piracy resulting from this legal vacuum left the authorities with the task of finding an alternative for printing privileges without reinstating the old monopolies, and it was from this perspective, that the first copyright statutes were adopted in the 18th century.

In the following section, I will discuss the developments leading up to and resulting from the enactment of the first English and French copyright statutes. Inspired by the idea of promoting the creation and dissemination of literary works without creating unrestricted monopolies, both statutes were typical for their

---

40. Feather, at 377.
41. Darnton at 185; Dock, at 168.
42. Darnton, at 186; Feather, at 378; Patterson, at 9; Ploman/Clark Hamilton, at 11; Saunders, at 49.
43. Patterson, at 10, 11; Ploman/Clark Hamilton, at 12.
44. Patterson, at 11; Ploman/Clark Hamilton, at 11.

time.[45] Although these statutes sowed the seeds for what we now call the *droit d'auteur* and *copyright* systems, we will see that their most distinctive characteristics result from later developments.

2.7 From privilege to copyright

The first statute ever to refer to the author as the beneficiary of protection was the *Statute of Anne*, enacted by Queen Anne of Great Britain in 1710.[46] As the Preamble states, this statute intended to stop the practice of printing and publishing without the author's or proprietor's consent 'to their very great detriment and too often to the ruin of them and their families', and to encourage 'learned men to compose and write useful books'.[47] The immediate reason for legislation, however, was the need to restore order in the national book trade, which was suffering from unbridled piracy after the House of Commons had refused to reconfirm the Stationers' monopoly in 1695.

The Stationers' Company's monopoly had been upheld in the second half of the 17th century by means of a number of Acts of Parliament designed to maintain government control over the printing press.[48] The monopoly allowed the Company to decide which books to print, in what number and at what price. A succession of governments accepted this constraint on competition, as long as they could use the Stationers' Company as a means of exercising censorship. But as the government became more tolerant towards the printing press, the negative effects of the Stationers' monopoly gradually became intolerable, and in 1695, the House of Commons finally refused to renew the statutory monopoly of the Stationers' Company. Piracy flourished from that year on, and the Stationers immediately launched a campaign to regain a legal basis for their monopoly, which they still had *de facto*. One of their arguments was that parliament should protect 'literary property' from piracy. The Stationers did not specify this notion of 'literary property' in further detail, and they advanced it as a basis for their own protection from piracy, not as an author's right.[49]

---

45. Printing privileges continued to be granted in the various German states until the middle of the 19th century and these were complemented in many states by statutory protection against copying. The first state statutes which vested rights in the author emerged at the end of the 18th century. In 1870, the German Union enacted a statute on author's rights in literary, dramatical and musical works and illustrations. The German Reich adopted this statute in 1871, based on its constitutional power to legislate the protection of 'intellectual property'. *See infra* 2.15 on the transition from privilege to copyright in the Netherlands.

46. 8 Anne c. 21, An Act for the Encouragement of Learning, by Vesting the Copies of Printed Books in the Authors or Purchasers of such Copies, during the Times therein mentioned. Reprinted in Latman/Gorman/Ginsburg, before p. 1.

47. *Id.*

48. The hybrid nature of these acts is reflected in the titles used to designate them: Licensing Act, Printing Act, Press Regulation Act.

49. Feather, at 379. Prescott, at 453, explains that the Stationers' lobby stemmed from a desire to restrict competition from Scottish publishers who, unhampered by any guild regulations, were starting to compete with the London Stationers. It was not until the 1707 Act of Union, however, that Parliament was able to bring the Scottish publishers within its copyright jurisdiction.

In 1710, Parliament finally adopted statutory protection for future publications as well as for books that were already in print. Contrary to the Stationers' wishes, however, this protection was open to all publishers and valid for a limited time only: Parliament had sought to regulate the book trade, not to perpetuate the Stationers' monopoly. The Statute of Anne granted 'the Author of any Book or Books already Composed and not Printed and Published, or that shall hereafter be Composed, and his Assignee, or Assigns' an exclusive right to print and reprint a book for a 14-year period after its first publication. After expiry of this period, an author could renew the copyright for another 14-year period, provided he was still alive when the first term expired.[50] Registration in the Stationers' Register was necessary to enforce the copyright and for documentation purposes. Nine copies of the book were to be deposited in a library. The statute furthermore contained rules to prevent publishers from selling books at 'High and Unreasonable' prices.

Protection thus for the first time vested in the author and, therefore, could arise only if there was an author. Although of great importance to the development of copyright law, this did not yet fundamentally change the position of authors, as an author was considered to have assigned his rights to the publisher upon the sale of his manuscript. The Stationers, in the meantime, continued their monopoly on the basis of a provision in the Statute of Anne according to which works published before April 10, 1710 would be protected for a period of 21 years. After expiration of this 21-year period, the Stationers' market position was seriously threatened for the first time. In a series of law suits against Irish and Scottish publishers who flourished on cheaper editions of works which were formerly printed under the Stationers' monopoly, the London publishers claimed to have a perpetual right in common law to the works they had published. To support their claims, they invoked John Locke's 'labour theory',[51] which the contemporary legal scholar William Blackstone elaborated in respect of literary works.[52] Locke had postulated a theory that every man has a natural right of property to the fruits of his labour.[53] On the basis of this theory, the Stationers claimed to have a perpetual exclusive right in common law to publish and sell copies acquired from the authors who had sold them their manuscripts. The London publishers thereby defended the idea of a natural right of property for the

---

50. Although the reversion of copyright to the author for the second term seemed to be in the author's interests, legal literature has suggested other motives for the renewal. Patterson, at 13, argues that by being granted a renewal, authors were being used as an instrument against monopolists. Curtis, at 802, argues that it was merely a legislative omission. The House of Lords had added the second 14-year term in order to extend the term of protection, but had forgotten to declare this extension explicitly applicable to assigns. The Court of Chancery later interpreted the two-term protection in such a way that a transfer of all interests implied a transfer for both terms, so that the copyright did not revert to the author upon expiry of the first term. Carnan v. Bowles, 29 Eng.Rep. 45 (Ch. 1786). See infra 2.14 on renewal of copyright in U.S. law.

51. Locke, Second Treatise, Chapter V. See also infra 2.9.

52. W. Blackstone, II Commentaries on the Laws of England, 405 (1765).

53. Locke, Second Treatise, Chapter V, § 27. See infra 2.8.

author, with the apparent aim of perpetuating their own monopoly.[54] In the 1769 case of *Millar v. Taylor*,[55] the King's Bench accepted the argument in favour of perpetual protection in common law. However five years later, the House of Lords took a different view in *Donaldson v. Becket*,[56] after having referred the case to the justices of the King's Bench, Common Pleas and Exchequer for an opinion. Although the reports on this advisory opinion are anything but unanimous,[57] a small majority of the judges is said to have acknowledged that a perpetual right existed in common law, but also that the Statute of Anne, with its limited term of protection, superseded this protection once the work was published. Subsequently voting on the case, the full House of Lords denied the injunction invoked by Becket, based on the argument that the common law did not recognize a perpetual copyright at all, and that such a right should not be recognized either, in view of the threat which a perpetual monopoly might pose to public access to science and literature.[58]

Sixty-five years later, the same issue of common law and statutory protection was brought before the Supreme Court of the United States of America. On the basis of its constitutional mandate 'to promote the progress of the science and the useful arts, by securing for limited times to authors and inventors the exclusive rights to their respective writings and discoveries',[59] Congress adopted its first copyright statute in 1790.[60] Following the example of the Statute of Anne, this statute offered protection for a 14-year period, commencing upon publication, and with an opportunity to renew the protection for another 14-year period. In 1831, the first term was extended to 28 years.[61] Protection could be forfeited if the work was published without timely recordation at the district court's office, publication of the record in a newspaper and deposit of a copy of the work with the U.S. Secretary of State.

In 1834, Supreme Court reporter Henry Wheaton sued Richard Peters for the publication of case reports previously published by Wheaton. The reports published by Peters included notes, abstracts and other materials written by Wheaton. Wheaton based his claims on a perpetual property right at common law to the copies of his works as well as on the copyright statute. In response, Peters challenged the validity of Wheaton's copyright, arguing that Wheaton had not

---

54. This indicates that producers may well have an interest in defending a natural right of the creator to his work, because this generally implies broader and longer protection than a statutory monopoly.
55. 4 Burr. (4th ed.) 2303, 98 Eng.Rep. 201 (K.B. 1769).
56. 4 Burr. (4th ed.) 2408, 98 Eng.Rep. 251 (H.L. 1774).
57. *See* Abrams, at 1166-1171.
58. Discussions in the House preceding the vote are reported in 17 Parl.Hist. Eng. 953, 992-1003 (H.L. 1774). *See* Abrams, at 1161-1171.
59. U.S. Const. art. I, § 8, cl. 8. *See also infra* 2.14.
60. Act of May 31, 1790, 1 Stat. 124, for the encouragement of learning, by securing the copies of maps, charts and books, to the authors and proprietors of such copies, during the times therein mentioned. Ginsburg, *A Tale of Two Copyrights*, at 145, mentions that state statutes preceding the first federal copyright statute mentioned as arguments for protection both the encouragement of learning as well as every man's right to the fruits of his intellectual labour.
61. 4 Stat. 436.

16

complied with the formalities required by the statute. The U.S. Supreme Court held that, although an author has a right in common law to oppose the disclosure of his work without his consent, it is only possible to have an exclusive right to publish and sell copies after the work has been made public under an act of Congress.[62] According to the court, copyright is a creation of statute for which Congress can set the conditions on the basis of its constitutional mandate and can therefore only be invoked if all the statutory requirements are complied with.[63]

The *Donaldson* and *Wheaton* decisions effectively prevented courts from further elaborating on the protection of published works in common law,[64] thus casting the die for Anglo-American copyright law in the years to come: statutory protection upon publication of the literary work, whereby the requirements for and the scope and duration of protection were determined solely by statute.[65]

Returning to the 18th century, we see that the transition from printing privileges to copyright in France was also a reaction against the government-maintained monopoly of the publishers' guild. The Paris Community of Book Sellers and Printers, whose monopoly had been confirmed by several ordinances during the 17th and 18th centuries,[66] confined itself to publishing limited numbers of books according to the guild's strict quality rules and the rules of censorship. This limited supply did not meet the national demand for literary works. There was a huge, unexplored market in the province, but the provincial booksellers did not have the privileges to serve it, at least not legally. As a result, the Parisian publishers were in constant conflict with provincial booksellers, with the latter arguing that it would not be in the public interest to renew the privileges of the Parisian publishers. Like the London Stationers, the Parisian guild invoked Locke's labour theory to defend its monopoly. Louis d'Hericourt, hired to state

---

62. Wheaton v. Peters, 33 U.S. (8 Pet.) 591 (1834).

63. *Id.*

64. *See e.g.* Beckford v. Hood, 7 T.R. 620 (1798); Jefferys v. Boosey, 4 H.L.C. 815 (1855). *But see* Goldstein v. California, 412 U.S. 546 (1973): states have not, under the Constitution, relinquished all power to grant authors exclusive rights, even if these exclusive rights are unlimited in time. State legislation is permitted in areas which Congress has not provided for, as is the case with sound recordings made before February 15, 1972. The Act of October 15, 1971, Pub. L. no. 92-140, 85 Stat. 391 (1971) grants federal protection to sound recordings made after this date, while any rights and remedies at common law and state legislation have been preempted (§ 301(c) USCA). Patterson, at 16, and Nimmer, § 4.02[B], 4.03, have argued that the *Donaldson* decision should not have been interpreted so as to preclude common law protection of published works. *But see* Abrams, at 1128, arguing that this view is based on the idea that the decision in *Donaldson* was given by the judges of the King's Bench, Common Pleas and Exchequer, whereas the actual decision was given by the full House of Lords, the majority of whom voted that a common law copyright did not exist. Bowker, at 26, also refers to the vote of the House of Lords as the *Donaldson* decision, but he also argues that it might have been possible for the English legislature to 'restore' the common law rights, in view of the fact that it had already done so to a certain extent in 1775, when it granted perpetual copyrights to the English and Scottish universities and the Eton, Westminster and Winchester colleges for all works bequeathed to and printed by them. *Id.* at 34. This perpetual protection was abolished under the 1988 British Copyright, Designs and Patents Act.

65. Bowker, at 7: 'Literary and like property to this extent lost the character of copy-*right*, and became the subject of copy-*privilege*, depending on legal enactment for the security of the private owner.'

66. Notably in 1666, 1686, 1723 and 1744. *See* Darnton, at 185-186.

the guild's case, argued that an author has a natural right of property to the fruits of his labour, which he has transferred to the publisher and of which the royal privilege is merely a confirmation.[67] Denis Diderot, subsequently hired to support the guild's position, even argued that literary property was the most inviolable form of property, because it originates in the mind of the author and is not, like land and wine, the result of appropriation and cultivation of something which is already there in nature.[68]

The conflict was settled in 1777 by a number of royal edicts designed to regulate the book trade. The publishers' arguments in favour of perpetual protection had made some impression, but had failed to convince the King fully. An author was granted a perpetual privilege to publish his work, but this privilege would be replaced upon publication by a privilege for the publisher which was limited in time so as not to unduly restrain the competition in the book trade.[69] A situation similar to that for which the majority of the judges had voted three years earlier in their advisory opinion to the House of Lords in *Donaldson v. Becket*.[70]

In 1789, the Revolution eradicated all the characteristic elements of the 'Ancien Régime', including the system of privileges and the corporatistic structure of the book trade. The resulting vacuum created such chaos in the book trade that the revolutionaries feared it would endanger the dissemination of ideas and thoughts, one of the reasons why they had abolished the privileges.[71] Against this background, a number of decrees on the freedom of theatre and on reproduction rights were enacted. Article 3 of the Decree of 13-19 January 1791 provided that theatrical performances were subject to the author's consent, and article 1 of the Decree of 19-24 July 1793 granted writers, composers, artists and designers the right to sell and distribute their works and to assign their property in whole or in part.

Although the revolutionaries embraced the concept of property as a human right,[72] literary and dramatic works were not granted the perpetual nature of a natural law-based property right. Not only would that have made the anti-guild measures illusory, the idea of literary property as a perpetual, natural right had also lost much of its political impact after government censorship had been abolished.[73] Instead of supporting the freedom of ideas and thoughts, literary property now came to be weighed against the public interest of encouraging the

---

67. Dock, at 188.
68. Diderot, 'Lettre Historique et politique sur le commerce de la librairie', in: *Oeuvres complètes*, Vol. 5, 331 (1978), discussed by Hesse, at 114, 115.
69. An amendment of the Act one year later allowed the author to publish his work without losing the perpetual privilege, but only if he had the work printed and published at his own expense and risk. *See* Dock, at 196.
70. *See supra* notes 56-58 and accompanying text.
71. Ginsburg, *A Tale of Two Copyrights*, at 175. See also Hesse, at 109-137, discussing the different legislative proposals issued between 1789 and 1791 to redress piracy.
72. Article 17 of the Declaration of the Rights of Man and of the Citizen of 29 August 1789.
73. *See* Hesse, at 125; Ginsburg, *A Tale of Two Copyrights*, at 171.

dissemination of thoughts and ideas.[74] The 1791 Decree restricted the protection to five, and the 1793 Decree to ten years *post mortem auctoris*.[75] These terms were just about enough to bring the works of authors such as Rousseau, Voltaire, Molière and Racine in the 'public domain', thus finally ending the monopoly of the Paris Community of Printers and Booksellers and the Comédie Française.[76]

Case law following the enactment of the 1791 and 1793 Decrees reflects the incentive arguments of the revolutionary legislators and reveals a number of decisions in which protection was denied on account of a failure to comply with statutory formalities such as deposit of copies at the Bibliothèque Nationale or publication within French territory.[77] In view of these cases, it is unclear whether the act of creation or the compliance with formalities gave rise to statutory protection,[78] which indicates that the protection granted to authors was still far away from the present concept of *droit d'auteur*: a recognition of an author's natural right to claim protection of the moral and economic rights to his works.[79] Whereas the Anglo-American concept of *copyright* had already largely crystallized as a result of case law proclaiming the primacy of the statute over common law, the French concept of *droit d'auteur* had only just begun to develop.

---

74. Le Chapelier, whose reports formed the basis for the two decrees, is often cited as expressing the essence of the French author's right: 'The most sacred, the most legitimate, the most inattackable, ... the most personal of all properties, is the work which is the fruit of a writer's thoughts.'. *Le Moniteur Universel*, 15 January 1791, quoted in: Ginsburg, *A Tale of Two Copyrights*, at 159. Ginsburg points out, however, that Le Chapelier's words referred to unpublished works and that he went on to state that, in his view, the public interest should prevail over the interests of the author and the publisher once the work had been published. *Id.* at 159.

75. Article 2 Law of 13-19 January 1791; Article 2 Law of 19-24 July 1793.

76. *See* Ginsburg, *A Tale of Two Copyrights*, at 157; Hesse, at 120, 131. A Decree of 30 August 1792, which was repealed one year later, reduced the duration of the theatrical performance right to ten years commencing upon first publication and made protection dependent on the author reserving his rights in the play by way of a notice to be printed on every copy and to be deposited with a notary.

77. Compare the cases discussed by Ginsburg, *A Tale of Two Copyrights*, at 185-199, 203-227. A case concerning the Dictionaire de l'Académie Française is of particular interest to this study. The plaintiffs who had acquired the right to publish a fifth edition of the Dictionary from a publisher who had been assigned this right by the revolutionary authorities, brought an infringement action against a competing edition of the Dictionary which was based on the fifth and earlier editions. Under the 1793 Decree, only 'true owners' could claim damages. The defendant argued that the publisher was not a 'true owner', because the 1793 Decree only protected the actual writers and not the State. The plaintiffs replied that under the 1793 Decree an 'author' also included those who had commissioned others to write certain works, which is what the State did when it commissioned the Académie Française to write the Dictionary. The court upheld the plaintiffs' claim stating that they were the 'true owner', since only their interests were being prejudiced by the infringement. Case cited by Ginsburg, *A Tale of Two Copyrights*, at 283, n. 85.

78. *See* Ginsburg, *A Tale of Two Copyrights*, at 197: '[T]he role of the deposit of copies with the Bibliothèque Nationale as constitutive or merely declaratory of the author's right remained ambiguous throughout the revolutionary and Napoleonic periods. If deposit constitutes, rather than simply proves copyright, then the right cannot arise out of the mere act of authorship.'

79. *See* Françon, at 10.

19

2.8 John Locke's labour theory and the creator doctrine of copyright law

In an effort to restrict despotic power over the individual, the 17th century English philosopher John Locke postulated the idea that every man has certain natural rights and that these rights do not require the government's consent.[80] One of these natural rights was the property of one's own body. Locke argued that if a man combines his human labour with natural objects and adds something of his own, the result automatically becomes his property[81] and may not be taken away from him without his consent:[82] 'Thus the Grass my Horse has bit; the Turfs my Servant has cut; and the Ore I have digg'd in any place where I have a Right to them in common with others, become my *Property*, without the assignation or consent of any body.'[83]

The idea that every man has a natural right to the fruits of his labour, hereinafter to be referred to as the labour theory, has greatly influenced copyright thinking. In the foregoing paragraph, we have seen that authors and publishers invoked this theory as a basis for perpetual protection against copying in situations in which statutory protection was not available, either because the required formalities had not been complied with or because statutory protection had expired.[84] We have also seen that the highest English and American courts decided that published works could be protected by virtue of legislation only.[85] According to the U.S. Supreme Court in *Wheaton v. Peters*, statutory copyright was not a confirmation of an existing property right to the fruits of labour, but a new right of limited scope and duration, designed to achieve the constitutional objective of promoting the progress of science and the arts.[86]

Vesting as it did upon the work's first publication, statutory copyright did not protect an author's fundamental interest to decide if, when and by whom his works should be disclosed to the public. Not pre-empted by the copyright statute, courts were willing to protect this interest based on the principle that every man has a right to the fruits of his labour.[87] According to this combined system of common law protection of unpublished works - somewhat confusingly referred to

---

80. Locke, Second Treatise, Chapter V. On Locke, see also Strowel, 179-190.
81. Locke, Second Treatise, Chapter V, § 27.
82. *Id.* §§ 138, 139, 193.
83. *Id.* § 28.
84. *See supra* 2.7.
85. Donaldson v. Becket, 4 Burr. (4th ed.) 2408, 98 Eng.Rep. 251 (H.L. 1774); Wheaton v. Peters, 33 U.S. (8 Pet.) 591 (1834).
86. Wheaton v. Peters, 33 U.S. (8 Pet.) 591 (1834).
87. Wheaton v. Peters, 33 U.S. (8 Pet.) 591 (1834). *See also* Prince Albert v. Strange, 2 DeG. & Sm. 652, 64 Eng. Rep. 293, 79 Rev. Rep. 307, *aff'd* 1 Mac. & G. 25, 41 Eng. Rep. 1171 (1849). *Cf. also* Baker v. Libbie, 210 Mass. 599, 97 N.E. 109 (1912): 'It is generally recognized that one has a right to the fruits of his labor. This is equally true whether the work be muscular or mental or both combined. Property in literary productions, before publication and while they rest in manuscript, is as plain as property in the game of the hunter or in the grain of the husbandman.'

as 'common law copyright'[88] - and statutory copyright protection of published works,[89] an author or the person whom the author had authorized to publish the work could secure copyright protection by publishing the work in compliance with formalities.

It is only possible to speculate what the situation might have been if the English and American courts had allowed themselves to elaborate on the idea of common law protection for published works. It has been argued that this might have led to an early statutory recognition of an author's right upon creation,[90] even to a body of law for the protection of an author's moral interests before and after the work's publication.[91] The fact is, that when the U.S. Copyright Act of 1909 defined 'author' so as to include employers in case of works made for hire,[92] it did so in confirmation of court decisions that presumed that the employer owned the common law copyright to a work created by an employee and that the employer was therefore automatically entitled to secure copyright protection.[93] The specific nature of intellectual labour apparently did not prevent the courts from applying Locke's principle that the results of a servant's labour automatically become the property of the master (master and servant principle).[94]

Looking at the development of copyright law in the 20th century, it seems that the Anglo-American countries have somewhat returned to the path which the *Donaldson* and *Wheaton* decisions blocked off so rigorously. In conformity with the 1908 Berlin revision[95] of the Berne Convention to which the United Kingdom had become a party in 1887, the British Copyright Act of 1911 shifted the starting point of protection from the moment of first publication to the moment of creation and abolished all formalities to which copyright protection was subject. The 1988 British Copyright, Designs and Patents Act of 1988 for the first time

---

88. *Cf.* Estate of Hemingway v. Random House, 23 N.Y.2d 341, 244 N.E.2d 250, 296 N.Y.S.2d 771 (1968): 'Common-law copyright is the term applied to an author's proprietary interest in his literary or artistic creations before they have been made generally available to the public. It enables the author to exercise control over the first publication of his work or to prevent publication entirely - hence, its other name, the "right of first publication".'

89. § 2 U.S. Copyright Act 1909: Nothing in this title shall be construed to annul or limit the right of the author or proprietor of an unpublished work, at common law or in equity, to prevent the copying, publication, or use of such unpublished work without his consent, and to obtain damages therefor.

90. *See* Bowker, at 4, 34.

91. *See* Patterson, at 18.

92. § 26 U.S. Copyright Act 1909.

93. *See* Bleistein v. Donaldson Lithographing Co., 188 U.S. 239, 248 (1903): 'There was evidence warranting the inference that the designs belonged to the plaintiffs, they having been produced by persons employed and paid by the plaintiffs in their establishment to make those very things.' *See also* Colliery Engineer Co., v. United Correspondence Schools Co. et al., 96 F. 152, 153 (C.C.S.D.N.Y. 1889): 'It seems equally clear that, under this contract, which made it Ewald's duty while a salaried employé of complainant, inter alia, to compile, prepare, and revise the instruction and question papers, the literary product of such work became the property of complainant, which it was entitled to copyright, and which, when copyrighted, Ewald would have no more right than any stranger to copy or reproduce.' *See also infra* 2.14.

94. Locke, Second Treatise, Chapter V, § 28. *See supra* note 83 and accompanying text.

95. *See* Ricketson, at 87-96.

grants moral rights protection to authors of literary, dramatical, musical and artistic works and to directors of films, albeit still with many exceptions.[96]

In American copyright law, a similar development seems to have set in with the adoption of the Copyright Act of 1976 and the U.S. adherence to the Berne Convention in 1989.[97] Under the 1976 Act, the number of cases in which the creator is not the first copyright owner has been considerably reduced in comparison to the situation under the 1909 Act.[98] The exceptions to the creator doctrine that still exist, however, are not likely to disappear completely in the near future. Both Congress and the Supreme Court recently reiterated that the primary objective of copyright law is not to reward the labour of authors, but to 'promote the Progress of Science and useful Arts'.[99] As long as this constitutional purpose remains the primary justification for copyright protection, the 'creator' doctrine will not be as imperative as it would be if a reward for labour or the bond between creator and work were considered the primary justification for copyright protection.[100]

Although the first continental-European copyright statutes also intended to stimulate the dissemination of knowledge and culture, the idea of a natural law-based right to published works was not resisted as strongly as in England and the United States.[101] Continental-European courts, doctrine and legislators continued to elaborate on this concept, with the result that statutory copyright protection is now, more than in the Anglo-American countries, perceived as a recognition and

---

96. §§ 77-83, 86-89, 94, 95 BCA. For a critical discussion, see Ginsburg, *Moral Rights*, at 128-129.

97. *See infra* 2.14.

98. *See infra* 2.14.

99. Feist Publications, Inc. v. Rural Telephone Service Company, Inc., 111 S.Ct. 1282 (1991). *See also* House Report to the Berne Convention Implementation Act of 1988, H.R. Rep. No. 100-609, 100th Cong., 2d Sess., 22 (1988).

100. *See infra* 2.14. In English copyright law, legislative discretion in defining authorship has even increased with the adoption of the 1988 Act. According to this Act, authorship may extend to sound recordings, typographical arrangements of works, broadcasts, cable programmes and computer-generated works, i.e. works generated by computer in circumstances such that there is no human author (§ 178 BCA). Author of a sound recording, film or computer-generated work is the person by whom the arrangements necessary for the creation of the work are undertaken (§§ 9(2)(a), 9(3) BCA). Author of a broadcast is the person making the broadcast (§ 9(2)(b) BCA), while the author of a cable programme is the person providing the cable programme service in which the programme is included (§ 9(2)(c) BCA). Author of the typographical edition of a work is the publisher (§ 9(2)(d) BCA). For critical comments, see Ricketson, *People or Machines*, at 29.

101. Compare the policies underlying the protection accorded by the Publication of the Government of the Batavian Republic of July 3, 1803 to the person who first published a literary work and who had obtained the right of copy thereto: promoting the enlightenment of the sciences and securing that the book trade is not restricted more than is strictly necessary for maintaining every person's legal right of property. *See* Memorandum of the Government of the Batavian Republic of January 10, 1803 to the legislative body of the Batavian Commonwealth, discussed by De Beaufort (1909), at 41. *See also infra* 2.15.

elaboration of an author's natural[102] or human[103] right to the economic and moral fruits of his creation.

In certain respects, this natural law approach to author's rights goes further than Locke's concept of natural property rights. For Locke, qualifying property as a natural right was not an end in itself, but a means of curtailing the power of absolutist monarchs. He furthermore believed that property only existed in sofar as there was enough left over for others.[104] The idea that the natural scope of author's rights is *limited* rather than *determined* by the public interest,[105] therefore does not go back to Locke.[106]

Other differences concern the first owner and the alienability of the right. According to the natural law approach to author's rights, statutory protection can only vest in the originator of the intellectual creation, whereas Locke had argued that the result of a servant's labour belongs to his master.[107] Locke also argued that, in the nature of things, a man does not need more property than he needs for his own survival and that he is robbing others if he takes more. He however recognized that society had come to agree that a person could own more than he could consume in exchange for money.[108] By allowing goods to be exchanged for money, Locke recognized that property in the results of labour is alienable. As Peter Laslett stated in his comment on Locke: 'We cannot alienate any part of our personalities, but we can alienate that with which we have chosen to mix our personalities.'[109] This probably explains best why, in some systems, author's rights are not considered to be completely alienable like property in tangibles and why such rights can only vest in the actual creator: because there is more of a

---

102. *See* Françon, at 10; Hubmann, at 47, 54, 75; Schricker/Loewenheim, at 205; Ulmer, at 65. In Dutch doctrine, De Beaufort (1909), at 85, and Meijers, Hand. II, 1952-1953, at 2918 (10 September 1953), make explicit reference to natural law.

103. *See* Memorandum to the EC Council Directive on rental right, lending right, and on certain rights related to copyright, COM(90) 586 final - SYN 319, 41 (1991); Dietz, *The concept of author*, at 44; Hirsch Ballin, at 42; Klaver, at 125; Smit, at 1068; Woltring, *Wetenschapsbeoefening*, at 68, all referring to Article 27(2) of the Universal Declaration on Human Rights, according to which every man has a right to obtain protection for the moral and economic interests resulting from the creation of scientific, literary and artistic works. *See also* Ricketson, *People or Machines*, at 34 and Dietz, *Thesen*, at 24, referring to Article 15(1)(c) of the International Covenant on Economic, Social and Cultural Rights, providing that the parties to the Covenant recognize every man's right to benefit from the protection of the moral and material fruits of any scientific, literary or artistic work of which he is the author.

104. Locke, Second Treatise, Chapter V, § 27.

105. *See* Judgment of May 18, 1955, BGH, Germany, 20 UFITA 314, 324, 325 (1955) (Gema v. Grundig), discussed *infra* 2.9. *See also* Hirsch Ballin, at 166; Nordemann, at 38, 53; Schricker, at 56; Ulmer, at 6-7.

106. Compare Article 27 of the Universal Declaration on Human Rights, providing in subsection 1 that everyone has a right to participate in the cultural life of the community, to enjoy the arts and to share in the benefits of scientific advancement, to be followed in subsection 2 by the provision that everyone has the right to the protection of the moral and material interests resulting from any scientific, literary or artistic production of which he is the author. Grosheide, at 292: not the isolated individual, but the collectivity of individuals is at the centre of Article 27.

107. *See supra* note 83 and accompanying text.

108. Locke, Second Treatise, Chapter V, §§ 46-51.

109. Laslett, in: Locke, at 116.

man's personality in the results of his intellectual labour, than there is in the grain which he has harvested or in the bread he has baked.[110]

Although discernible in every modern continental-European statute on author's rights, this view of an intellectual creation as something personal to the creator has not been elaborated uniformly. While the author's right is generally believed to encompass economic and moral attributes, differences occur with respect to the alienability of the author's right. For a better understanding of the various approaches, I will first discuss three 18th and 19th century theories which have influenced the development of the modern continental-European theories on author's rights.[111] All three theories presuppose that a creator has an exclusive right to control the use of his work, but differ on the place which this right should occupy in the system of civil law.

2.9 Property rights

Ever since protection other than by privileges was first contemplated, theorists in civil law countries have tried to classify this protection under existing civil law concepts. The first attempt, as we have seen, was to qualify literary works as property.[112] Although efforts were made from the outset to distinguish 'literary property' from the public domain,[113] the threat of monopolization proved to be too great to accept intellectual creations as property without restriction.[114] Even the French revolutionaries, who saw property as a key to civil liberty, issued decrees to specify what prerogatives literary property gave to authors and for

---

110. Bowker, at 3-4: 'If Farmer Jones does not raise potatoes from a piece of land, Farmer Smith can; but Shakespeare cannot write "Paradise Lost" nor Milton "Much Ado" ... It was the very self of each, *in propria persona*, that gave these form and worth, though they used words that had come down from generations as the common heritage of English-speaking men.' *See also* Kuypers, at 10; Wijnstroom/Peremans, at 8, both arguing that the bond between the creator and his work constitutes an independent justification for author's rights. *But see* Kohler, at 201 and De Beaufort (1932), at 54, endorsing the application of the master and servant principle to works of authorship in spite of their natural right approach to authors' rights. Their view on the nature of the author's right differs from most modern continental-European theories, however, in that they regard the author's right as an economic right, which is not specifically directed at the author's intellectual interests in the work. *See infra* 2.10-12.

111. For a more comprehensive discussion of these and other 18th and 19th century continental-European theories on the legal nature of author's rights, see e.g. De Beaufort (1909), 70-125; Grosheide, 146-168; Saunders, 109-121; Strömholm, I; Strowel, 97-106, 517-522.

112. *See supra* notes 49, 54, 62 and accompanying text. *See also* Bappert, at 266; Schricker/Vogel, at 77, 78.

113. For a discussion of eighteenth century authors who tried to define literary property (or in German doctrine: intellectual property) from the public domain, see Bappert, at 279, 280; De Beaufort (1909), at 111-113; Hesse, at 114-117; Schricker/Vogel, at 78.

114. *But see* Decree of November 27, 1795 of the Assembly of Provincial Representatives of the People of Holland, reprinted in: *Letterkundig Eigendomsrecht*, at 12, granting perpetual protection to publishers who had acquired the 'right of copy', in order to protect their 'lawful property'. Hirsch Ballin, at 17, characterizes this Decree as an expression of the ideas of the French Revolution, diverted into capitalistic channels under the influence of seventeenth century Dutch calvinism.

how long.[115] This same notion of property as a guarantee for personal freedom,[116] rather than as property in the legal sense, explains why the French Law of March 11, 1957 still refers to 'literary and artistic property',[117] whereas in many other countries such as Germany and the Netherlands, the incompatibility of intellectual creations with the absolute, perpetual nature of property has caused the term 'literary property' to disappear from statutory language long ago.[118]

But even here, 'property' is still used in its 'emotive meaning', i.e. as a reference to the strongest legal position possible.[119] In German case law and doctrine, the term 'intellectual property' every now and then crops up to express the notion that the economic protection of authors is not necessarily restricted to the rights defined in the statute, but should, where possible, extend to any use.[120] In a post-war upheaval of the natural law theory, the Bundesgerichtshof in a 1955 decision extended the economic protection of authors beyond the scope defined in the statute, stating that an author's control over his work is not attributed to him by the legislator, but follows from the nature of things, from his intellectual property, of which the statute is merely a recognition and elaboration.[121] This fundamental right to the economic fruits of an author's intellectual

---

115. *See supra* text accompanying notes 71-76.

116. *See* Grosheide, at 295: the primary meaning of the qualification of authors' rights as 'property' is the protection of the results of intellectual labour from government interference.

117. § 1(1) of the Law of March 11, 1957 on literary and artistic property provides that the author of a work of the mind enjoys, by sole virtue of its creation, an exclusive, incorporeal right of property in his work, that is opposable to others. This right involves attributes of an intellectual and moral nature, as well as attributes of an economic nature, that are determined by this Act. To emphasize every person's freedom to express his personality in a work of authorship, the 1957 Act furthermore provides that the enjoyment of the rights recognized in § 1(1) is not in any way affected by the existence of an employment contract or a contract of commission (§ 1(2) FCA).

118. Although the Constitution of 1871 gave the German Reich legislative authority to regulate the protection of 'intellectual property', all German legislation which has been adopted since, refers to 'Urheberrecht' rather than to intellectual property. According to the German system of civil law, the term 'property' is reserved for tangible objects. In the Netherlands, the term 'literary property' was last used in statutory language in the Decree of January 24, 1814, no. 1, S. 17, concerning provisions on the book trade and property in literary works. Under the old Civil Code, author's rights were qualified as moveable goods (§ 2(1) DCA (1912); § 559 BW (old)), but under the new Civil Code (effective January 1, 1992) the term 'property' is reserved for tangible objects (§ 3:1; § 5:1 BW) and author's rights are qualified as patrimonial (economic) rights.

119. Grosheide, at 273. Troller, I, at 91, uses the term 'intellectual property' to express an author's power to control the use of his work ('Herrschaftsmacht'), both with respect to his economic as well as to his intellectual interests. Compare also Cohen Jehoram, *Opportuniteit*, at 65, arguing that the notion of property can adequately express an author's encompassing claim to economic protection as recognized by the Hoge Raad in its Judgment of June 22, 1990, NJ 1991, 268 note Spoor ('Zienderogen Kunst'). *But see* Verkade, *Rechtsbeginselen*, at 147, arguing that the reward-concept is not strong enough in Dutch law to speak of a general legal principle on the basis of which an author has the right to claim protection of his economic interests.

120. *See* Hubmann, at 57; Nordemann, at 52; Schricker, at 58; Ulmer, at 108.

121. Judgment of May 18, 1955, BGH Germany, 20 UFITA 314, 323 (1955) (Gema v. Grundig). *But see* Hirsch, at 15, arguing with reference to the *Donaldson v. Becket* and *Wheaton v. Peters* decisions (*supra* notes 56, 62), that the court has exceded its discretion in determining the scope of protection with respect to published works. More positively: Von Gamm, at 73-78; Hubmann, at 47, 54; Schricker, at 58; Schulze, at 47; Ulmer, at 108.

25

creation is also protected as 'property' under Article 14 of the German Constitution.[122] Although primarily intended for defining the scope of protection in relation to the public interest, some German commentators have also invoked the notion of 'intellectual property' and the constitutional guarantee of property to support legislation on author's contracts aimed at ensuring that creators adequately participate in the proceeds from the exploitation of their works.[123]

There is yet another aspect of the qualification of intellectual creations as the subject matter of a property right which requires mention. The ultimate consequence of property in an intellectual creation implies that transferring the manuscript does not, in itself, transfer the property in the intellectual creation. Although not yet recognized by statute or case law, this distinction between property in the manuscript and property in the intellectual creation inspired theorists to argue that an author might retain control over his work while authorizing others to exploit it at the same time. One of the early protagonists of this concept was the German scholar Johann Gottlieb Fichte, who, in a 1793 article, argued that an author has an inalienable and exclusive right to his intellectual property, i.e. the form in which he has expressed his thoughts, and that it would suffice for a book to be published that the author granted the publisher the usufruct of his intellectual property.[124]

The idea that an author does not relinquish all his rights upon handing over the manuscript to the publisher, gave authors a personal interest in the discussion on piracy of books, whereas, before, their role had been mainly to justify the protection of publishers.[125] It was not until the beginning of this century, however, before courts and legislators fully recognized that the transfer of an unpublished manuscript does not imply an assignment of the author's right.[126]

---

122. *See* Judgment of July 7, 1971, BVerfG, Germany, 63 UFITA 279 (1972) ('collections for church and educational use'). Article 14 of the Constitution also protects the interests of performing artists and producers of phonograms, but this protection is less extensive than the protection granted to authors. According to the court, authors perform creative labour, whereas the labour of performing artists is 're-creative' and the activities of producers of phonograms are of a technical and organizational nature. *See* Judgment of July 8, 1971, BVerfG, Germany, 63 UFITA 306, 316 (1972) ('Bearbeiter-Urheberrecht'); Judgment of October 3, 1989, BVerfG, Germany, 92 GRUR 183, 185 (1990) ('"no rental" reservation').

123. *See* Katzenberger, at 410, 411. *See also* Wandtke, at 140, arguing that the theory of intellectual property as adopted by the Bundesgerichtshof is a decisive step towards an author's claim for remuneration on the basis of copyright law. *See also infra* 2.13.

124. Fichte, 'Beweis der Unrechtmäßigkeit des Büchernachdrucks', 21 *Berlinische Monatschrift* 443, 457 (1793), discussed in Bappert, at 270; De Beaufort (1909), at 111; Schricker/Vogel, at 78.

125. For a sceptical view on the effects this development has had on the position of authors in relation to their publishers, see Dommering, at 10: the replacement of the printing privilege by a right which referred to an author's intellectual creation created a permanent conflict between authors and those who produce and distribute their works. While the author became the first owner of the right in a legal sense, the publisher remained its main economic beneficiary. *Id.*

126. In Germany, the distinction between the author's right and ownership of the original copy of the work was first recognized by the Law of 9 January 1907 concerning author's rights to artistic and photographical works, and was later extended to all categories of works. According to § 44(1) GCA, an author, by handing over the original copy of a work, is not presumed in case of doubt to have granted a right to use the work embodied in it. The Dutch Copyright Act of 1912 does not contain a similar provision, but § 2(2) DCA stipulates that full or partial assignments must be effected in a written instrument. *See infra* 2.15.

2.10 Immaterialgüterrecht

In 1880, the German professor Josef Kohler published a treatise in which he emphasized the incorporeal nature of literary works and elaborated on the relationship between authors and publishers.[127] Although he acknowledged that author's rights and patents were based on the same basic assumptions as property in corporeal goods, Kohler qualified author's rights and patents as 'rights to incorporeal goods' ('Immaterialgüterrechte'), a new category which would seem to assume a position beside property in the system of civil law.[128] Rationale for these rights to incorporeal goods was Locke's labour theory: every man has a natural right to the goods he creates.[129] In line with the labour theory, Kohler argued that an author's right vests in the creator or, if the creator has put his intellectual labour at another's disposal, in that other person.[130] He made a distinction between commissioned works and works made in the course of employment, arguing that an artist who makes a painting or sculpture on commission has an obligation to deliver a work, not to put his labour at the disposal of someone else.[131]

Kohler saw a publisher as an intermediary between an author and the public, rather than as a successor in title.[132] He argued that a publisher who undertakes the contractual obligation to publish a work does not become owner of the author's right, but acquires an exclusive, enforceable right to use the work.[133] This 'publishing right' ('Verlagsrecht') could be limited in scope, duration and territory[134] and would only be transferable as part of a transfer of the publisher's entire business.[135] A modified version of this 'publishing right' has been incorporated in the German Publishing Act of 1901, which is still in force today.[136]

2.11 Persönlichkeitsrecht

In his 1895 treatise on civil law, the German scholar Otto von Gierke categorized author's rights among the 'rights of personality' ('Persönlichkeitsrechte').[137] Although the term 'Persönlichkeitsrecht' has often been used to refer to an

---

127. Kohler, at 1 *passim*.
128. *Id.* at 1, 2. Kohler's theory has been prominently advocated by the Dutch scholar De Beaufort in his 1909 treatise on author's right. De Beaufort (1909), at 78, 122.
129. Kohler, at 98.
130. *Id.* at 201. *See also* De Beaufort (1932), at 54.
131. Kohler, at 202. In his view, the author's right vests in the commissioning party only if the work depicts his life or portrait. *Id.* at 202, 203.
132. *Id.* at 285.
133. *Id.* at 283.
134. *Id.* at 292.
135. *Id.* at 286.
136. Law of 19 June 1901, RGBl. p. 217, on publishing right, as amended by the Act on Author's Right and Related Rights of 9 September 1965, BGBl. p. 1273. *See infra* 2.13; 4.3.
137. Von Gierke, at 705.

author's intellectual, immaterial interests in relation to his work,[138] Von Gierke used the term to indicate that an author has an exclusive right to control the publication and reproduction of his creation as being a part of his personal sphere.[139] He argued that, by exercising the right to decide if and how his work should be disclosed to the public, an author would be able to enjoy the intellectual and economic fruits of the publication of his work.[140] This view of an author's right as protecting both his intellectual and economic interests must be understood in the light of his statement that certain 'Persönlichkeitsrechte' may coincide with economic rights ('Immaterialgüterrechte'), but that these economic rights should not be considered to prevail, or to be wholly separate from the 'Persönlichkeitsrecht'.[141]

In his perception of the relationship between an author's economic and intellectual interests, Von Gierke differs from his contemporaries Kohler and De Beaufort, who saw the author's right as a patrimonial right and who argued that an author's intellectual interests are protected by his 'individual right'.[142] Although they acknowledged that certain acts may infringe on an author's individual right as well as on his patrimonial right,[143] they made a point of presenting them as separate rights with different characteristics: the author's right as a right to an incorporeal good detached from its creator, and an individual right as a right to personal goods, which exists regardless of the existence, duration and validity of the author's right.[144]

2.12   The monistic v. the dualistic concept of the author's right

By the time the Berne Union for the Protection of Literary and Artistic Works was founded in 1886,[145] most continental-European countries had statutorily recognized an author's exclusive right to his literary or artistic work. The limited protection which these statutes afforded to an author's intellectual, non-pecuniary

---

138. Compare Ulmer, at 111, stating that 'Persönlichkeitsrechte' generally serve to protect intellectual interests, whereas an author's right also serves to protect the author's economic interests.
139. Von Gierke, at 702, 748. *See also* Troller, I, at 87: von Gierke designated the author's right as a 'Persönlichkeitsrecht' to indicate that a work originates in a person, but he regarded it as a right to an incorporeal good and distinguished it from other 'Persönlichkeitsrechte' such as the right to one's life, honour and reputation.
140. Von Gierke, at 759.
141. Von Gierke, at 259.
142. De Beaufort (1909), at 121-125; (1932), at 25 ('persoonlijkheidsrecht'). Kohler, at 123 ('Individualrecht').
143. De Beaufort (1909), at 125; Kohler, at 156.
144. De Beaufort (1909), at 125; Kohler, at 154, 155.
145. *See generally* Ricketson, 3-125.

interests in relation to his work, was complemented by judicial protection.[146] This protection of what came to be known as the author's 'droit moral'[147] was recognized in 1928 by the inclusion in the Berne Convention of the rights of ((attribution and integrity, i.e. the right of the author, even after the transfer of his economic rights, to claim authorship of the work and to object to any distortion, mutilation or other derogatory action in relation to the work which would be prejudicial to his honour or reputation (Article 6bis BC).[148] Although the Convention did not require these rights to be part of the author's right,[149] the doctrine continued to elaborate on the idea that the author's right should protect not only an author's economic interests, but also his intellectual interests in relation to the work.[150] Two mainstream theories developed as a result, and most modern continental-European copyright laws are based on these: the monistic and the dualistic concept of author's right.

According to the monistic or unitary concept of the author's right adopted in the Austrian[151] and German Copyright Acts,[152] Kohler's dual concept of author's right and individual right is rejected by arguing that it is impossible to distinguish between the protection of an author's economic and intellectual interests.[153] The author's right therefore cannot be qualified as either a patrimonial or a personal right. Rather, the author's right is conceived as a *sui generis* right, a unitary, encompassing right of the author to claim protection for his intellectual and economic interests in the work.[154] Because of the inextricable link with the economic interests, it is only fully possible to guarantee an author protection of his personal and intellectual interests ('Urheberpersönlichkeitsrecht') if the unity of the author's right is maintained.[155] The author's right as a whole as well as the exploitation rights and moral rights which constitute a part thereof, are therefore considered to be inalienable during an author's lifetime.[156] Exploitation

---

146. *See e.g.* Judgment of June 8, 1912, RG, Germany, RG 79, 397 (1912) ('Felseneiland mit Sirenen'), in which the German Reichsgericht upheld a claim against a defendant who commissioned a painter to repaint naked sirens which were part of a mural made by the plaintiff on the defendant's commission. For a discussion of early French and German case law, see e.g. Dietz (1968) 15-21; Gerbrandy (1988), 285-286; Quaedvlieg, 1-5; Strömholm, I; Strowel, 482-489, 522-527; Saunders, 102-105.

147. On the terms 'droit moral', 'moral rights' and 'rights of personality', see Kernochan IV, at 103-104; Quaedvlieg, at 2 n. 3; Saunders, at 120-121. Kernochan IV, at 103, argues that the reluctance of the American courts to accept the notion of 'droit moral' partly results from the fact that 'moral' in English refers to what is right and wrong in behaviour.

148. Rome Act 1928. *See also infra* 5.5, 5.6.

149. *See* Ricketson, at 475.

150. *See* Dietz (1968), 15-21; Strömholm, I, 438-490.

151. Federal Law No. 375 of 9 April 1936 on Author's Rights in Literary and Artistic Works and on Related Rights, öst. BGBl. Nr. 111.

152. *See infra* 2.13.

153. Ulmer, at 114.

154. Ulmer, at 113, 118.

155. Ulmer, at 357.

156. Ulmer, at 114, 207, 357. § 29 GCA; § 23 ACA. The Swiss Copyright Act of 9 October 1992 also underlies a monistic view on author's right. However, while the early drafts were based on the concept of an inalienable author's right, the final text provides that the author's rights are fully alienable (§ 16(1) SCA). Dessemontet, at 184, mentions that some Swiss theorists have interpreted this provision so as to imply that the 'droit moral' is susceptible to transfer,

of the work is not based on a transfer of ownership, but on a grant by the author of an exclusive or non-exclusive right to use the work in a particular way.[157] The unity of the author's right is furthermore maintained in the term of protection: the exploitation rights and the moral rights expire simultaneously.[158]

According to the dualistic concept of the author's right as elaborated in the French Law of March 11, 1957, the author's right also protects an author's economic and intellectual interests in relation to the work. Unlike the monistic theory, however, the economic interests are considered to be protected by alienable, patrimonial rights, whereas the intellectual, non-economic interests are protected by inalienable and unwaivable personal rights, springing from the author's 'droit moral'.[159] Since an author's personality is considered to live on through his works, the 'droit moral' is perpetual and, therefore, survives the limited exploitation monopoly.[160] The 'droit moral' also precedes the exploitation monopoly, because the exploitation monopoly only arises if the author, by exercising his right to first publication ('droit de divulgation'), decides to disclose his work to the public.[161] The 'droit moral' furthermore prevails over the exploitation monopoly in that it allows the author to withdraw or modify the work after indemnifying the assignee.[162]

Most continental-European statutes on author's rights[163] follow the dualistic concept in that they provide that the author's right encompasses inalienable moral rights and alienable rights of exploitation.[164] Differences exist, however, with respect to the scope of the moral rights and the formal requirements to which a transfer of exploitation rights is subject (written instrument, notarial act, specification in the agreement of the modes of exploitation, etc.).

2.13 The creator doctrine in German copyright law

While, under the German Acts of 1901[165] and 1907,[166] the author's right was still fully transferable[167] and did not in all cases vest in the actual creator,[168]

---

while others have argued that this provision merely implies that the author can authorize others to bring moral rights actions on the author's or on their own behalf.

157. §§ 29(2), 31 GCA; §§ 23(2), 24 ACA. *See also infra* 2.13.
158. Ulmer, at 115. § 60 ACA: 70 years *p.m.a.* § 64 GCA: 70 years *p.m.a.*
159. Desbois, at 470. § 1(2), 6 FCA.
160. Desbois, at 470.
161. *Id.* at 276, 468.
162. *Id.* at 276, 469. § 32 FCA.
163. *See generally* Dietz (1978); Dietz (1984); Dietz (1989).
164. *See e.g.* §§ 9(1), 40, 43(1), 44 Portuguese Law No. 63/1985 of 14 March 1985 on Author's Rights and Related Rights; §§ 1, 14(1), 43(1) Spanish Law No. 22/1987 of 11 November 1987 on Intellectual Property. On the relationship between the economic and moral rights in Dutch copyright law, see *infra* 2.15.
165. Law of 10 June 1901 relating to author's rights in literary, musical and dramatical works, RGBl. 227.
166. Law of 9 January 1907 relating to author's rights in artistic and photographical works, RGBl.7.
167. § 8 Law of 19 June 1901; § 10 Law of 9 January 1907.

the German Copyright Act of 1965, with its monistic concept of author's rights, can be qualified as the ultimate manifestation of the creator doctrine.[169] The author's right vests upon creation and remains vested in the author until his death, after which it passes to his heirs or testamentary beneficiaries.[170] The 'author' ('Urheber') is defined as the 'creator of the work' (§ 7 GCA), and if a work is created jointly by two or more persons and their individual contributions cannot be exploited in isolation from each other, they are considered to be co-authors of the work (§ 8(1) GCA).[171] A 'work' is a 'personal, intellectual creation' (§ 2(2) GCA), a perceptible expression of individual,[172] intellectual and human[173] activity.

The author's right protects the author in his personal, intellectual bond with the work ('Urheberpersönlichkeitsrecht') as well as in respect of the exploitation of the work (§ 11 GCA). This protection is elaborated in a non-limitative list of moral rights,[174] exclusive exploitation rights[175] and a number of remuneration rights,[176] all of which remain with the author throughout his life. A producer therefore cannot acquire title by means of a transfer of ownership of one of these rights.[177] Instead, the author may grant an exclusive or non-exclusive right to use the work in a certain way ('Einräumung von Nutzungsrechten').[178] An exclusive right to use a work authorizes the owner to sue for infringement independently,[179] while the owner of a non-exclusive right to use a work is dependent on the cooperation of the author or the owner of an exclusive right-to-

---

168. Public bodies which published a work without identifying an author, were considered to be the author of that work (§ 3 Law of 10 June 1901; § 5 Law of 9 January 1907). The editor was considered author in the case of collective works. If the work did not specify an editor, the publisher would be considered to be the editor (§ 4 Law of 10 June 1901; § 6 Law of 9 January 1907).

169. See Dietz, *Thesen*, at 18.

170. §§ 28, 29 GCA.

171. See also *infra* 3.2.2; 3.3.2.

172. See Judgment of February 28, 1991, BGH, Germany, 35 GRUR 425 (1991) ('technical drawings'): a technical drawing may be protected if it reflects an individual, intellectual activity and, as such, distinguishes itself from the everyday production of technical drawings. See also Schricker/Loewenheim, at 97; Ulmer, at 133: 'personal, intellectual creation' presupposes a certain scope for personal input.

173. See Judgment of May, 30, 1989, LG Berlin, Germany, 92 GRUR 270 (1990) ('satellite photograph'): 'Author' in the sense of § 2 GCA can only be a natural person, because only a natural person is capable of personal, intellectual creation. See also Nordemann/Vinck, at 57; Schricker/Loewenheim, at 91, 206.

174. § 12 GCA: right of first publication; § 13: right of attribution; § 14: right of integrity; § 39 GCA: the owner of a right to use a work is only entitled to alter the work if the author cannot reasonably refuse it; § 42 GCA: right of withdrawal in case of changed conviction. See also *infra* 5.4; 5.5.1; 5.6.1.

175. §§ 15-24 GCA. *Cf.* Memorandum to 1965 Act, 45 UFITA 241 (1966): it is a basic principle of the law on author's rights to define an author's exclusive rights in such a way that an author is able to control, where possible, every use of his work.

176. §§ 26, 37, 46, 47, 49, 52, 54 GCA.

177. Although remuneration rights are inalienable, actual remuneration claims, including future claims, seem to be transferable under the terms of § 398 BGB. See Hubmann, at 203; Rossbach, at 117; Schricker, at 414.

178. § 31(1) GCA.

179. § 97 GCA. Ulmer, at 368. See also *infra* 3.3.7.

use to redress infringement.[180] Unless agreed otherwise, the owner of a right-to-use can only transfer this right to a third party with the author's consent.[181] If the reason why such a right-to-use was granted has ceased to exist, e.g. if the underlying contractual relationship has been terminated, the right-to-use automatically reverts to the author, and the latter's right then regains its full strength.[182] And if a work no longer reflects the author's convictions, so that he cannot be expected to tolerate its continued exploitation, he may withdraw the right to use the work in return for compensating the owner (§ 42 GCA). The object of this system is to ensure that creators can retain control over their works after they have delegated the exploitation to someone else.[183]

The purpose of enabling a creator to retain the greatest degree of control possible over his work not only serves to protect his intellectual interests in the work after he has delegated the exploitation to a producer, but also to ensure that he can share in the proceeds from exploitation as adequately as possible (*participation principle*).[184] To this end, the 1965 Act contains a number of provisions on the scope and duration of rights-to-use, the most important of which is the provision that the scope of a grant must be determined according to its purpose in case the uses which the grant is supposed to include have not been defined separately in the agreement (§ 31(5) GCA).[185] This *purpose transfer rule* ('Zweckübertragung'), which is complemented by the provision that grants of rights to unknown uses are void (§ 31(4) GCA), provides courts with a

---

180. In this respect, a non-exclusive right to use a work resembles a contractual license to use a work in a manner which would otherwise constitute an infringement. Unlike a mere contractual license, however, a non-exclusive right-to-use may be invoked against a third party to whom the creator subsequently grants an exclusive right-to-use (§ 33 GCA). *See also infra* 3.3.7. On the nature of non-exclusive rights-to-use, see Nordemann/Hertin, at 199; Ulmer, at 368.

181. §§ 31(1), 31(4) GCA. An author's consent is not required if the right-to-use is granted in conjunction with a right to use a collective work in which the work has been incorporated (§ 34(2) GCA) or together with the business of the owner of the right-to-use (§ 34(3) GCA). If the author's consent is not required in law or under the agreement, the transferee is liable for the obligations arising from the agreement between the author and the first owner of the right-to-use (§ 34(5) GCA). *See also infra* 3.3.7.

182. Explicitly, § 9(1) Publishing Act 1901, stipulating that the 'publishing right' arises upon the handing over of the work and expires when the publishing relationship ends. Nordemann/Hertin, at 173; Schricker, at 424; Ulmer, at 359, also recognize the dependency of a right-to-use on the underlying contractual relationship in respect of contracts other than publishing contracts.

183. Memorandum to 1965 Act, 45 UFITA 243 (1966).

184. Judgment of April 23, 1954, BGH, Germany, 18 UFITA 206 (1954) ('theatrical performance contract'); Judgment of May 18, 1955, BGH, Germany, 20 UFITA 314 (1955) (Gema v. Grundig); Judgment of July 7, 1971, BVerfGE, 63 UFITA 279 (1972) ('collections for church and educational use'). *See also supra* 2.9.

185. *Cf.* Judgment of April 26, 1974, BGH, Germany, 72 UFITA 324 (1975) ('Anneliese Rothenberger'); Judgment of November 7, 1975, BGH, Germany, 78 UFITA 179 (1977) ('Kaviar'): purpose transfer rule is designed to secure the author a possibly extensive participation in the economic exploitation of his works. Section 37 GCA provides that, in case of doubt, (1) a grant of a right to use a work does not include the right to exploit adaptations, (2) a grant of a right to use a work does not include the right to record the work by mechanical means, and (3) a grant of a right to publicly perform a work does not entitle the grantee to publicly perform the work by technical means outside the premises for which the right has been granted. About the relationship between § 31(5) and § 37, see *infra* 6.2.2.

considerable scope for weighing up the interests of the creator and producer in a particular case.[186]

To prevent creators from committing themselves to one producer for the rest of their creative lifes, grants of rights to future works which are unspecified or merely indicated by a category must be in writing and may be cancelled by either party after five years (§ 40 GCA).[187] If the owner of a right-to-use does not exploit the work or exploits it inadequately and, by doing so, considerably prejudices the author's interests, the author has the right to withdraw the right-to-use in return for compensating the owner, provided that the inadequate exploitation is not due to circumstances within the author's control (§ 41 GCA). As ultimate remedy to secure adequate participation, the author has an unwaivable right to demand an adjustment of his contract with the producer in case the actual revenues of exploitation turn out to be grossly disproportionate to the negotiated remuneration (§ 36 GCA).[188]

Although adequate participation is considered by German doctrine as a major purpose of legislation on author's rights,[189] the German legislator has not undertaken additional action in respect of contracts between creators and producers. In 1989, the federal government took the position that the existing provisions in the 1965 Act provide creators with sufficient safeguards, and that creators should seek to further strengthen their position in the collective administration of their rights and in collective agreements.[190]

In view of the purpose transfer rule (§ 31(5) GCA), a producer has most certainty on the scope and exclusivity of his rights if he opts for a written agreement detailing every mode of exploitation. A failure to make such an express agreement however does not necessarily leave the producer without any

---

186. *See e.g.* Judgment of March 20, 1986, BGH, Germany, 88 GRUR 885 (1986) ('Metaxa'): the purpose of the agreement must be determined according to the circumstances of the case and in consideration of principles of good faith and trade practice. *See also* Schricker, at 477. *But see* Nordemann/Hertin, at 205: trade practice can not be construed as reflecting the parties' intention at the time of contracting.

187. *See infra* 3.3.4.

188. Judgment of June 27, 1991, BGH, Germany, 93 GRUR 901 (1991) ('horoscope calendar'): the disproportionality between the negotiated remuneration and the exploitation revenues must be unexpected. This situation is presumed to exist if the negotiated remuneration considerably deviates from what would have been a modest compensation under the circumstances.

189. *See* Dietz, *Transformation of authors rights*, at 53; Katzenberger, at 410; Nordemann, *Vorschlag*, at 2; Schricker/v. Ungern-Sternberg, at 276.

190. Statement of the Federal Government on the effects of the 1985 revision of the copyright law and questions on author's and neighbouring rights law, July 7, 1989, 113 UFITA 242. In response to the German government's position, Nordemann proposed to amend the substantive provisions on author's contracts in the 1965 Act, as well as certain provisions in other statutes relating to author's contracts. Nordemann, *Vorschlag*, 1-10. According to this proposal, authors would have an unwaivable right to remuneration for every use of their work, unless this were grossly inappropriate under the circumstances, as may be the case in employment relationships directed at extensive exploitation of creative works in return for fixed, regular payments. The proposal furthermore includes a right to terminate a grant after 30 years, the exclusion of collective agreements in the field of author's rights from certain anti-trust provisions, as well as an obligation for collecting societies to distribute the largest part of the collected fees to authors and performers.

rights. A grant of a right-to-use is not subject to formalities[191] and, therefore, may be effected by oral agreement or even be inferred from the circumstances, as is generally considered to be the case in respect of works made by employees in the course of their employment.[192] In the absence of an express agreement, an employer is generally presumed to have acquired the rights necessary for his business purposes.[193] This presumption has not been codified, but is implied from the general provision that the provisions on contracts (§§ 28-44 GCA) are applicable to works created in the fulfilment of an employment contract, *unless the import and essence of the employment relationship determine otherwise* (§ 43 GCA).[194]

In the case of periodical collections and film works, the 1965 Act also accomodates producers, in that it makes presumptions on the scope and exclusivity of the rights granted to the publisher and film producer in case of doubt.[195] The 1901 Publishing Act furthermore stipulates that if a person undertakes to publish a literary, dramatical or musical work, he acquires an exclusive right to reproduce and distribute that work, including the right to sue in case of infringement ('publishing right').[196]

On top of these presumptions in favour of producers, the 1965 Act contains an elaborated system of rights related to author's rights ('verwandte Schutzrechte'). In the case of performances of works of authorship (§§ 73-84 GCA), scientific publications (§ 70 GCA) and photographs which do not qualify as a work of authorship (§ 72 GCA), a related right vests in the natural person who performs the labour: the performing artist, the writer, the photographer.[197] In the

---

191. A written agreement is only required in case of a grant of rights to use an unspecified, future work (§ 40 GCA). *See supra* note 187 and accompanying text. *See also infra* 3.3.4.

192. Memorandum to § 43 GCA, 45 UFITA 277 (1966).

193. *See* Judgment of October 26, 1951, BGH, Germany, 54 GRUR 257 (1952) ('patient card index'); Judgment of February 22, 1974, BGH, Germany, 76 GRUR 480 (1974) ('Hummelrechte'); Judgment of September 13, 1983, BAG, Germany, 86 GRUR 429, 431 (1984) note Ulmer ('statistical programs'); Judgment of February 6, 1985, BGH, Germany, 87 GRUR 529 (1985) ('Happening'); Judgment of May 27, 1987, OLG Karlsruhe, Germany, C&R 763, 767 (1987) ('computer program'). *See also* Memorandum to § 43 GCA, 45 UFITA 241 (1965); Dietz, *The Relation Employer - Employee*, at 38; Nordemann/Vinck, at 250; Rehbinder, *Recht am Arbeitsergebnis*, at 492, 494; Schricker/Rojahn, at 577; Ulmer, at 405. *But see* Judgment of September 27, 1990, BGH, Germany, 93 GRUR 523 (1991) ('excavation material'): if an employee performs research for and in the interest of the employer, the results of research must generally be submitted to the employer for use, but not in case of the university professor who may have a duty to perform research and to publish, but who is free to choose the subject matter of research and whose research is not subject to supervision and control ('Zweckfreie Forschung').

194. To implement the EC Council Directive of 14 May 1991 on the legal protection of computer programs, Off.J.Eur.Comm. No. L 122/42 (1991) [hereinafter: Software Directive], a new provision will be introduced that allocates exclusive exploitation rights to the employer in case of computer programs made in the course of employment.

195. §§ 38, 88, 89 GCA. *See infra* 4.3; 6.2.

196. §§ 1, 8, 9 Publishing Act of 1901. *See also infra* 4.3.

197. § 70 GCA ('Verfasser'); § 72 GCA ('Lichtbildner'); §§ 73 GCA ('ausübende Künstler'). If a performance has been made in order to fulfil the duties of an employment contract, the import and essence of the employment relationship determine the extent and conditions under which the employer may exploit the performance (§ 79 DCA). This is generally understood to imply that the employee, in the absence of an express agreement, has granted those rights which are necessary for the purpose of the employer's business. *See* Schricker/Rojahn, at 924. In the case of a performance by a choir, orchestra or theatre, the group's board or, in the absence of a

case of an edition of a posthumous public domain work (§ 71 GCA), the production of a sound recording (§ 85 GCA), a broadcast (§ 87 GCA) or the production of a film (§§ 94, 95 GCA),[198] a related right vests in the person *or* entity responsible for the activity.[199]

With the author's right as the creator's inalienable right, related rights for producers, and relatively extensive provisions on contracts, some of which are intended to protect the creator's and others the producer's interests, the German copyright law has a differentiated approach in balancing the interests of creators and producers. The collective administration of rights is an additional factor affecting the relationships between creators and producers. Under the 'Wahrnehmungsgesetz' of 1965,[200] which governs the activities of collecting societies on German territory, collecting societies have an obligation to distribute the fees collected according to fixed rules that prevent arbitrariness.[201] The Act does not specify, however, how the collected fees should be distributed in those cases in which a creator has granted exclusive rights to the collectively administrated mode of exploitation to a producer.[202] In 1987, the President of the German Patent Office stated as supervising authority[203] that collective administration is an independent means of realizing the principle of participation, especially with respect to additional uses which producers do not need in order to realize their commercial objectives, and that collecting societies should therefore distribute the royalties to creators and producers in an appropriate manner, irrespective of their individual contractual obligations.[204]

---

board of directors, the group's leader is authorized to exercise the group's rights (§ 80 GCA).

198. § 94 GCA: production of a film which qualifies as a work of authorship; § 95 GCA: production of a film which does not qualify as a work of authorship.

199. According to § 71 GCA, the related right to the edition of a posthumous work vests in the person 'who has the work published'. *See* Nordemann/Hertin, at 320; Schricker, at 853: § 71 GCA refers to the editor of the work, who or which may be a natural person or a legal entity. The related right to sound recordings vests in the producer of the phonorecord ('Hersteller des Tonträgers'), who or which may be the owner of an enterprise if the recording is made within that enterprise (§ 85 GCA). The related right to broadcasts vests in the broadcasting organization (§ 87 GCA). The related right to a film vests in the 'Hersteller' (§§ 94, 95 GCA), who or which is generally understood to be the owner of the enterprise if the film was made within that enterprise. *See* Nordemann/Hertin, at 276; Schricker/Katzenberger, at 1007. *See also infra* 7.6.

200. Law of 9 September 1965 on the administration of author's rights and related rights, BGBl. 1294 (WahrnG).

201. § 7 WahrnG.

202. A collecting society has an obligation to adequately represent the rightholders (§ 6 WahrnG). Schricker/Reinbothe, at 1355: 'rightholder' includes owners of rights-to-use. *But see* Nordemann, at 460, arguing that producers need not be included, because creators could entrust their rights to the collecting society just as easily.

203. §§ 18-20a WahrnG.

204. Letter of August 7, 1987, reprinted in: 33 ZUM 506, 508 (1989). *Cf. also* Dietz, *Transformation of authors rights*, at 55: 'Thus, in sense of the idea it embodies of a balance of interests, the law relating to collectives societies, with its distribution principles, goes beyond the conventional categories of contractual freedom in copyright and prevails over them.' On collective administration, see also *infra* 3.3.6; 6.4.

2.14 The creator doctrine in U.S. copyright law

The legislative authority of the U.S. Congress in the field of copyright law is enshrined in the U.S. Constitution: 'The Congress shall have Power...to promote the Progress of Science and useful Arts by securing for limited Times to Authors and Inventors the exclusive Right to their respective Writings and Discoveries.'[205] Like the first European copyright statutes, this clause reflects the idea that an exclusive right to literary works may serve the public interest by ensuring a broad dissemination of knowledge and culture, provided this right is limited in scope and duration.[206] Unlike most other countries, however, the United States has maintained this incentive rationale as the primary reason for copyright protection to this very day.[207] More than in countries with a prevailing natural right approach to author's rights, copyright legislation in the U.S. is therefore open to the argument that producers' interests must be taken into consideration in order to promote the production and dissemination of creative works.[208]

Because of the underlying incentive rationale, statutory copyright traditionally protects works from the moment they are made available to the public.[209] Under the 1909 Copyright Act, a producer could secure copyright protection in his own name by publishing a work with the required copyright notice,[210] provided he had acquired the common law copyright to the work.[211] An assignment of common law copyright did not need to be in writing and could be implied from the sale of the manuscript or original copy of the work.[212] In keeping with the common law presumption that the employer had the common law copyright to works made by an employee within the scope of an employment contract,[213] the 1909 Act designated the employer as 'author' in case of 'works

---

205. U.S. Const. art. I, § 8, cl. 8 (Patent-Copyright Clause).

206. *See supra* 2.7.

207. *See* Feist Publications, Inc. v. Rural Telephone Service Company, Inc., 111 S.Ct. 1282 (1991); Sony Corporation of America v. Universal Studios, Inc., 104 S.Ct. 774 (1984). H.R. Rep. No. 100-609, 100th Cong., 2d Sess., 22 (1988). As a result of this incentive rationale, American copyright doctrine, more than continental-European doctrine, focuses on the question whether copyright is necessary, i.e. whether it is the appropriate instrument for promoting the advancement of science and arts. *See* Breyer; Gordon; Landes/Posner.

208. *See* Curtis, at 818-819; Katzman, at 876-877; Ladd, at 93. For similar arguments in continental-European literature, see Asscher, *What publishers need*, at 12; Auf der Maur, at 66; Strowel, at 665. The argument of public availability every now and then crops up in case law on copyright ownership. *See e.g.* Bartsch v. M.G.M., Inc., 391 F.2d 150 (2d Cir. 1968): an additional reason for enabling an assignee of motion picture rights to control the telecasting of the motion picture, is that it prevents the assignor from refusing its authorization to show the motion picture over the new medium. *See also* Hardy, at 195-226, arguing with support of lower court decisions prior to the 1989 Supreme Court decision in *CCNV v. Reid*, 109 S.Ct. 2166 (1989) that courts have always interpreted the definition of 'work made for hire' in such a manner that ownership would be allocated in the person best suited to exploit the work.

209. *See supra* 2.7; 2.8.

210. § 9-10 Copyright Act 1909.

211. On common law copyright, see also *supra* 2.7, 2.8.

212. *See* Pushman v. New York Graphic Society, Inc., 287 N.Y. 302, 39 N.E.2d 249 (1942). Under California and New York state statutes, delivery of a work of fine art was not considered to transfer the common law copyright in the work. *See* Nimmer § 10.03[B] n. 34.

213. *See* Colliery Engineer Co. v. United Correspondence Schools Co. et al., 96 F. 152, 153 (C.C.S.D.N.Y. 1889); Bleistein v. Donaldson Lithographing Co., 188 U.S. 239, 248 (1903).

made for hire'.[214] The Act furthermore provided that the employer would be entitled to renew the copyright in a 'work made for hire' for a second 28-year period.[215]

In the period following the enactment of the 1909 Act, many courts presumed that the copyright to a work made on commission by an independent contractor vested in the commissioning party unless the independent contractor had expressly reserved copyright ownership.[216] In the 1960s, courts even started to designate works made by independent contractors as 'works made for hire' under the 1909 Act, which entailed that the commissioning party was considered to be the 'author'. In order to qualify as a 'work made for hire', it was held sufficient for the work to have been prepared at the instance and expense of the hiring party,[217] or for the hiring party to have had a right to direct and supervise the manner in which the work was being performed.[218] With the result that, by the time the new Copyright Act was adopted in 1976, there was an 'almost irrebutable presumption that any person who paid another to create a copyrightable work was the statutory "author" under the "work for hire" doctrine.'[219]

As we will see later on, the U.S. Copyright Act of 1976 does not follow this extensive interpretation of the 'work for hire' doctrine under the 1909 Act.[220] On other important issues, the 1976 Act also constitutes a major break with the past. Copyright now vests upon creation[221] and, consequently, includes the right

---

214. § 26 Copyright Act 1909.
215. § 24 Copyright Act 1909. For works in their first term on 1 January 1978: § 304(a) USCA. The copyright could be renewed after 28 years by the author or his successors in title, or by the proprietor in the case of (1) works made for hire which had been copyrighted by the employer, (2) posthumous or composite works (periodicals, encyclopaedias) copyrighted by the proprietor, and (3) works copyrighted by a corporate body otherwise than as assignee of the individual author (§ 24 Copyright Act 1909). Originally, the proprietor of a composite work could renew the copyright to his own editorial contributions as well as the copyrights to the individual contributions to the composite work, unless these copyrights had been secured by the contributors in their own name. In the case of *Stewart v. Abend*, however, the successor in title of the author of a contribution to a periodical was allowed to renew the copyright to that contribution, despite the fact that the author had not secured the copyright to his contribution by way of a copyright notice in his own name. 100 S.Ct. 1750 (1990).
216. *See* Lumière v. Robertson-Cole Distributing Corp., 280 F. 550 (2d Cir. 1922); Yardley v. Houghton Mifflin Co., 108 F.2d 28 (2d Cir. 1939); Lin-Brook Builders Hardware v. Gertler, 352 F.2d 298 (9th Cir. 1965).
217. Brattleboro Publishing Co. v. Winmill Publishing Corp., 369 F.2d 565 (2d Cir. 1966); Picture Music, Inc. v. Bourne, Inc., 457 F.2d 1213 (2d Cir. 1972); Siegel v. National Periodical Publications, Inc., 508 F.2d 909 (2d Cir. 1974); Bernstein v. Universal Pictures, Inc., 379 F.Supp. 933 (1974). *See also* Katzman, at 890: 'The ... test rewarded commissioning parties entirely on the basis of their initial contribution of inspiration, initiative and assumption of economic burden of risk.'
218. Scherr v. Universal Match Corp., 417 F.2d 497, 500 (1969); Picture Music, Inc. v. Bourne, Inc., 314 F.Supp. 640 (S.D.N.Y. 1970), *aff'd* 457 F.2d 1213 (2d Cir. 1972); Epoch Producing Corp. v. Killiam Shows, Inc., 522 F.2d 737, 744 (2d Cir. 1975); Schmid Bros. v. W. Goebel Porzellanfabrik, 589 F.Supp. 497 (1984). *See also* Murray v. Gelderman, 566 F.2d 1307 (5th Cir. 1978), in which the court stated that a hired party can not simply circumvent the 'work for hire' doctrine by stipulating creative freedom in a situation in which the hiring party has no intention of exercising control.
219. Easter Seal Society for Crippled Children and Adults of Louisiana, Inc., v. Playboy Enterprises, 815 F.2d 323, 335 (1987), *cert. denied* 485 U.S. 981 (1988).
220. *See infra* notes 230-238 and accompanying text; 7.2.
221. § 302(a) USCA.

of first publication.[222] The common law protection of unpublished works which are fixed in a tangible medium of expression has been abolished,[223] including the doctrine according to which the transfer of an unpublished manuscript or other original copy implies a transfer of the common law copyright to the work.[224] Copyright expires 50 years after the author's death or, in the case of an anonymous or pseudonymous work or a work made for hire, 75 years after first publication or 100 years after creation, whichever expires first.[225] The term of protection therefore is no longer dependent on renewal of the copyright 28 years after the work's first publication.[226] The 1976 Act has furthermore reduced the cases in which a failure to include a copyright notice in copies of the work invalidates the copyright (§ 405 USCA), while a copyright notice is no longer a requirement for the validity of copyrights to works distributed after the effective date of the Berne Convention Implementation Act of 1988.[227]

Copyright initially vests in the 'author' or the 'authors' of the work (§ 201(a) USCA). The authors of a joint work are coowners of the copyright (§ 201(a) USCA).[228] According to the U.S. Supreme Court, 'author' is, as a general rule, the party who actually creates the work, that is the person who translates an idea into a fixed, tangible medium of expression entitled to copyright protection.[229] The major exception to this rule is the provision that in the case of a work made for hire, the employer or other person for whom the work was prepared is considered to be the author and, unless the parties have expressly agreed otherwise in a written instrument signed by them, owns all the rights comprised in the copyright (§ 201(b) USCA). A 'work made for hire' is defined in § 101 USCA as follows:

---

222. The right of first publication is guaranteed by the exclusive right of the copyright owner to distribute copies of the work to the public (§ 106(3) USCA). *See* Harper & Row Publishers, Inc. v. Nation Enterprises, 105 S.Ct. 2218 (1985). *See also infra* 5.4. The old common law protection of unpublished works still shines through in the provision that unpublished works fixed in a tangible medium of expression are protected under the Copyright Act without regard to the nationality or domicile of the author (§ 104(a) USCA).

223. § 301(a) USCA. Statutory copyright protection subsists in original works of authorship fixed in any tangible medium of expression (§ 102(a) USCA). State or common law protection of works of authorship that are not fixed in any tangible medium of expression is not pre-empted by the Copyright Act (§ 301(b)(1) USCA).

224. H.R. Rep. No. 94-1476, 94th Cong., 2d Sess., 124 (1976). § 202 USCA: transfer of ownership of any material object, including the copy or phonorecord in which the work is first fixed, does not of itself convey any rights in the copyrighted work embodied in the object.

225. § 302 USCA.

226. For copyrights in their first term on 1 January 1978, § 304 USCA contains special renewal provisions intended to extend the term of protection to 75 years from the moment of first publication. As from 26 June 1992, all works published before 1978 and currently in their first term of copyright will automatically be renewed for another 47 years. Registration for renewal can still occur, however. If renewal is automatic, the author's grantee gets the second term. If the author's heirs register for renewal during the first term, they get the benefit of the second term, thus cutting off the author's grantee. Act of 26 June 1992, Pub.L. No. 102-307, 106 Stat. 264. *See generally* Sobel, 3-11.

227. Act of 31 October 1988, Pub.L. 100-568, 102 Stat. 2853, amending § 405(a) USCA.

228. About joint authorship, *see also infra* 3.2.2; 3.3.3; 7.3.

229. Community for Creative Non-Violence v. Reid, 109 S.Ct. 2166, at 2171 (1989).

(1) a work prepared by an employee within the scope of his or her employment;[230] or

(2) a work specially ordered or commissioned for use as a contribution to a collective work, as a part of a motion picture or other audiovisual work, as a translation, as a supplementary work, as a compilation, as an instructional text, as a test, as answer material for a test, or as an atlas, if the parties expressly agree in a written instrument signed by them that the work shall be considered a work made for hire. For the purposes of the foregoing sentence, a 'supplementary work' is a work prepared for publication as a secondary adjunct to a work by another author for the purpose of introducing, concluding, illustrating, explaining, revising, commenting upon, or assisting in the use of the other work, such as forewords, afterwords, pictorial illustrations, maps, charts, tables, editorial notes, musical arrangements, answer material for tests, bibliographies, appendixes, and indexes, and an 'instructional text' is a literary, pictorial, or graphic work prepared for publication and with the purpose of use in systematic instructional activities.

This definition is part of a larger compromise reached in 1965 between creators' and producers' representatives on the ownership provisions in the bill for a new copyright law.[231] The Register of Copyrights' original proposal to specifically exclude commissioned works from the definition[232] had been vigorously contested by producers in light of another proposal to allow authors of works other than 'works made for hire' to terminate their transfers after a certain time.[233] In the final compromise adopted by Congress, authors of works other than a 'work made for hire' have an inalienable, unwaivable right to terminate their transfers

---

230. Copyright protection is not available for U.S. Government works (§ 105 USCA), which means that works made by employees of the U.S. Government in the scope of their employment are not protected. The U.S. Government is not precluded, however, from holding copyrights to works made by independent contractors, which have been assigned to the Government.

231. Joint Memorandum of American Book Publishers Council, Inc., American Guild of Authors and Composers, American Society of Composers, Authors and Publishers, American Textbook Publishers Institute, the Authors League of America, Inc., Composers and Lyricists Guild of America, Inc., Music Publishers' Protective Association, Inc., Music Publishers Association of the United States, Re H.R. 4347, Hearings Before Subcommittee No.3 of the Committee on the Judiciary, H.R. Rep., 89th Cong., 1st Sess. 1965, CLR Part 5, 134 (1965). A proposal by screenwriters' and composers' representatives to provide that an employer acquires a right to use works made by employees to the extent needed for the purposes of his regular business, similar to the judicial presumption in German copyright law, was rejected by Congress. H.R. Rep. No. 94-1476, 94th Cong., 2d sess., 121 (1976).

232. Register of Copyrights, Preliminary Draft for Revised U.S. Copyright Law and Discussions and Comments on the Draft, CLR Part 3, 15, n. 11 (1964).

233. Id. at 15-16. The Register of Copyrights proposed two alternatives, one of which would automatically terminate a transfer after 25 years, and one which would enable an author to bring an action for reformation or termination of a transfer after 20 years if the profits should turn out to be strikingly disproportionate to the compensation negotiated.

after 35 years,[234] and the 'work made for hire' definition was extended to include the nine categories of commissioned works described above.[235]

Since the enactment of the 1976 Act, several bills have been introduced in Congress to restrict the scope of the 'work made for hire' provisions,[236] but none were adopted. The U.S. Supreme Court has however sought to ensure that the definition of a 'work made for hire' is not interpreted more extensively than originally intended when the 1976 Act was drafted. In 1989, the court held that a work can only be a work made for hire if it meets the requirements of § 101(2) USCA, or if it is made by an employee within the scope of his employment, 'employee' to be understood according to its meaning in the general common law of agency.[237] With this decision, the U.S. Supreme Court disqualified more extensive interpretations of the term 'employee' that would allow commissioned works to be considered as works made for hire even though they did not meet the requirements of the second subsection of the 'work made for hire' definition.[238]

Notwithstanding the U.S. adherence to the Berne Convention in 1989,[239] the introduction of moral rights protection for works of visual arts[240] and case law reflecting a more intellectual concept of authorship,[241] the 'work for hire' doctrine still stands within the limitations set by the Supreme Court. The 'work for hire' provisions have been found to be compatible with the Berne Convention with the argument that the Convention does not define the word 'author', while other Berne countries such as the Netherlands also vest authorship in the employer.[242] Congress furthermore has taken the position that the obligation arising under Article 6bis BC to guarantee authors of foreign works the rights of integrity and attribution, is covered by the existing provisions of the 1976 Act and the protection provided under common law and state statutes.[243] Every

---

234. § 203, 304(c) USCA.

235. *Cf.* Dumas v. Gommerman, 865 F.2d 1093, 1101, (9th Cir. 1989): 'By gaining passage of § 101(2), the movie and publishing industry obtained the power to bargain for "work for hire" status for certain types of work. These are categories where such designations are especially crucial to buyers, principally owing to the number of workers involved in producing the final product.'

236. S. 2044, 97th Cong., 2nd Sess. (1982); S. 2138, 98th Cong., 1st Sess. (1983); H.R. 5911, 98th Cong., 2d Sess. (1984); S. 2230, 99th Cong., 2d Sess. (1986); S. 1223, 100th Cong., 1st Sess. (1987); S. 1253, 101st Cong., 1st Sess. (1989). For a discussion of these proposals, see Fidlow, at 618-619; Hamilton, at 1306; Kernochan, *After U.S. Adherence*, at 167.

237. CCNV v. Reid, 109 S.Ct. 2166 (1989). *See also infra* 7.2.2.

238. *See also infra* 7.2.1.

239. Effective 1 March 1989. The Berne Convention is not self-executing in American law. The obligations arising under the Convention are considered to be executed by the amendments to the Copyright Act of 1976 implemented in the Act of 31 October 1988, Pub.L. 100-568, 102 Stat. 2853 (Berne Convention Implemention Act), and the law as it exists on 31 October 1988. For a discussion of the amendments, see Baumgarten/Meyer; Ginsburg/Kernochan.

240. *See infra* notes 244-246 and accompanying text.

241. Feist Publications, Inc. v. Rural Telephone Service Company, Inc., 111 S.Ct. 1282 (1991). *See infra* note 249 and accompanying text.

242. Ad Hoc Working Group, at 102-103.

243. Article 2(3) Berne Convention Implementation Act 1988. H.R.Rep. No. 100-609, 100th Cong., 2d sess., 34 (1988). Sceptical: Dietz, *The United States*, at 226. On moral rights protection in the U.S., see Ginsburg, *Moral Rights*, at 21; Kernochan, IV, at 109-113, 143-188. *See also infra* 5.4-5.6.

initiative to introduce specific moral rights protection within the copyright statute has been successfully blocked by producers, with the exception of one initiative which affects the commercial exploitation of copyright works only marginally. As from 1 June 1991, authors of works of visual art enjoy a right of attribution and integrity under the Copyright Act.[244] Both rights are inalienable, but may be waived by contract.[245] Excluded from protection are authors of posters, maps, globes, charts, technical drawings, diagrams, models, applied art, audiovisual works, books, magazines, newspapers, periodicals, databases, electronic information services, electronic or similar publications, merchandising items, authors of any advertising, promotional, descriptive, covering or packaging material or container, and authors of works made for hire.[246]

In the past, doubts have been voiced about the constitutionality of the 'work for hire' doctrine in view of the fact that the U.S. Constitution explicitly states that exclusive rights should be secured to 'Authors'.[247] In the 1989 decision of *Community for Creative Non-Violence v Reid*,[248] the only time the U.S. Supreme Court spoke out on the 'work for hire' provisions in the 1976 Act, the court did not refer to the copyright clause in the Constitution, which may suggest that it did not think that the Constitution was at issue. A 1991 Supreme Court decision on the protection of compilations of facts has however once again stirred up the discussion. In this case, the Supreme Court held that the Constitution's

---

244. § 106A USCA. Title VI of Act of 1 December 1990, Pub.L. 101-650, 104 Stat. 5128. S. 1198, 101st Cong., 1st Sess. (1989); H.R. 2690, 101st Cong., 1st Sess. (1989). *See also* Ginsburg, *Moral Rights*, at 125-126.

245. § 106A(e)(1) USCA. The language of § 106A indicates that the exclusive rights comprised in the copyright and the rights of attribution and integrity are separate rights (dualistic approach). § 106A(a) USCA: 'Subject to section 107 and independent of the exclusive rights provided in section 106, ...' § 106A(b) USCA: 'Only the author of a work of visual art has the rights conferred by subsection (a) in that work, whether or not the author is the copyright owner...' The rights of attribution and integrity expire in the case of works created after 1 June 1991 upon the death of the (last surviving) author. In case of works created before 1 June 1991, protection expires simultaneously with the exclusive rights (§ 106A(d) USCA).

246. § 101 USCA (definition of 'work of visual art'). *Cf.* Ginsburg, *Moral Rights*, at 125: '[W]hile moral rights in general may inspire trepidation among major exploiter groups, such as motion picture producers and periodical publishers, the subject of this bill, essentially works of painting and sculpture, could be seen as discrete. Hence, protecting these works from mutilation and destruction could achieve a socially desirable goal with minimal disruption to most copyright owners' interests.'

247. Scherr v. Universal Match Corp., 417 F.2d 497, 502 (2d Cir. 1969)(Justice Friendly dissenting) *cert. denied* 397 U.S. 936: '[B]oth in the Constitution and in the Copyright Act, the emphasis is on protecting "the author" and that any principle depriving him of copyright and vesting this in another without his express assent must thus be narrowly defined...' Referring to Judge Friendly's dissenting opinion, a New York court held that an employer, in order to be considered author, must presumably make some significant contribution to the work and, in any event, have the right to control and supervise the actual performance of the work. Schmid Brothers, Inc. v. W. Goebel Porzellanfabrik KG., 589 F.Supp. 497 (S.D.N.Y. 1984). *See also* Vitaphone Corp. v. Hutchinson Amusement Co., 28 F.Supp. 526 (D.Mass. 1939)(dictum). *But see* Childress v. Taylor, 945 F.2d 500, 506 (2d Cir. 1991): conferring 'authorship' status on employer is not constitutionally suspect. *See also* Nimmer, § 1.06 [C] 1-40: § 201(b) USCA passes constitutional muster, because it allows the parties to make an agreement to the contrary. The fact that, in the case of employment works, an agreement to the contrary is only possible with respect to copyright ownership but not with respect to authorship, is not considered relevant by Nimmer, although he does refer to the termination of transfers provisions in a note. Nimmer, § 1.06[C] n. 25.

248. 109 S.Ct. 2166 (1989)

reference to 'Author' implies that, in order for a work to qualify for copyright protection, it must show a minimum degree of creativity, of intellectual production.[249] Whether this intellectual concept of authorship renders the 'work for hire' provisions unconstitutional as has been contended,[250] remains to be seen.[251] Fact is, that the 'work for hire' provisions are not undisputed,[252] leading producers to vigourously defend the *status quo* in the copyright law.[253]

The 'work for hire' rule is the only provision in the 1976 Act which directly allocates exclusive rights to producers. Unlike German copyright law, American copyright law does not recognize related or neighbouring rights for producers. Since the Patent-Copyright Clause in the Constitution authorizes Congress to secure to 'Authors and Inventors the exclusive Right to their respective Writings and Discoveries',[254] it is doubtful whether Congress has power to introduce a *sui generis* regime for products of labour which cannot be qualified as either a 'writing of an author' or the 'discovery of an inventor'.[255] This, combined with the fact that the required degree of authorship is determined by the Constitutional objective of advancing the progress of science and art,[256] explains why new products such as motion pictures, sound recordings and computer programs, in

249. Feist Publications, Inc. v. Rural Telephone Service Company, Inc., 111 S.Ct. 1282 (1991).

250. *See* comment of Cohen Jehoram, Proceedings of the 58th Conference of the ALAI, Aegean Sea, 19-26 April 1991, at 240.

251. Ginsburg has argued that the contention that the 'work for hire' rule is unconstitutional may be consistent with *Feist*'s logic, but that this rule is so deeply-rooted in American copyright law, that it is not likely to be easily overturned. Proceedings of the 58th Conference of the ALAI, Aegean Sea, 19-26 April 1991, at 258.

252. *See* Kastenmaier, at 21; Kernochan, *After U.S. Adherence*, at 163-167; Kernochan, *Moral Rights*; Kernochan, *Works-Made-For-Hire*; Landau. *See also infra* 5.1.

253. *See* Statement of Michael Klipper on behalf of the Committee for America's Copyright Community, Hearings on Moral Rights and S. 1253 before the Subcommittee on Patents, Copyrights and Trademarks, Senate Judiciary Committee, 101st Cong., 1st. Sess. (1990): 'Current law enhances public access to creative works. It allows the producers and publishers of collaborative works, such as educational and training audiovisual works, educational books and materials, and motion pictures, the freedom to meld together the efforts of work-for-hire employees and freelancers in ways that (1) take into account the special nature of these particular industries, and (2) are calculated to take full advantage of the opportunities made possible by technological change.' Kernochan, *After U.S. Adherence to Berne*, at 172, remarks about the production and publishing companies which this Committee for America's Copyright Community represents: 'They wield redoubtable political power in the USA. A number of them control the main means by which members of Congress communicate with their constituents.'

254. U.S. Const. art. I, § 8, cl. 8.

255. Ginsburg, *No "Sweat"?*, at 375, 388, argues that Congress has discretion to decide what 'Writings' of 'Authors' serve to 'promote the Progress of Science' and that the U.S. Supreme Court should be extremely reticent in reviewing the congressional findings in this respect. Ginsburg furthermore argues that Congress may have power under the 'Commerce Clause' in the Constitution to enact an anticopying statute that departs in significant ways from the traditional copyright scheme. *Id.* at 383, 388.

256. *See* Feist Publications, Inc. v. Rural Telephone Service Company, Inc., 111 S.Ct. 1282, 1290 (1991). In this case, the Supreme Court thought it better for the progress of science and art not to protect compilations of facts aside from their possibly creative selection or arrangement. *Id.* at 1290.

the end, have all been found to pass constitutional muster and have been accepted as works of authorship under the copyright statute.[257]

Whereas, in Dutch and German law, performers and producers have separate related rights to their respective contributions to a sound recording, ownership of the copyright to a sound recording under the 1976 Act is determined according to the general provisions on copyright ownership.[258] Depending on whether their contributions involve authorship, the performer and the record producer[259] may be sole or joint authors of the sound recording (§ 201(a) USCA), unless their contribution was made within the scope of employment, in which case the employer is considered to be (co-)author (§ 201(b) USCA).[260]

To prevent multiple infringement suits by holders of different rights to a work, an old judicial doctrine presumed that a copyright could only be assigned as a whole and that, as a consequence, the holder of a particular exclusive right, as a mere 'licensee', did not have standing to sue for infringement.[261] To facilitate the increasingly diversified exploitation of copyright works, the 1976 Act has

---

257. Motion pictures: Act of 24 August 1912, 37 Stat. 488. Sound recordings: Act of 15 October 1971, Pub.L. 92-140, 85 Stat. 391. Computer programs: Act of 12 December 1980, Pub.L. 96-517, 94 Stat. 3028. Motion pictures and sound recordings are included as separate categories in the list of works of authorship (§ 102(a) USCA). Computer programs are protected as literary works to the extent that they reflect authorship in the programmer's expression of original ideas, as distinguished from the ideas themselves. H.R. Rep. No. 94-1476, 94th Cong., 2d sess., 56 (1976). *Cf. also* H.R.Rep. No. 92-487, 92nd Cong., 1st Sess., 5 (1971): 'The committee believes that, as a class of subject matter, sound recordings are clearly within the scope of the "writings of an author" capable of protection under the Constitution, and that the extension of limited statutory protection to them is overdue.'

258. H.R.Rep. No. 94-1476, 94th Cong., 2d Sess. 56 (1976).

259. H.R. Rep. No. 94-1476, 94th Cong., 2d Sess. 56 (1976): authorship of the record producer may result from his responsibility for setting up the recording session, capturing and electronically processing the sounds, and compiling and editing them to make the final recording. *But see* Nimmer § 2.10[A][b] 2-146-147 (1990), arguing that the record producer can not become author based on these activities, because these activities, if creative, are performed by others (sound engineers, etc.). In this sense also Cohen Jehoram, *The Nature*, at 88. The interpretation of 'author' by the Supreme Court in *CCNV v. Reid*, 109 S.Ct. 2166 (1989), would indeed seem to restrict authorship to the person who actually performs the creative labour or, in the case of a work made for hire, to that person's employer or commissioning party. This does not exclude the possibility, however, that a record producer becomes (joint) author by dictating the manner in which the sounds should be captured, mixed and edited. *See infra* 3.3.3.

260. The only right which is independent from the general ownership provisions is the right to share in the levies on digital audio equipment. Two-thirds of the total royalty income is distributed to performers and record companies (Sound Recording Fund) and one-third to composers/songwriters and music publishers (Musical Works Fund). Performers have a direct claim vis-à-vis the Copyright Office for 40% of (96% of) the Sound Recording Fund against the record companies 60 %. Act of 28 October 1992, Pub.L. 102-563 of 106 Stat. 4237.

261. *See e.g.* New Fiction Pub. Co. v. Start Co., 220 F. 994 (S.D.N.Y. 1915). This rule of 'indivisibility' also implied that, if an author granted someone the right to publish his work in a particular medium, the work could fall into the public domain if that person first published the work in that medium without a copyright notice in the author's name. In case law under the 1909 Act, this result has been modified. *See* Goodis v. United Artists Television, Inc., 425 F.2d 397 (1970): the primary rationale of the doctrine of indivisibility, prevention of multiple infringement suits, is not at issue if the author sues for infringement. The consequence of the indivisibility, namely that plaintiff's novel has fallen into the public domain because it has been first published by a publisher to whom plaintiff has granted serialization rights, should therefore be avoided, especially since the novel has been published in a magazine with a copyright notice in the publisher's name, so that it could be clear to the public that plaintiff had no intention to surrender the fruits of his labour.

abolished this principle of indivisibility of copyright.[262] Copyright may now be transferred in whole or in part (§ 201(d)(1) USCA), and the owner of any particular exclusive right is entitled, to the extent of that right, to all the protection and remedies accorded to copyright owners (§ 201(d)(2) USCA).[263] An exclusive license is considered to be a transfer of ownership of a particular exclusive right,[264] which means that an exclusive licensee may sue for infringement independently.[265]

Unlike many continental-European copyright laws, the 1976 Act does not provide extensive rules on copyright contracts.[266] Instead of regulating the terms of contracts, the American legislator has sought to ensure that creators are aware of their rights from the outset, so that they can settle on the price of the work and the ownership of the rights in it.[267] For this reason, transfers of copyright ownership, including exclusive licenses, must be in writing.[268] If a transfer nevertheless turns out to be unremunerative for the author, the author, or after his death, his widow and children, may terminate the transfer after 35 years (§ 203 USCA), so that they can renegotiate the terms of the transfer or attempt to get a better deal elsewhere.[269] According to the House Report, this is necessary '[b]ecause of the unequal bargaining position of authors, resulting in part from the impossibility of determining a work's value until it has been exploited.'[270] In order not to strain the exploitation of creative works too much, however, the 1976 Act provides that termination of a transfer of ownership in an underlying work does not affect the exploitation of already existing derivative works.[271] The 1976 Act furthermore provides that the termination provisions are not

---

262. H.R. Rep. No. 94-1476, 94th Cong., 2nd Sess., 123 (1976).
263. Registration and copyright notice are still reserved to the 'copyright owner' (§§ 401, 408 USCA). An assignee of a particular exclusive right is not considered the copyright owner. If a producer only needs a specific exclusive right, but nevertheless wants to register the copyright in his name and put his name on the copyright notice, the author will have to assign the whole copyright, after which the publisher has to reassign the rights he does not need.
264. § 101 USCA (definition of 'transfer of copyright ownership').
265. §§ 201(d)(2), 501(b) USCA. See also H.R.Rep. No. 94-1476, 94th Cong., 2nd Sess., 123 (1976).
266. Aside from the introduction of inalienable moral rights for visual artists in 1991, the only provision on the scope of a transfer is the provision that the owner of the copyright in a collective work, in the absence of an express transfer of copyright ownership, has only acquired a non-exclusive right to reproduce and distribute the contributions in the collective work, in a revision of that work, or in a later collective work of the same series (§ 201(c) USCA).
267. CCNV v. Reid, 109 S.Ct. 2166, 2177-2178 (1989).
268. § 204(a) USCA. See Effects Associates v. Cohen, 908 F.2d 555, 556 (9th Cir. 1990), cert.denied 111 S.Ct. 1003 (1991): argument of defendant that film industry is exempted from the writing requirement because 'moviemakers do lunch, not contracts' rejected. § 204 USCA ensures that the creator of a work will not give away his copyright inadvertently and forces a party who wants to use the copyrighted work to negotiate with the creator to determine precisely what rights are being transferred and at what price.
269. Applicable to works made after 31 December 1977, the first terminations will take place in 2014. For works first published before 1 January 1978, § 304(c) USCA allows authors or other executors of a grant to terminate a grant 65 years after the date copyright was originally secured or 65 years after 1 January 1978, whichever is later.
270. H.R.Rep. No. 94-1476, 94th Cong., 2d Sess., 124 (1976).
271. § 203(b)(1); § 304(c)(6)(A) USCA. See also infra 3.3.6.

applicable to works made for hire,[272] thereby excluding a large part of all creators from invoking the most important author-protective measure in American copyright law.[273]

2.15 The creator doctrine in Dutch copyright law

Lacking an explicit constitutional basis or underlying theory on the nature of copyright,[274] Dutch copyright law traditionally represents a pragmatic mixture of continental-European and Anglo-American concepts. During the Batavian Revolution of 1795, the Province of Holland abolished the system of printing privileges. In its place came a perpetual copyright which, upon publication, vested in the publisher who had lawfully acquired the 'right of copy'.[275] Unlike their London and Paris counterparts,[276] the Amsterdam publishers thus succeeded in obtaining perpetual statutory protection against copying. Although this perpetual protection was replaced by limited protection in 1803,[277] and substituted by an exclusive right of the author in 1817,[278] the publisher would remain the primary beneficiary of protection *de facto* until the Copyright Act of 1912 abolished all formality requirements and explicitly required that full and partial

---

272. § 203(a) USCA; § 304(c) USCA. Even if works made for hire would not be explicitly excluded from the termination provisions, the actual creators would still not be able to benefit from them, because they are not considered 'authors' and, as such, can not execute a grant which they might want to terminate.

273. Goldstein I, at 485: 'Presumably, Congress rested the exclusion of these works from the termination of transfer provision on the premise that employees will rarely need protection from unremunerative transfers.'

274. There is however a discussion on the nature of copyright protection. *See* e.g. De Beaufort (1909), at 78-95, discussing whether copyright is a matter of expediency or right. De Beaufort adheres to the latter view, arguing that authors would be able to claim damages in case of unauthorized use of their works even if there were no statutory copyright protection. *Id.* at 90. In modern literature, Cohen Jehoram, *Opportuniteit*, at 63-65, argues that the economic protection of authors is subject to the property guarantee of the First Protocol to the European Convention for the Human Rights, while Verkade, *Rechtsbeginselen*, at 147, argues that a certain moral rights protection may be based on the constitutional principle of freedom of expression, but that there is no legal principle which presupposes an author's economic protection. Grosheide, at 302-303, takes an instrumental approach to copyright. He argues that the scope and nature of copyright are determined by its underlying objectives, which are multiform and may vary from case to case. In defining the minimum-threshold, scope and characteristics of protection, courts and legislators should differentiate according to these objectives, thus creating a tailor-made law of copyright. *Id. See also* Grosheide, *Paradigms*, at 232; Grosheide, *Auteurswet*, at 126; Hugenholtz, at 178.

275. Decree of the Assembly of Provisional Representatives of the People of Holland of 27 November 1795; Publication of the Provincial Government of Holland of 8 December 1796.

276. *See supra* 2.7.

277. Publication of the Government of the Batavian Republic of 3 July 1803. This law accorded a copyright of limited duration to the person who first published a work and who had obtained the right of copy thereto. This person could be the 'draughtsman' or the person who had obtained the right of copy from the 'draughtsman' (Article 2).

278. After the Dutch Provinces had been under French rule for several years and, as such, had been subject to the French Decrees of 1791 and 1793, the old publishers' protection was reinstated by the Restoration Decree of 24 January 1814, S. 17. In 1817, a new statute was enacted to bring legislation in line with the southern Provinces which followed a more French-oriented course. Act of 25 January 1817, S. 5, concerning the rights which may be exercised in the Netherlands with respect to the printing and publishing of literary and artistic works.

assignments of author's rights be executed in a written instrument signed by the assignor (§ 2(2) DCA).

The 1817 Act accorded to 'authors and their successors in title' an exclusive right to print and publish literary and artistic works which expired 20 years after the author's death.[279] The author's right could only be invoked if the work had been printed by a Dutch printer and published by a Dutch publisher, if the work made mention of the publisher's name and if three copies had been deposited at the publisher's local government at the moment of first publication.[280] In a 1840 case about reprints of Royal Decrees to which the State had invested itself with copyrights by Royal Order, the Hoge Raad (the Netherlands Supreme Court) held that the State did not have an exclusive right to print because the 1817 Act did not give it such a right, nor had the State complied with the formalities required by this Act.[281] The court furthermore stated that the State was not an 'author', because 'author' could only be a natural person under the 1817 Act.[282]

The hybrid concept of an author's right which could be forfeited in case of a failure to deposit copies, was maintained in the Act of 28 June 1881 on author's rights.[283] Like other contemporary statutes on author's rights,[284] the 1881 Act treated certain producers as 'authors'. An entrepreneur was considered to be an 'author' in respect of works consisting of multiple creative contributions (collective works),[285] and public institutions, associations, foundations and corporations were considered 'authors' in respect of works supplied by them, i.e.

---

279. § 3 Act of 25 January 1817.
280. § 6 Act of 25 January 1817.
281. Judgment of September 8, 1840, HR, Netherlands, W. 122 (1840). This decision seems to suggest that the court considered the protection granted to published works to be a creation of statute rather than a confirmation of the creator's natural right. Cf. Donaldson v. Beckett, 4 Burr. (4th ed.) 2408, 98 Eng.Rep. 251 (H.L. 1774); Wheaton v. Peters, 33 U.S. (8 Pet.) 591 (1834). See supra 2.7. In 1987, the Hoge Raad was once again required to adjudicate on a case about copying of Royal Decrees published by the Government Printing Office. This time, the Printing Office had invoked the theory of misappropriation, which, in a previous case, the Hoge Raad had considered to be applicable to results of labour similar to those products that have been considered eligible for protection under the copyright or patent statutes. Judgment of June 27, 1986, HR, Netherlands, NJ 1987, 191, note Van Nieuwenhoven Helbach (Holland Nautic v. Decca). The Hoge Raad held that copying of a Royal Decree, in itself, is not unlawful, but that it could become unlawful in the light of the circumstances of the case. The Hoge Raad however added that, in drawing such a conclusion, a court should take into account that the copyright statute specifically excludes statutes and decrees from copyright protection (§ 11 DCA) so as to ensure public access. Judgment of November 20, 1987, HR, Netherlands, NJ 1988, 311 note Wichers Hoeth (Staat v. Den Ouden).
282. Judgment of September 8, 1840, HR, Netherlands, W. 122(1840). In this respect, the 1817 Act was closer to an author's right in the purest sense of the word, than the subsequent 1881 and 1912 Acts which grant authorship to legal entities in certain cases. The 1817 Act furthermore specificly excluded from protection almanacs, bibles and calendars, while the 1912 Act extends protection to all writings, including those which do not have personal character. See infra notes 301-306 and accompanying text.
283. S. 124. Two copies had to be deposited at the Department of Justice within one month after the first publication in print in the Netherlands (§§ 10, 11 Act of 28 June 1881).
284. See supra 2.13 note 168. See also the German Act of 11 June 1870, which considered universities to be the first owner of the author's right in the case of works published under their name.
285. § 2(1)(a) Law of 28 June 1881. Unless agreed otherwise, the contributors retained the author's right to their own contribution (§ 2(2)).

works made at their commission and published in their name.[286] While such departures from the creator doctrine have been abolished in most continental-European copyright laws, the Dutch Copyright Act of 1912 still reflects a certain legislative scope in defining the 'author'.

Under the 1912 Act, an author's right vests in the 'maker' of the work (§ 1 DCA).[287] 'Maker', hereinafter translated as 'author',[288] is generally understood to refer to the creator of a work in the sense of the 1912 Act,[289] specified by the Hoge Raad as a work with an individual, original nature bearing the author's personal imprint.[290] This principle also applies to the author of a collective work as defined in § 5 DCA,[291] the author of a work prepared according to the plan and under the supervision and direction of another person defined in § 6 DCA,[292] and to the author of a film work as defined in § 45a DCA.[293] Departures from the creator doctrine occur, however, with respect to works made by an employee within the scope of an employment contract and works published in the name of a legal entity.

§ 7 DCA: If the labour performed in the service of another person entails making specific literary, scientific or artistic works, the person in whose service the works were made is considered to be the author of these works, unless the parties have agreed otherwise.[294]

---

286. § 2(1)(b) Law of 28 June 1881.
287. *See generally* Cohen Jehoram, *the Netherlands*, § 4.1; F.W. Grosheide, P.B. Hugenholtz, J.M.B. Seignette, W.F.F. Oppenoorth, P.H. Ariëns Kappers, 'The Determination of the Author', National Report, the Netherlands, in: *Copyright and Industrial Property*, Report of the ALAI Conference, 19-26 April 1991, Aegean Sea, 375-386 (1991).
288. The use of the term 'maker' instead of 'auteur' was not a matter of principle. 'Maker' was preferred because it could refer to both literary as well as artistic works, whereas the general public still mainly perceived 'auteur' as referring to the writer of a book. Memorandum in Reply, Parl.Gesch. 1.5 (1912).
289. *See* Memorandum to § 6 DCA, Parl.Gesch. 6.3 (1912): 'creator of the work'. Memorandum to § 45a, Parl.Gesch. 45a.9 (1985): 'creator of an original work'. *See also* Hirsch Ballin, at 79; van Lingen, at 23; Quaedvlieg (1987), at 27 n. 68; Spoor/Verkade, at 21.
290. *See* Judgment of June 1, 1990, HR, Netherlands, NJ 1991, 377 note Verkade (Kluwer v. Lamoth); Judgment of January 4, 1991, HR, Netherlands, NJ 1991, 608, note Verkade (Romme v. Van Dale); Judgment of February 21, 1992, HR, Netherlands, NJ 1993, 164 note Spoor ('Barbie').
291. § 5(1) DCA: 'Without prejudice to the author's right in every individual work, is considered author of a literary, scientific or artistic work which consists of independent works by two or more persons, the person under whose supervision and direction the entire work was prepared or the person who compiled the various works.' [translation JS] *See* Van Lingen, at 30: the collection must, however trivial, bear the personal imprint of the collector. *See also* Spoor, *De filmkwestie*, at 21: 'creative collector's labour'. *See also infra* 3.3.3.
292. § 6 DCA: 'If a work has been prepared according to the plan and under the supervision and direction of a third party, that party is considered to be the author.' [translation JS] *See infra* 3.3.3; 7.5.
293. § 45a(2) DCA: 'Without prejudice to sections 7 and 8, are considered authors of a film work the natural persons who made a contribution of a creative nature to and intended for the realization of the film work.' [translation JS] Memorandum, Parl.Gesch. 45a.9 (1985). *See also infra* 3.2.2.
294. [translation JS] Notice the shift in terminology in comparison with § 2(2) of the 1881 Act, which read: 'Are equated with "authors" ...' *See also infra* 4.2; 6.3; 7.4.

§ 8 DCA: If a public body, association, foundation or corporation first publishes a work as if it originated from that body and without naming a natural person as its author, that body is considered to be the author of that work, unless it is demonstrated that publication under these circumstances was unlawful.[295]

The rationale behind § 7 DCA is the principle that the employer has a right to the fruits of his employee's labour,[296] while § 8 DCA intends to ensure that legal entities can prove title to their reports, announcements, etc.[297] The method applied to realize these objectives, attribution of the legal status of 'author' to the employer or legal entity, has been criticized in legal doctrine, in particular because § 25 DCA grants moral rights to the 'author' (rather than to the creator).[298] So far, the majority of lower courts has decided that 'author' in § 25 DCA refers to the statutory author, whether this is the creator, an employer or a legal entity.[299]

Another example of the discretion which the 1912 legislator allowed itself in defining authorship, is the protection granted to writings under § 10(1) DCA, including those that do not meet the general standard of authorship.[300] The

---

295. [translation JS] *See also infra* 4.4; 6.3; 7.5.
296. Parl.Gesch. 7.4 (1912). *See also infra* 4.4; 5.2.
297. Parl.Gesch. 8.3 (1912). *See also infra* 4.4.
298. *See* De Beer, at 423; Du Bois, *Enkele aspecten*, at 58; Cohen Jehoram, *Grenzen*, at 526; Gerbrandy, at 290-291; Hirsch Ballin, at 102; Kuypers, at 9; Van Lingen, *Morele Rechten*, at 191; Quaedvlieg (1992), at 52; Verkade/Spoor, at 241. Limperg, at 517; Van Lingen/Van Niftrik, at 55; Schuijt, *Schrap artikel 7*, at 22, 24; Smit, at 1067; Woltring, *Wetenschapsbeoefening*, at 68, reject § 7 DCA *per se*. Compare also the Report of the Committee on the Revision of the Copyright Act, at 23 (1952), proposing to substitute § 7 DCA by a legal assignment of those rights that necessarily follow from the nature and purpose of the employment conditions. Approval with §§ 7 and 8 DCA as a matter of law, principle and practice: De Beaufort (1932), at 54-57; Maeijer, at 352, 353; Vermeijden, at 142. Explicitly with respect to § 7 DCA also Verkade, *Het beste artikel 7*, at 9-19; Spoor/Verkade, at 34. *See also infra* 5.2.
299. *See* Judgment of May 24, 1978, Ger. 's-Hertogenbosch, Netherlands, 53 BIE 99, 102 (1985) (Van Gunsteren v. Lips); Judgment of August 20, 1987, Pres.Rb. Amsterdam, Netherlands, 12 Informatierecht/AMI 18 note Cohen Jehoram (Zeinstra v. Van den Hoek); Judgment of July 12, 1988, Pres.Rb. Leeuwarden, Netherlands, 13 Informatierecht/AMI 17 (1989) note Cohen Jehoram (Bonnema v. Gemeente Tietjerksteradeel); Judgment of April 13, 1989, Commissariaat voor de Media, Netherlands, 14 Informatierecht/AMI 12 (1990) note Verkade ('credits television programs'); Judgment of May 27, 1992, Rb. 's-Gravenhage, Netherlands, 17 Informatierecht/AMI 94 (1993) note Quaedvlieg (Gorter v. PTT). In its Judgment of February 10, 1970, NJ 1971, 130 ('The Forgers'), the Amsterdam Court of Appeals held that moral rights may only be invoked by the person who has given the work its personal, individual character. But see Judgment of February 28, 1991, Ger. Amsterdam, Netherlands, 60 BIE 128 (1992) (Chanel v. Maxis), in which the Amsterdam Court of Appeals examined whether the moral rights of a French corporation had been infringed (*quod non*).
300. § 10(1) DCA: '[b]ooks, brochures, newspapers, periodicals and all other writings...' The protection of 'all writings' served to continue the 19th century practice of protecting writings with a useful purpose. Parl.Gesch. 10.5 (1912). *See generally* Van Engelen, 35-46; Van Engelen, *Geschriften-bescherming*, 243-250; Holtzer, 63-67; Hugenholtz, 41-51. The bill introduced in Dutch Parliament to implement the EC Directive for the legal protection of computer programs explicitly excludes computer programs from the protection as 'writing' and introduces 'computer program' as a separate category. TK 1991-1992, 22531, no. 1, at 2. Critically: Dommering, *De software richtlijn*, at 85-86, arguing that this approach may have a negative effect on the protection of electronic databases as 'writings'. *See also infra* 4.4, on the 'author' of impersonal writings.

inconsistency of protecting 'impersonal' writings under a regime with extensive economic and moral protection has been mitigated by the Hoge Raad by adjusting the scope of protection according to the degree of authorship involved.[301] Writings with little or no personal character are only protected if they are published or intended to be published. The protection is restricted to copying from the writing itself, provided the structure of the text is not changed drastically.[302] Further application of the 1912 Act to impersonal writings depends on the purpose of each, individual provision,[303] which probably means that the moral rights guaranteed by § 25 DCA are not necessarily applicable.[304] Legal doctrine in the meantime remains divided over the question whether this tailor-made protection for impersonal writings belongs in a statute on author's rights.[305]

Doctrine is also divided as to whether sound recordings can qualify as works of authorship,[306] while it is commonly agreed that performances, recorded or unrecorded, may involve authorship.[307] The Dutch legislator has taken the position, however, that neither performances nor sound recordings qualify as works of authorship in the sense of the 1912 Act.[308] Since 1 July 1993, performances, sound recordings (phonograms) and broadcasts are statutorily protected as the subject matter of neighbouring rights.[309] To implement the 1992 EC

---

301. Judgment of June 25, HR, 1965, NJ 1966, 116 note Hirsch Ballin ('radio program listings').
302. Id. at 181, 182.
303. Id. at 181. See also infra 4.4, on allocation of copyright ownership in impersonal writings.
304. See Hugenholtz, at 47, designating the protection of impersonal writings as a copyright without moral rights. But see Quaedvlieg (1992), at 31: if there is a need, courts will probably nevertheless grant moral rights protection to writings without an individual character.
305. Negative: De Beaufort (1932), at 77; Cohen Jehoram, Schrap één onzalig woordje, at 1542; Gerbrandy (1988), at 76: 'anachronism'; Hirsch Ballin, 83-84 ('author's right without an author'); Van Lingen, at 52; Report of the Committee on the Revision of the Copyright Act, at 6 (1952). Van Engelen, at 46: 'unwritten intellectual property right', 'sui generis protection'. Affirmative: Dommering, Introduction, at 38; Holtzer, at 64; Hugenholtz, at 172, 178; Verkade, Gegevensbescherming, at 52. Cf. also Grosheide, at 306, favouring differentiation with respect to the notion of 'work' in a common-law like manner.
306. Negative: Cohen Jehoram, The Nature, at 88; Hirsch Ballin, 77-92. Affirmative: Mak, at 119 (as a derivative work); Komen/Verkade, at 44; Spoor/Verkade, at 482. See also Grosheide, Auteurswet, at 126: since it is one of the objectives of copyright protection to regulate competition and since the different objectives of copyright do not have to be translated into law uniformly, there is no reason why the activities of phonogram producers, film producers, publishers and broadcasting organizations should not be protected by the copyright law. See also Seignette, Het wetsontwerp, at 6-7: in view of the existing differentiation within the copyright law as to the definition of authorship and the scope of protection offered to various categories of works, the protection of performances and sound recordings does not necessarily require regulation under a separate regime.
307. Cohen Jehoram, The Nature, at 88; Dommering, De sportprestatie, at 11; Van Engelen, Uitvoerende kunstenaars, at 83; Hirsch Ballin, at 90; Heevel, Wet 1991?, at 128; Komen/Verkade, at 43; Van Lingen, at 41; Spoor, De auteursrechtelijke positie, at 324; Spoor/Verkade, at 481. But see Gerbrandy (1988), at 116: performing artist is not an author.
308. TK 1988-1989, 21244, no. 3, at 4.
309. S.1993, 178 (WNR). Before this took effect, the unauthorized copying of performances and sound recordings was redressed under a theory of unfair competition. See Judgment of February 24, 1989, HR, Netherlands, NJ 1989, 701 note Wichers Hoeth (Elvis Presley I); Judgment of April 2, 1993, HR, Netherlands, NJ 1993, 573 note Verkade (NVPI v. Snelleman). See Van Engelen, at 319-322; Heevel, Leistungsschutz, at 204; Roos/Seignette, at 178.

Directive on rental, lending and on certain rights related to copyright,[310] a neighbouring right will also be introduced for the producer of the first fixation of a film.[311]

Unlike the 1965 German Copyright Act, which grants performing artists limited moral rights protection, the Dutch Act on Neighbouring Rights guarantees performing artists virtually the same moral rights protection as the 1912 Act does to authors.[312] The neighbouring right to a performance vests in the performing artist(s) (§§ 1a, 2 WNR), and can be exercised in the event of a collective performance by a representative elected by a majority of the performing artists (§ 12 WNR).[313] In the event of a performance made by an employee, the performing artist's employer is entitled to exploit the performance to the extent permitted under the employment contract, by custom or on the basis of the principles of reasonableness and equity (§ 2a WNR). The first owner of the neighbouring right to a sound recording (phonogram) is the phonogram producer (§§ 1(d), 5 WNR), i.e. the natural or legal person responsible for organizing and financing the recording.[314] First owner of the neighbouring right to a broadcasted television or radio program is the broadcasting organization (§§ 1(e), 7 WNR).

Since its enactment in 1912, the Dutch Copyright Act has been frequently amended, without fundamentally changing its basic structure. The introduction of the rights of attribution and integrity in the Berne Convention in 1928[315] did not require systematic changes, because the 1912 Act already contained a number of provisions directed at the protection of moral interests.[316] On other issues, the 1912 Act has also proved to be flexible. According to § 1 DCA, the author's right encompasses the exclusive right of reproduction ('verveelvoudiging') and

---

310. Council Directive 92/100/EEC of 19 November 1992 concerning rental and lending rights and certain related rights in the field of intellectual property, O.J.Eur.Comm. No. L 290/9 (1993).

311. TK 1992-1993, 23247, nos. 1-2, at 5. On neighbouring rights for film producers, see also Grosheide, *Auteurswet*, at 123-124. *See also supra* 6.4.

312. § 4 WNR. The text of § 4 WNR is based on § 25 DCA with the exception of § 25(4), which entitles the author to make changes to the work after assignment of the author's right, to the extent permitted according to principles of good faith. § 83 GCA only grants protection against mutilation or other distortions of the performance.

313. The individual artists are entitled to independently enforce their neighbouring rights in the collective performance.

314. § 1(d) WNR. Memorandum, TK 1988-1989, 21244, no. 3, at 10. *But see* Report of the Dutch Copyright Society on the Bill on Neighouring Rights, March 1990, at 11, and Supplementary Report of 13 April 1992, at 2, proposing to strike the element of financial responsibility as being misleading, unnecessary, and not in conformity with the definition of producer of phonograms in other countries.

315. *See supra* 2.12.

316. Under § 25 DCA (1912), alterations to works other than architectural works as well as alterations to the title of the work or the name of the author identified on the work were subject to the authorization of the author, even after he had assigned his author's right. The author was furthermore entitled to modify the work after assignment of the author's right, unless this were contrary to the principles of good faith. In 1931, § 25 DCA was amended so as to remove the exception for architectural works. Parl.Gesch. 25.10-12 (1931). § 25 DCA was further amended in 1972 (S. 579) and 1989 (S. 282).

the exclusive right of communication to the public ('openbaarmaking').[317] By interpreting and amending the provisions in which the scope of these rights have been defined (§§ 12-25a DCA), courts and legislators have been able to adapt to the technological developments and to comply with obligations under international treaties without having to revert to a systematic, integral legislative revision.[318]

While most copyright laws have been integrally revised in the course of this century, the basic structure of the Dutch Copyright Act of 1912 has thus remained the same. The structure and terminology of the 1912 Act, in fact, are reminiscent of Kohler and De Beaufort, who argued that the 'author's right' is a patrimonial right and that the creator's moral interests are protected as personal rights.[319] According to the Act, the 'author's right' encompasses the exclusive rights of reproduction and communication to the public (§ 1 DCA) and may be assigned in whole or in part (§ 2 DCA). The rights of attribution and integrity are categorized as limitations to the author's right and may be invoked by the author even after he has assigned his 'author's right' (§ 25(1) DCA).[320] Although the 1912 Act does not specifically say so,[321] the latter provision has often been interpreted as a statement that the rights of attribution and integrity are inalienable.[322]

In regulating the contractual relationships between creators and producers, the Dutch legislator seems to take a more reserved attitude than most other continental-European legislators.[323] Proposals to statutorily restrict the duration of

---

317. § 12 DCA: communication to the public; §§ 13-14: reproduction; §§ 15-25a DCA: limitations. On communication to the public, see Mom, 9-114. On reproduction, see generally Spoor.

318. *See* Spoor/Verkade, at 139.

319. *See supra* 2.11. De Beaufort (1932), at 22-26. Within the system of the Dutch Civil Code, authors' rights are categorized as patrimonial rights. *See* Meijers, at 169; Grosheide/Hartkamp, at 212.

320. *See also* Gerbrandy (1988), at 289; Van Lingen, at 91. Quaedvlieg (1992), at 42, argues that protection of the right of integrity is based on theories of contract law and torts and, as such, may well be protected without reference to the author's right. Grosheide, at 301: since new expressions of cultural information may not be compatible with the concept of moral rights, it could be in the interest of the development of copyright law to replace the moral rights provisions in the copyright law by special provisions of contract law or tort, or to restrict moral rights protection to the protection guaranteed under national constitutions and international human rights conventions. *See also* Grosheide, *Paradigms*, at 232. On the nature of the rights of integrity and attribution, see also infra 5.5.3, 5.6.3.

321. *See* Spoor/Verkade, at 301, 302: the wordings of § 25 DCA do not preclude assignment of the rights of integrity and attribution. Vermeijden, at 147: assignment of the 'droit moral' is possible.

322. Du Bois, *Enkele aspecten*, at 56; Cohen Jehoram, *Grenzen*, at 524; Kuypers, at 10; Van Lingen, at 18, 91; Quaedvlieg, at 19. *See also* Memorandum to § 25 DCA, Parl.Gesch. 25.15 (1972).

323. *See* Boytha, *National Legislation on Authors' Contracts*, at 199, comparing the number of provisions on contracts: Germany 60 (including the Publishing Act of 1901), France over 30 and the Netherlands 3 (§§ 2, 23, 24 DCA). It should be noted, however, that Boytha has not taken into account §§ 7, 8, 25 and the provisions on contracts between authors and producers of film works (§§ 45e-g DCA). In favour of legislation on contracts between creators and producers: Du Bois, *Het contractenrecht*, at 102; Cohen Jehoram, *The Author's Place*, at 390 and *Uitgaveovereenkomst revisited*, at 48, with approval of Gerbrandy, at 21; Grosheide, *Contractuele exploitatie*, at 421; Van Lingen, at 19.

assignments[324] as well as initiatives to regulate publishing contracts within the framework of the new Civil Code[325] have been fruitless up till now.[326] There are, however, a few provisions in the 1912 Act which are designed to prevent authors from bargaining away their rights too easily. Full and partial assignments of the author's right must be executed in a written instrument signed by the assignor (§ 2(2) DCA).[327] Licenses to use a work may be granted orally or be implicit in the circumstances,[328] but the licensee can only legally enforce them against third parties if he has expressly stipulated the right to do so in an agreement with the author or his successor in title.[329]

An assignment only extends to the rights which are specified in the written instrument or those which necessarily follow from the nature and purpose of the title (§ 2(2) DCA).[330] This provision resembles the German 'purpose transfer rule' (§ 31(5) GCA),[331] but is not as frequently invoked[332] and has not led to

---

324. *See* proposals made by members of the Committee on the Judiciary, TK 1964-1965, 7877, 7889 (R446), no. 5, at 2. *See also* Cohen Jehoram, *Uitgaveovereenkomst revisited*, at 52, proposing to introduce a right whereby an author could terminate a publishing agreement after three of five years if the publisher failed to exercise the exclusive publishing right.

325. Bill for a new Civil Code, Book 7, Title 8, in: Meijers, at 288. *See generally* Alberdingk Thijm, 51-58; Cohen Jehoram, *Uitgaveovereenkomst revisited*, at 48-56; Soetenhorst, 91-100.

326. TK 1968-1969, 7877, 7889 (R 446), no. 6, p. 2: a limit on the duration of assignments is not necessarily favourable for authors, because it may remove the incentive to publish works by young, unknown authors. If assignments are limited in time, publishers run the risk that their work will not sell, while they can only profit from succesful works for a limited period.

327. The bill for a new law on author's right, introduced to parliament in 1911, only required a written instrument in the event of a full assignment. Parl.Gesch. 2.3 (1912). According to the Memorandum, a partial assignment could be implied from the circumstances, e.g. in case of photographs commissioned for inclusion in an industrial catalogue. Parl.Gesch. 2.3 (1912). With reference to this example, the Minister of Justice rejected a proposal to provide that a transfer of the title to a physical object does not imply an assignment of the author's right. Parl.Gesch. 2.7 (1912). Members of parliament replied that it would be possible to allow the exploitation of a work without assigning any rights, so that a writing requirement for partial assignments would not lead to impracticalities. Parl.Gesch. 2.4-5 (1912). Parliament subsequenly adopted a proposal to extend the writing requirement to partial assignments. Parl.Gesch. 2.16 (1912).

328. *See e.g.* Judgment of March 20, 1992, HR, Netherlands, NJ 1992, 563 note Verkade (Veld v. Suthormo): receiver sells the assets of a bankrupt corporation to defendant, including a trademark designed by plaintiff. There was no written agreement between the corporation and the plaintiff dealing with author's right. HR: the appellate court's ruling must be interpreted so as to imply that, by selling the trademark design and allowing the corporation to do with it what it pleased, the plaintiff intended not to exercise his author's right (if any) vis-à-vis the corporation or those who derive title to the trademark from the corporation. This ruling does not violate any rules of law. Spoor/Verkade, at 358: this interpretation implies that the sale of the trademark design to the corporation with the permission to use it as it pleased, had the same effect as an outright assignment of the author's right.

329. § 27a(2) DCA. *See also infra* 3.3.7.

330. This provision has been incorporated in the final text of the statute based on an amendment proposed by representative Drucker, Document 8, I, 12 June 1912, Parl.Gesch. 2.9 (1912). *See generally* Soetenhorst, at 55-58.

331. *See* Cohen Jehoram, *Netherlands*, § 4[2][c]. *But see* Spoor/Verkade, at 358: § 2(2) DCA should not be understood in the sense of the purpose transfer doctrine, i.e. as a restriction of the scope of an assignment to the modes of exploitation primarily envisaged by the parties. The nature and purpose of the agreement may imply that a 'full assignment of the author's right' must be understood as an assignment of all rights. *See also* Gerbrandy, at 30. *See also infra* 3.3.6.

standard contracts with the same degree of detail as the German 'purpose transfer rule'.[333]

The only exception to the requirement of a written instrument for an assignment is the provision that the authors of a film work, with the exception of the author of the film music, are presumed to have assigned to the producer the exclusive right of communication to the public, the right of reproduction by way of fixation on a physical object intended for performance or exhibition, as well as the right to dub and subtitle the work, unless they have agreed otherwise in a written instrument (§ 45(d) DCA).[334] In 1993, § 45d DCA has been amended so as to oblige the producer to pay an equitable remuneration to the authors for every mode of exploitation, existing and future, to be agreed upon by written agreement (§ 45d DCA).[335] The object of this amendment is to prevent the producer from acquiring the rights to all modes of exploitation by one, lump sum payment.[336]

2.16 Evaluation: author's right vs. copyright

To illustrate the various concepts of authorship and copyright ownership in the various national copyright laws, I will briefly summarize the most distinctive characteristics of the two major systems of copyright which have developed since the breakdown of the system of printing privileges. In reading, it should be borne in mind that modern developments have taken the edge off both systems, gradually leveling out copyright laws worldwide.[337]

---

332. For interpretation of the scope of a grant according to the nature and purpose of the agreement, see e.g. Judgment of December 29, 1990, Rb. Maastricht, Netherlands, 7 IER 30 (1991) ('Anton Pieck'); Judgment of October 9, 1987, Pres.Rb. Haarlem, Netherlands, 12 Informatie-recht/AMI 63 (1988) (Fimla v. van Driel) *Cf. also* Judgment of March 25, 1949, HR, Netherlands, NJ 1950, 643 note Veegens ('La belle et la bête'): the movie theatre's argument that the nature and purpose of an agreement to compose film music imply that the film producer acquires the right to perform the music as a part of the film dismissed because an authorization to publicly perform the music may just as easily be obtained from the performing rights society in the country of exhibition.

333. Compare Schricker, at 473, stating that in Germany author's contracts reflect a factual, case-oriented approach which is unusual for continental-European law.

334. Act of May 30, 1985, S. 307. *See infra* 3.2.2; 4.3; 6.2; 7.6.

335. S. 1993, 178. Until the 1993 amendment, the obligation to pay a remuneration only existed with respect to modes of exploitation that were unforeseeable at the moment the producer decided that the film was ready for public performance.

336. TK 1989-1990, 21244, no. 6, at 35. The producer must pay the remuneration to the 'authors or their successors in title' (§ 45d DCA). However, the producer is the successor in title on the basis of the presumption of assignment. The requirement that the remuneration must be agreed in a written instrument furthermore would seem to be at odds with the statutory presumption of assignment. According to the legislative reports, a failure to make a written agreement on remuneration could entail nullity. TK 1989-1990, 21244, no. 5, at 35. What this means in general and also in the specific situation in which the parties have not made a written agreement at all and the authors, consequently, are presumed to have assigned their exploitation rights to the producer, is unclear.

337. On the divergence and convergence of 'droit d'auteur' and 'copyright' see, in particular, Strowel.

In the *natural right approach to author's rights* which is prevalent in continental Europe, statutory protection of creators is considered a recognition of their natural claims to the economic and intellectual benefits arising from their intellectual creations. The natural right approach manifests itself in:

1. the statutory recognition of an exclusive right of the author in his personal, intellectual creation. Authorship and first ownership are inherently restricted to the originator of the intellectual creation.[338]
2. statutory protection upon creation which is not dependent on the compliance with formalities.
3. the term of protection is related to the life of the author.
4. the formulation of inalienable and universally protected moral rights recognizing the permanent bond between an author and his work.
5. a tendency to regard the public interest as limiting rather than determining the scope of protection. The statutory author's right is considered to be an elaboration of an author's all-encompassing right to the fruits of his intellectual labour, rather than being a limited enumeration of exclusive rights. Exploitation rights are formulated in a broad and flexible manner in order to include new modes of exploitation.
6. the natural right approach does not preclude regulation of transfers. Legislation on the scope, duration and exclusivity of transfers is considered a means to enable the author to preserve his work's integrity and to secure a fair share of the proceeds from exploitation.

According to the *instrumental approach of copyright* which is traditionally manifest in Anglo-American copyright legislation, copyright serves as an economic incentive for creators and producers to engage in the creation and dissemination of new works. The instrumental approach manifests itself in:

1. statutory protection vesting upon publication which is dependent on the compliance with formalities, thereby restricting statutory monopolies to works which are accessible to the public and for which protection is actually sought.
2. copyright protection is secured by the person who first publishes a work with the author's permission and upon compliance with statutory formalities.
3. the protection commences upon first publication and is valid for a fixed term. Renewal for a second term is possible if certain formalities are complied with before expiry of the first term.
4. the copyright domain and the scope of protection are determined according to the purpose of copyright protection, as expressed in a limitative enumeration of exclusive rights and broadly formulated exceptions.
5. a copyright is fully alienable. It is attached to the work more than to its creator.
6. a reticence in extending protection to foreign works.

---

338. *See e.g.* Nordemann, at 88-89; Schricker/Loewenheim, at 205-206; Ulmer, at 183. *See also* Ricketson, *People or Machines*; Dietz, *The concept of author*, both arguing that the Berne Convention underlies a human centred notion of authorship.

In the course of this century, the Anglo-American copyright laws have abandoned characteristics 1, 2, 3 and 6 of the instrumental approach and have adopted characteristics 2, 3 and, to a certain degree, also 4 of the natural right approach.[339] While they have thus embraced the creator doctrine as a basic rule for attributing copyright ownership, they have also codified common law doctrines which presumed that employers and certain commissioning parties had the common law right of first publication, by qualifying them as author and/or first owner of the copyright. This legislative discretion in defining authorship and copyright ownership still distinguishes the Anglo-American copyright laws from continental-European copyright laws which consider the creator as 'author' and first copyright owner *per se*.

The continental-European copyright laws, for their part, have never elaborated the concept of the author's right as a natural right of the creator to its full consequence. While most countries to some extent accord moral rights protection to creators without regard as to their nationality,[340] economic protection only extends to creators who meet the general criteria of applicability (nationality, first publication, etc.).[341]

The principle that ownership automatically vests in the creator of the work, furthermore, is somewhat stretched by the generally accepted rule that co-authors enjoy an undivided ownership interest in the co-authored work, because this rule implies that a co-author acquires an ownership interest in the results of another person's creative labour. Compared to the American copyright law, however, which recognizes co-authorship if the parties have an intention to merge their contributions into interdependent or inseparable parts of a unitary whole (§ 101 USCA), the German copyright law as major representative of the natural right approach does remain closer to the creator doctrine by limiting co-authorship to

---

339. Strowel, at 591, argues that, although the provisions on moral rights in the Anglo-American copyright laws are still limited in scope, the introduction of these provisions may lead courts to elaborate on the idea that the intellectual interests of creators can impinge on the rules of commerce.

340. In German copyright law, the rights of first publication (§ 12 GCA), attribution (§ 13 GCA), and integrity (§ 14 GCA) may be invoked by all foreign authors (§ 121(6) GCA). Article 1 cl. 2 of the French Law of 8 July 1964, provides that authors enjoy protection under French law for the integrity of their work regardless of the country of first publication. *See also* Judgment of May 28, 1991, Cass.Civ. 1re, France, 149 RIDA 197 (1991) (Huston v. La Cinq), discussed *infra* 3.4; 6.3. *Cf. also* § 104(a) USCA, according protection to unpublished works, regardless of the nationality or domicile of the author. In Dutch copyright law, foreign authors cannot invoke the Copyright Act if they do not meet the general criteria for applicability (§ 47 DCA, Article 3 BC), but they may enjoy protection of their moral interests under theories of contract or torts law. *See e.g.* Judgment of November 30, 1961, Pres. Rb. Rotterdam, Netherlands, NJ 1962, 169 ('The enemy general'): publication in the Netherlands of an abridged and translated version of an American novel without the original title and without identification of the names of the author and copyright owners is considered unlawful towards the authors and copyright owners, even though the novel does not meet the criteria for applicability under § 47 DCA. *See also infra* 5.3.

341. Article 3 BC; § 47(1) DCA; § 121(1) GCA.

mergers of contributions which are inexploitable standing alone (§ 8(1) GCA).[342]

More important than the issues of universal protection and co-authorship, is that the continental-European legislators have all to some extent accomodated economically important industries by lowering the protection treshold for certain categories of works, by introducing neighbouring rights for producers and by adopting presumptions of transfers and restrictions on the moral rights protection for specific categories of works.

Looking at the German and American copyright laws as representatives of the natural right and instrumental approaches, we could say that the German Copyright Act demonstrates a 'split right' approach in allocating rights between creators and producers, and the U.S. Copyright Act an 'all or nothing approach'. The 'split right' approach of German copyright law is expressed in a combined system of inalienable author's rights and presumptions on the scope of grants of rights-to-use, complemented in certain cases with related rights for producers.

In American copyright law, any rule on the scope of transfers runs counter to a deeply-entrenched commitment to contractual freedom.[343] Therefore, rather than regulating what rights are presumed to have been transferred to the producer and what rights remain with the creator, the 1976 Act reveals *integral* shifts of copyright ownership, such as the 'work made for hire' rule and an author's unwaivable right to terminate a transfer after 35 years. The introduction of inalienable but waivable moral rights for authors of works of visual art has only marginally affected this 'all or nothing' approach.

The Dutch copyright law combines both approaches. While the attribution of authorship to employers and legal entities demonstrates an 'all or nothing' approach to allocating rights, the 1912 Act also reveals a 'split right' approach in providing that the scope of an assignment is limited to the rights specified in the agreement or the rights which follow from the nature or purpose of the title, and also in the presumption that the film producer has acquired certain, specified exploitation rights from the authors of the film work in the absence of an agreement to the contrary.

---

342. On the requirements for co-authorship under Dutch law, see *infra* 3.2.2; 7.5. The ability of co-owners under American law to independently license uses and to transfer their copyright interest in the work also goes further than the German and Dutch copyright laws, which do not allow the co-owner to individually exploit the co-owned work. *See infra* 3.3.2. § 8(2) GCA provides that the co-authors can only decide on first publication and alteration of the work collectively. Whether the co-authors may independently enforce the right of integrity or attribution, is unclear under German law. Affirmative: Schricker/Loewenheim, at 212; Ulmer, at 193. In Dutch copyright law, independent enforcement of moral rights by a co-author seems to be accepted. *See* Spoor/Verkade, at 399. For a discussion of the enforcement of moral rights by co-authors under American copyright law, see Karlen, 242-275.

343. *See* Report of the Register of Copyrights on the General Revision of the U.S. Copyright Law, CLR Part 2, 93 (1961): 'We would not favor a statutory specification of the terms and conditions of transfer agreements, or a prohibition of transfers on any particular terms. Transfers are made in a wide variety of situations; terms that may be unfair in some cases may be appropriate in others. And statutory specifications or prohibitions may hamper authors, as well as potential users, in arranging for the exploitation of copyright works.'

Chapter 3

The impact of the creator doctrine on the exploitation of creative works

3.1 Introduction

In Chapter 2, we saw how the creator doctrine has developed into a world-wide accepted basic principle of copyright law. It will however be clear from the description of the American, Dutch and German copyright laws at the close of the chapter that legislators and courts do not always accept the implications of the doctrine in full. There are departures from the creator doctrine on all kinds of levels, varying from provisions which treat the producer as author and first owner of the copyright, to provisions which treat the producer's domicile as point of attachment for protection under the national copyright law.

In most cases, these departures from the creator doctrine are designed to eliminate certain consequences of this doctrine. In this chapter, I will discuss these consequences and examine how they affect the exploitation of works of authorship. The chapter opens with a discussion of the general problem of identifying the first owner of the copyright (§ 3.2), followed by an analysis of the problems producers may encounter when they seek to acquire and prove title to works of authorship. In order to structure the analysis, I will distinguish between problems connected with security in copyright transactions (§ 3.3), problems connected with international copyright transactions (§ 3.4), and problems connected with efficiency in the process of acquiring and establishing title (§ 3.5). The American, Dutch and German copyright laws will serve as points of reference throughout the discussion.

3.2 Identifying the first copyright owner according to the creator doctrine

3.2.1 WHO IS THE AUTHOR?

In order for creative works to be distributed to the public and for copyright owners to profit from the use of their works by the public, the identity of the copyright owner must be clear. This is still true for most uses, although the techniques for controlling the mass consumption of creative works increasingly disconnect the relationship between the individual copyright owners and the remuneration paid for the use of their works.

According to the creator doctrine, copyright vests in the 'author', and the 'author' is the natural person who created the work. As logical as this may seem, this attribution rule is not always easy to apply in practice. Many works are commissioned by a person who has certain wishes and ideas as to what the work should look like or do. The creative process furthermore often involves a large number of people who contribute to the work simultaneously or successively in a more or less creative manner. In either situation, it may be difficult to establish who created the work.[1] While it may be evident that a work qualifies for copyright protection, it may not be clear who actually created it. Firstly, it is necessary to establish who actually contributed what, and then to establish whose contribution merits authorship and whose does not. In order to be able to do this, it must be clear which elements of the work constitute authorship, and this is still one of the most difficult questions of copyright law.[2]

Identification of the author(s) is even more difficult if a work does not reflect an identifiable personal expression or has been designed with the aid of a technical device. Was it the computer program or the human being who made the work? Was the human contribution sufficiently creative to qualify as an independent work of authorship? Etc.[3] And even if it is clear who made a creative contribution, it may still be unclear how the contributions relate to one another: as original and derivative works, as contributions to a collective work, as contributions to a work of co-authorship, etc.

Copyright ownership is only of value to the owner if he is aware of his status of title-holder and if he can prove it to others.[4] Uncertainty about the identity of the author(s) is therefore likely to disadvantage creators in relation to producers, and producers in relation to financiers, buyers and infringers. Creators are not always in a position to enforce their alleged rights vis-à-vis producers, let alone to seek a declaratory judgment on the authorship status to support their claims for remuneration. Producers, in their turn, may fail to prove title in respect of buyers or infringers of their products if the author's identity is disputed. In practice, producers often try to get around this risk by requesting contributors to sign standard agreements stipulating broad transfers if copyrights should arise from their contributions. This may indeed provide the producer with full title, but it does not guarantee that the actual creators will be treated any differently than the product's other contributors when it comes to defining the terms of their agreements.[5]

---

1. *See* Larese, at 69, 118; Gerbrandy (1992), at 35; Ginsburg, *Moral Rights*, at 127; Grosheide, at 220; Ricketson, *People or Machines*, at 15.
2. See *infra* 7.3, 7.5, discussing American and Dutch case law on co-authorship.
3. *See e.g.* De Cock Buning, at 12-15; Gervais, at 643-654; Kabel, at 87-91, Spoor/Verkade, at 27.
4. Community for Creative Non-Violence v. Reid, 109 S.Ct. 2166, 2178 (1989): 'In a "copyright marketplace", the parties negotiate with an expectation that one of them will own the copyright in the completed work ... With that expectation, the parties at the outset can settle on relevant contractual terms, such as the price for the work and the ownership of reproduction rights.'
5. *See* Grosheide, *Auteurswet*, at 122; Larese, *Fragen*, at 194; Spautz, at 188; Verkade, *Het beste artikel 7*, at 16.

3.2.2 STATUTORY PRESUMPTIONS AND DEFINITIONS OF AUTHORSHIP

It will be clear from the above that attributing copyright ownership to a creator may cause problems if it is difficult to establish who created the work and what the legal status of the creative contributors is in relation to each other and in relation to other contributors. To facilitate proof of authorship, the Berne Convention as well as most national copyright laws provide that the person whose name is recorded on the work is presumed to be its author, unless proved otherwise (Article 15(1) BC).[6] The possibility of contrary evidence is inherent to the principle that the author is the person who created the work.

In order to facilitate proof of title to an anonymous or pseudonymous work without having to disclose the creator's identity or presume that a person is considered author who did not create the work, the Berne Convention and most national copyright laws presume that the publisher whose name is on the work is entitled to enforce the copyright on the author's behalf (Article 15(3) BC).[7] Although this presumption does not affect the attribution of copyright ownership, it may complicate proof of authorship for creators who decide to come out and enforce their rights personally.

Other means to facilitate proof of title are registration, deposit of copies or the placing of a copyright notice on copies of the work. These traditional features of American copyright law,[8] can only have evidentiary weight in the creator doctrine.[9] A certificate of registration issued by the U.S. Copyright Office upon application for copyright registration constitutes prima facie evidence of the validity of the copyright and of the facts stated in the certificate[10] and, as such, creates a presumption in favour of the person whose name appears on the certificate as the author. Without such a statutory presumption, registration can merely prove that the claimaint was aware of the work on the registration date.[11]

---

6. *See* § 4 DCA; § 10(1) GCA. Both the Dutch and German provisions require that the name of the presumed author is recorded on the work as being the author.

7. *See also* § 10(2) GCA: editor, or if the work does not refer to an editor, the publisher. § 9 DCA: the publisher, of if the work does not refer a publisher, the printer. According to the Memorandum to § 9 DCA, the publisher is entitled to do what the author is entitled to do. Parl.Gesch. 9.3 (1912). This would seem to include executing assignments of copyright ownership.

8. *See supra* text accompanying 2.7 note 61 and 2.14 note 210. For a discussion of the formality requirements in early Dutch and French copyright laws, see *supra* text accompanying 2.7 note 77 and 2.15 note 280.

9. In case of 'low authorship' works, (re-)introduction of formality requirements would seem to be admissible. *See also* Grosheide, at 307; Quaedvlieg (1987), at 155.

10. § 410(c) USCA). *See also* Article 4 of the Treaty on the International Registration of Audiovisual Works, 25 Copyright 177 (1989), creating a presumption that statements of ownership filed in the register administered by WIPO are true, unless proved otherwise or unless the statement is contradicted by a prior statement in the register or is invalid under national copyright law. An entry would be invalid under national law if it is stated that the producer is the first owner of the copyright, while the national law for which the presumption is invoked does not vest initial ownership in producers. *Id.* at 171.

11. Spoor/Verkade, at 47.

Identification of the author may also be facilitated by defining authorship with respect to a particular category of work or by regulating which contributors to a particular category of work are presumed authors. Most national copyright laws have done this with respect to audiovisual works.[12] The Dutch and German Copyright Acts have to some extent defined the authors of a film work in order to clarify the legal status of contributors to film works and, in particular, to distinguish between the author(s) of a film work and the authors of pre-existing works. This distinction is relevant because the authors of a film work are co-owner(s) of the copyright to that film and are presumed to have granted the producer exclusive exploitation rights (§ 45d DCA; § 89 GCA).[13]

The Memorandum to § 89 GCA refers to the director, photographer and film editor as authors of a film work.[14] These film authors are distinguished from other contributors to the film such as the script writer or composer. According to § 89(3) GCA, the statutorily presumed grant to the film producer does not affect works used for the making of the film, such as a novel, screenplay or music. With this system, the German legislator proceeds on the basis of the general rule that co-authorship is only possible if the work is made in collaboration and if the various contributions can not be exploited in isolation from the work (§ 8(1) GCA).[15]

Without prejudice to sections 7 and 8 DCA, the Dutch Copyright Act defines authors of a film work as the natural persons who have made a creative contribution with a view to realize the film work (§ 45a DCA).[16] The Memorandum refers to the director, screenwriter, composer and photographer as examples.[17] A contributor to a film work may therefore be co-author of the film work even if his contribution can be exploited independently, something which would not have been possible if the traditional rule that co-authorship is only possible if the individual contributions can no longer be assessed separately after they have been merged, is applied.[18] If a contribution to a film can be exploited independently, the creator is both co-author of the film work as well as sole author of his own

---

12. On the meaning of 'author' in the Berne Convention, see *infra* 3.4.

13. *See also infra* 4.3; 6.2; 7.6. Under § 88 GCA, the authorization by the author of a pre-existing work to use his work for the making of a film is also presumed in case of doubt as a grant of certain rights. This presumed grant is not as broad in scope, however, as the presumed grant by the authors of the film work. *See infra* 4.3.

14. 45 UFITA 318 (1965).

15. Nordemann/Hertin, at 365: as separately exploitable contributions, the screenplay, film music, set design, costume designs, choreography, architecture, etc. must be considered to be pre-existing works and, as such, are subject to the more restrictive presumption of § 88 GCA. *But see* Schricker/Katzenberger, at 1016-1017: every person who has made a creative contribution to and specifically made for the film work should be the film's co-author, even if his contribution is separately exploitable. These separately exploitable contributions should not be subject to the presumption of § 89 GCA, however.

16. Act of May 30, 1985, S. 307. For a discussion of authorship of film works created before 1 August 1985, see Cohen Jehoram, *Het filmrecht*, at 17-18; Dietz (1978), at 57-58; Spoor/Verkade, at 460-463; Vermeijden, at 76.

17. Parl.Gesch. 45a.9 (1985).

18. Judgment of March 25, 1949, HR, Netherlands, NJ 1950, 643 note Veegens ('la belle et la bête'): co-authorship is only possible if the collaboration between the co-authors is such that their individual contributions are no longer eligible for separate, artistic judgment. Since the enactment of § 45a DCA in 1985, this rule on co-authorship has been modified in case law. *See infra* 7.5.

individual contribution, and, as such, is entitled to exploit his individual contribution separately from the film, unless this should prejudice the exploitation of the film (§ 45f DCA).[19]

The EC directives on rental and lending, on satellite broadcasting and cable retransmission rights and on the term of protection all provide that the principal director of a cinematographic or audiovisual work shall be considered as its author or one of its authors and that the Member States may provide for others to be considered co-authors.[20] Although this would seem to require that the definition of 'author of a film work' in § 45a DCA is amended so as to provide that sections 7 and 8 DCA do not apply to the principal director of a film work, the Dutch government takes the position that the rules on authorship of film works in the Rental Directive are covered by the present language of § 45a DCA.[21]

Under the U.S. Copyright Act, most contributions to audiovisual works are 'works made for hire' of which the employer or commissioning party is considered to be the author (§ 101 USCA; § 201(b) USCA).[22] In all other cases, the author of an audiovisual work is determined according to the general rules on joint authorship. A 'joint work' is a work prepared by two or more authors with the intention to merge their contributions into inseparable or interdependent parts of a unitary whole (§ 101 USCA).[23] The 'intent requirement' implies that authors of pre-existing works which have not been specifically made for the film, cannot be co-authors of the film.

Although statutory presumptions of authorship may help a producer in proving title vis-à-vis third parties, he will still be required to prove that he acquired the necessary rights from the presumed author(s). The problems which producers may encounter in doing so are discussed in the following paragraphs.

---

19. Memorandum to § 45a DCA, Parl. Gesch. 45a.10 (1985). *See also* Vermeijden, at 97, 98.

20. Article 2(2) Council Directive 92/100/EEC of 19 November 1992 concerning rental and lending rights and certain related rights in the field of intellectual property, O.J.Eur.Comm. No. L 346/61 (1992) [hereinafter: Rental Directive]; Article 1(5) Council Directive 93/83/EEC of 27 September 1993 on the coordination of certain rules concerning copyright and rights related to copyright applicable to satellite broadcasting and cable retransmission, O.J.Eur.Comm. No. L 248/15 (1993) [hereinafter: Satellite Directive]; Article 2(1) Council Directive 93/98/EEC of 29 October 1993 harmonizing the term of copyright and certain related rights, O.J.Eur.Comm. No.L 290/9 (1993) [hereinafter: Duration Directive]. The definition does not apply to audiovisual or cinematographic works created before 1 July 1994 and must be implemented in national law before 1 July 1997. A proposal to define the authors of an audiovisual work as the natural persons who have made a creative contribution to the work, has not been adopted. *See* Article 1 bis of the amended proposal for a council directive harmonizing the term of protection of copyright and certain related rights, COM (92) 602 final - SYN 395, 7 January 1993. *See* Dworkin, at 155. *See also infra* 3.4.

21. Memorandum to the bill implementing the EC directive on rental and lending an on certain related rights in the field of intellectual property, TK 1992-1993, 23247, no. 3, at 3.

22. H.R.Rep. No. 1476, 94th Cong., 2d Sess., 120 (1976). *See also* 2.14; 7.6.

23. The House Report mentions a motion picture, opera and the words and music of a song as examples of a unitary whole consisting of 'interdependent parts'. H.R.Rep. No. 94-1476, 94th Cong., 2d Sess., 120 (1976). *See also infra* 7.3. *But see* Gilliam v. American Broadcasting Companies, Inc., 538 F.2d 14 (2d Cir. 1976), regarding scripts as underlying works and the television programs for which they were made as derivative works. On the basis of the formulation of the scriptwriter's agreement, the court held that the broadcasting of edited versions of the television programs infringed on the copyright in the scripts.

3.3 The impact of the creator doctrine on security in copyright commerce

3.3.1 INTRODUCTION

The creditworthiness of production and publishing companies, whether of books, electronic databases, television programs or computer software, rests for a large part on ownership of copyrights.[24] Security in copyright commerce therefore requires that the producer can prove title vis-à-vis potential financiers and buyers of his products and of his business as a whole. If for some reason proof is difficult to provide, the producer will have less opportunity to finance and sell his products, and pirates will have an easy defense in infringement suits.[25]

In the following paragraphs, I shall discuss in which respects the creator doctrine may affect a producer's ability to prove title to creative works. For the purpose of this analysis, I will take as a point of departure the situation in which the creator doctrine is carried through to its ultimate consequence: copyright vests in the work's creator(s) and none of the rights under the copyright are statutorily presumed to have been transferred to the producer.

3.3.2 ACQUISITION OF RIGHTS IN CASE OF MULTIPLE CREATIVE CONTRIBUTIONS

Although it may not always be easy to identify the authors if the creative process involves multiple contributors,[26] the producer has to contract with every contributor who qualifies as (co)author of that work or as author of a pre-existing work. In American copyright law, a certain concentration of rights has been realized by allowing joint authors, as co-owners of the copyright in the joint work, to individually transfer their ownership interest in the work[27] or to individually

---

24. On copyright as a piece of security, see Van Esch, at 63; Spoor, *Onzekere zekerheid*, at 359-361; Thole, at 243.

25. *See e.g.* Judgment of October 20, 1982, Ger. 's-Hertogenbosch, Netherlands, NJ 1983, 503 (Vlisco v. Dessina): an alleged infringer submitted the defense that the plaintiff had not established authorship. The plaintiff's action was upheld under § 8 DCA. U.S. case law indicates that a defense based on lack of standing tends to protract the lawsuit, because questions of ownership often bring up material issues of fact which cannot be solved on a motion for summary judgment. *See e.g.* Computer Data Systems, Inc. v. Kleinberg, 759 F.Supp. 10 (D.D.C. 1990). Dutch courts seem to be willing to try issues of fact connected with authorship and copyright ownership on a motion for summary judgment, provided the plaintiff's interests in a summary judgment are urgent and the facts of the case are not too complicated. *See* Judgment of December 28, 1983, Ger. 's-Gravenhage, Netherlands, 51 BIE 390 (1985) (Lintels v. Arcom).

26. *See supra* 3.2.1. *Cf. also* E.A. Sargoy, Motion Picture Association of America, Inc., Comment of 2 March 1962 on Report of the Register of Copyright of 1961, CLR Part 3, 359 (1962), about authorship of motion pictures: 'If it is not to be the picture's producer (corporate or individual), as the employer for hire, who will be the author or authors? Will it be one or more or all of the host of creative talents employed to contribute their artistic labors and intelligence to the copyrightable film production? Witness the rollcall of the variety of such talents nominated for Oscars this week.'

27. *See* Goldstein I, at 386; Nimmer § 6-11.

authorize the use of the joint work.[28] A producer may therefore become co-owner or obtain a non-exclusive license by contracting with one of the co-owners.

Under German copyright law, a work of co-authorship can be exploited collectively only, albeit that the co-authors may not unreasonably refuse their permission to exploit the work (§ 8(2) GCA). There is a similar provision with respect to combinations of separately exploitable contributions, such as choreography and music or text and illustrations. Although these combinations do not qualify for co-authorship under German law,[29] the authors may not unreasonably refuse their permission for the disclosure, exploitation or adaptation of the combination, once they have agreed to exploit their works as a combination (§ 9 GCA).[30]

Under Dutch copyright law, co-authors can not exploit the co-owned work individually.[31] It is arguable, however, that the principles of reasonableness and equity imply that a co-owner cannot always refuse the exploitation of the work desired by the other co-owners.[32]

3.3.3 THE PRODUCER AS AUTHOR

If a producer has been personally involved in the creative process, he may perhaps qualify as author or co-author. A producer may become sole author if he

---

28. *See* H.R. Rep. No. 1476, 94th Cong., 2d Sess., 121 (1976). *See also* Oddo v. Ries, 743 F.2d 630, 631 (9th Cir. 1984); Easter Seal Society for Crippled Children and Adults of Louisiana, Inc. v. Playboy Enterprises, 815 F.2d 323 (1987), *cert. denied*, 485 U.S. 981 (1988). To prevent the co-owners from competing with eachother, they are obliged to account to the other co-owners for profits made from the exploitation of the work. H.R. Rep. No. 1476, 94th Cong., 2d Sess., 121 (1976); Oddo v. Ries, 743 F.2d 630, 631 (9th Cir. 1984); Community for Creative Non-Violence v. Reid, 846 F.2d 1485, 1498 (D.C.Cir. 1988) *aff'd* 109 S.Ct. 2166 (1989). *See also* Nimmer, § 6.12[B] (1985). *See also infra* 7.3.

29. § 8(1) GCA. *See also supra* 3.2.2 text accompanying note 15.

30. *See e.g.* Judgment of June 9, 1982, BGH, Germany, 84 GRUR 743 (1982) ('joined works'): the composer of popular songs whose relationship with his publisher has been disturbed, cannot reasonably expect the writers of the lyrics to agree to terminate the publishing agreement in view of their financial interests in the agreement, their prospects for future assignments and their loyalty to the publisher.

31. *See e.g.* Judgment of June 14, 1990, Ger. Amsterdam, Netherlands, Computerrecht 194 (1990) (Vertimart v. JDS). The only statutory exception concerns authors of film music. The statutory presumption of assignment to the producer (§ 45d DCA) does not apply to the authors of the film music (§ 45d DCA) so as to enable them to individually authorize the reproduction and performance of their music as part of the film through their collecting societies.

32. *See* Judgment of November 27, 1985, Rb. Amsterdam, Netherlands, 15 Informatierecht/AMI 7 (1991) note Spoor, *rev'd on other grounds* Judgment of April 7, 1988, Ger. Amsterdam, Netherlands, NJ 1991, 377, *rev'd* Judgment of June 1, 1990, HR, Netherlands, NJ 1991, 377 note Verkade (Lamoth v. Kluwer): the relationship between co-authors is governed by the principles of reasonableness and equity. As co-author of photographs for a magazine article, the photographer could not reasonably refuse further exploitation of the photographs by the magazine publisher, the other co-author. The close relation between the text and photographs implied that the exploitation of the photographs was possible only in combination with the text, while the publisher would have been unreasonably prejudiced in his commercial activities by the photographer's refusal. *See also infra* 7.5. *But see* Verkade, *Het beste artikel* 7, at 19: since co-owners can veto an important transaction, initial ownership of the employer as provided for in § 7 DCA may serve to protect employees/teamworkers from each other.

creates a work entirely on his own. He may also become author if he dictates ideas and manner of expression to another person who subsequently translates the ideas into visually or orally perceptible form without adding anything substantially creative of his own. Although not specifically mentioned in the 1965 Act, it is generally understood in German copyright law that mere 'assistantship' ('Gehilfenschaft') does not merit (co)authorship.[33] U.S. case law also seems to recognize that authorship subsists in the intellectual creation rather than in the physical embodiment of that creation.[34]

In drafting the 1912 Act, the Dutch legislator specifically referred to the intellectual concept of authorship.[35] The Memorandum to the Act states that if the idea and manner of expression are dictated in a plan in such detail that it only needs mechanical execution to qualify as a work of authorship, the designer of the plan is the author.[36] A special provision was drafted to emphasize that authorship may also vest in the designer of a plan if the plan only contains a basic concept (e.g. sketch drawings) but is complemented by the designer's supervision and control of the manner in which the plan is executed: if a work has been prepared according to the plan and under the supervision and direction of another person, that other person is designated author (§ 6 DCA).[37] According to the Hoge Raad, this provision intends to solve the question of authorship in those situations in which the executors of the plan contribute in a more or less creative manner.[38] In this situation, the designer of the basic concept will only become author of the work if his supervision and control is such that the executors' contributions cannot be said to constitute individual creations.[39]

If the producer is sole author, he does not need the other contributors' permission to exploit the work. The same is true if the producer qualifies as a co-author and, as is the case in American copyright law,[40] the co-owners are allowed to exploit the work individually. The possibility of individual exploitation does not ensure,

---

33. *See* Judgment of February 6, 1985, BGH, Germany, 87 GRUR 529 (1985) ('Happening'): professor is sole author of a university happening based on a painting of Hieronymus Bosch. He provided the idea and choreography and directed the choreography, while the other contributors remained under his supervision and, as such, did not make a personal, intellectual contribution of their own. *See also* Schricker/Loewenheim, at 207; Ulmer, at 187.

34. *See* Andrien v. Southern Ocean County Chamber of Commerce, 927 F.2d 132 (3rd Cir. 1991); Lakedreams v. Taylor, 932 F.2d 1103 (5th Cir. 1991). *See also* Latman/Gorman/Ginsburg, Appendix, at 72, referring to the 'intellectual' conception of authorship as opposed to the 'economic conception' underlying the work for hire doctrine. *Cf. also* the definition of 'fixed' in § 101 USCA: a work is 'fixed' in a tangible medium of expression when its embodiment in a copy or phonorecord, by *or under the authority of the author*, is sufficiently permanent or stable to permit it to be perceived, reproduced, or otherwise communicated for a period of more than transitory duration (...) [Emphasis added]

35. Parl.Gesch. 6.3 (1912).

36. Parl.Gesch. 6.3 (1912). *See also* Hirsch Ballin, 77-92.

37. *See infra* 7.5, discussing case law on § 6 DCA.

38. Judgment of June 28, 1940, HR, Netherlands, NJ 1941, 110 note Meijers ('Fire over England I').

39. *Id.* at 163. *See also* Judgment of June 1, 1990, HR, Netherlands, NJ 1991, 377 note Verkade (Kluwer v. Lamoth), discussed *supra* 1.1 note 7. Courts do not easily assume authorship on the basis of § 6 DCA. See *infra* 7.3, discussing case law on authorship of commissioned works.

40. *See supra* 3.3.2 notes 27-28 and accompanying text.

however, that the other co-owner(s) will not engage in competing exploitations.[41]

If a producer adapts a work, or incorporates a work in a collection, the resulting adaptation or collection may perhaps qualify as a derivative or collective work.[42] Authorship of a collective or derivative work does not exempt the producer from acquiring title to the underlying work(s), however.[43] Although a non-exclusive license to use the pre-existing work as a part of the collective or derivative work would, strictly speaking, be sufficient, producers may want a broader transfer of rights in order to be able to license additional uses and to prevent competing exploitations.

Since, in many cases, it is difficult to assess whether the producer's contribution merits authorship and how his contribution relates to the contribution of the hired party, it is quite hazardous for producers to rely on their own creative contribution to acquire title to a work.[44] This is even more so if the actual creative contribution is not made by the producer in person, but by his employee(s), because the creator doctrine implies that a producer can only derive title from his employees' creative labour if he can prove that the employees granted him the necessary rights. It is obvious, therefore, that the majority of cases on co-authorship of commissioned works arise under regimes such as the American and Dutch copyright laws which consider the employer to be the author of works made by an employee within the scope of his employment. Under these copyright laws, a producer may become co-author of a work for which he hired an independent contractor, if his employees' combined input is sufficiently creative to qualify for co-authorship.[45]

3.3.4 ACQUIRING TITLE TO FUTURE WORKS

If a producer initiates the production of a work of authorship, he will have to find financiers and buyers before the creative process commences. Since copyright arises upon creation, it is however not possible to acquire and prove title

---

41. *See e.g.* Easter Seal, 815 F.2d 323, 337 (1987), *cert. denied*, 485 U.S. 981 (1988): the plaintiff, a charitable organization, hired a television station to videotape a staged parade and musical jam session. The television station licensed the defendant to use part of the tape in an adult film called 'Candy, the Stripper'. The court held that the plaintiff and the television station could be considered co-authors and that the television station, as a co-author, was entitled to license third parties to use the tape.

42. Collective works: § 5 DCA; § 4 GCA; § 103(a) USCA. Derivative works: § 10(2) DCA; § 3 GCA; § 103(a) USCA.

43. With respect to collective works: § 5 DCA; § 4 GCA; § 201(c) USCA. With respect to derivative works: § 13 DCA; § 23 GCA; § 103(a), § 106(2) USCA.

44. Compare the case of *Kluwer v. Lamoth*, Judgment of June 1, 1990, HR, Netherlands, NJ 1991, 377 note Verkade, dealing with authorship of photographs commissioned for incorporation in magazine articles. The editorial staff of the magazine selected and arranged the objects and the pictures were taken by a freelance photographer. The views of the parties, courts and commentators varied from (1) the photographer is the sole author, to (2) the publisher is the sole author on the basis of § 6 or § 7 DCA, to (3) the photographer and the publisher are co-authors, to (4) the publisher is author of the composition and the photographer is author of the photographical fixations (as derivative works). For a more detailed discussion of this case, see *supra* 7.5.

45. *See infra* 7.3; 7.5.

before the work has been created. The producer must therefore look for other ways to secure exclusivity at an early stage. He may try to purchase rights or take an option to purchase rights in a pre-existing work or acquire title to a preparatory work, such as a drawing, draft or treatment.[46] These measures do not however guarantee that the producer will acquire full title to the finished product. Especially if the production process requires several simultaneous or subsequent creative activities involving a large number of contributors, it may be difficult to identify the authors and to prevent conflicting transfers.

These problems may be avoided if it is possible to validly transfer future copyrights. In 1936, the Dutch Hoge Raad held that an assignment of author's rights to future works is not admissible under Dutch law.[47] It was therefore only possible to secure title to future works by stipulating an assignment to be executed upon delivery of the work, but such stipulation was not a watertight guarantee that the author would not assign his rights to someone else.[48] Under the new Netherlands Civil Code, the assignment of rights to future works is admissible, provided the work has been sufficiently specified at the moment the assignment is executed.[49] Although this requirement would at least seem to prevent authors from signing their lives away with one signature, it is still unclear how specific a work must be defined in order for the assignment to be valid.[50]

Under German law, it is possible to grant rights to use future works if the work can be specified at the moment the grant is executed.[51] The grant does not have to be in writing. A commitment to grant rights to use future unspecified

---

46. *Cf. e.g.* Judgment of January 23, 1992, Pres.Rb. Amsterdam, Netherlands, 16 Informatie-recht/AMI 112 (1992) ('Per wanneer kunt u beginnen'): idea for a television show may be eligible for copyright protection if it has been sufficiently elaborated and concretized (*quod non*). *See also* Schwarz, at 317. With respect to computer programs, Article 1(1) of the Council Directive of 14 May 1991 on the legal protection of computer programs provides that the term 'computer program' shall include preparatory design material. *See also* Van Esch, at 63-64, Dommering, *De software richtlijn*, at 86.

47. Judgment of February 13, 1936, HR, Netherlands, NJ 1936, 443 note Meijers ('Das Blaue Licht II'). *Critically*, Gerbrandy at 32; Meijers, NJ 1936, 443 at 884; Van Lingen, at 146-147; Verkade/Spoor, at 287, all arguing that an assignment of rights to future works should be possible with regard to works of which the nature can be more or less determined in advance. *See also* Van Engelen, *Overdracht*, at 48; Grosheide/Hartkamp, at 213; Vermeijden, at 107-116.

48. *See* Judgment of March 25, 1992, Rb. Amsterdam, Netherlands, 17 Informatierecht/AMI 34 (1993) (Vevam v. NOS II): freelance contributors to television programs have validly assigned their cable distribution rights to the broadcasting organization NOS, partly by express agreement and partly on the basis of the statutory presumption of assignment of § 45d DCA. The freelance authors therefore could not validly assign cable distribution rights to their collecting society Vevam, even though they had a contractual obligation to do so. The NOS does not act unlawful against Vevam by inciting the authors to breach their contractual obligation vis-à-vis Vevam.

49. *See* § 3:84(2); § 3:97 NBW. *See also* Van Engelen, at 48; Grosheide/Hartkamp, at 213; Spoor/Verkade, at 360-361; Thole, at 261.

50. Spoor/Verkade, at 361, mentions as examples of sufficiently specified works a book about a certain topic in a certain genre and a screen adaptation of an existing novel. *But see* Van Engelen, *Overdracht*, at 49, arguing that 'all the works an author will make' complies with the specificity requirement.

51. Schricker, at 419; Ulmer, at 360. *See also* Nordemann/Hertin, at 174-175: the work to which the grant applies must be specified to such an extent that it can not be exchanged for any other work under the circumstances. A 'report of the author's trip to Egypt' may and a 'novel on World War II' may not be sufficiently specified.

works or works which have only been specified according to category, however, must be in writing and may be terminated after five years (§ 40(1) GCA).

Under American copyright law, the validity of assignments of future copyrights does not seem to be an issue, although it has been argued that a transfer involving all future works an author will ever make, may be in breach of public policy.[52] Like any other transfer of copyright ownership, the title to future works must be transferred in a written instrument signed by the owner (§ 204(a) USCA). The 1976 Act does not require the work to be specified at the moment the transfer is executed. The possibility created under the Act to secure priority over later transfers by recording the transfer in the Copyright Office, does however require that the work to which the transfer pertains is specifically identified and registered (§ 205(c) USCA).[53]

A specificity requirement for transfers of rights to future works is probably less of a problem for a producer who contracts with an author for the exploitation of a particular work, than for a party who contracts with authors for the exploitation of multiple works on a long-term basis, such as an employer, music publisher or a collecting society.[54] This indicates that problems about conflicting transfers may very well arise between creators, producers and collecting societies. Can a creator validly transfer rights to a producer despite his commitment to a collecting society?[55] Can a collecting society exercise rights that have been previously transferred to a producer?[56] These questions will probably become increasingly

---

52. *See* Nimmer § 10.03[A].
53. *See infra* note 58 and accompanying text.
54. Schricker, at 535: § 40 GCA is applicable to exploitation contracts with collecting societies, but not to employment contracts. *Id.* Schricker/Rojahn, at 575. Nordemann/Hertin, at 231: § 40 GCA is applicable to exploitation contracts with collecting societies and to employment contracts with a copyright clause.
55. *See* Judgment of March 1, 1990, OLG Hamburg, Germany, 89 GRUR 599 (1991) ('broadcast commercial'): the granting of broadcasting rights in Henry Mancini's 'Pink Panther Theme' to a collecting society with the exception of the right to use the theme for commercials, does not entitle the collecting society to license a broadcasting organization to use the theme as background music to publicize its own television programs. The author has an interest in negotiating individually, because commercials represent a market that follows the principles of supply and demand, which allows the author to negotiate individually on a remuneration. *See also* Judgment of September 29, 1989, HR, Netherlands, NJ 1990, 307 note Verkade (Van Spijk v. Beeldrecht): collecting society's mandate to administer author's rights does not prevent the author/mandator from exercising his rights in his own name. In 1993, a provision has been included in the Civil Code, recognizing the possibility of a mandate to administer rights to the author's exclusion (§ 7:423 Civil Code).
56. Negatively: Judgment of March 25, 1992, Rb. Amsterdam, Netherlands, 17 Informatierecht/AMI 34 (1993) (Vevam v. NOS II). Judgment of November 28, 1941, HR, Netherlands, NJ 1942, 205: since the assignment of performing rights in the film music to the collecting society served to enforce and exploit these rights *in the author's interest*, the performance of the film in a movie theatre pursuant to a license granted by the film producer who, previously to the assignment to the collecting society, has been authorized by the author to perform the music as part of the film, does not infringe on the collecting society's rights. *But see* Judgment of March 25, 1949, HR, Netherlands, NJ 1950, 643 note Veegens: contractual agreement to compose film music does not necessarily imply authorization to publicly perform the film, because such an authorization may just as well be obtained from the performing rights society.

important in view of the expanding field of exploitation which is covered by collective administration.[57]

In case of conflicting transfers of rights to future works, the American copyright law gives priority to the transfer which is executed and recorded in the Copyright Office first in good faith.[58] According to Dutch and German law, priority will generally be given to the assignment or, in German terminology, the grant of rights-to-use, which was effected first.[59] Priority in time does not ensure, however, that the person invoking the later transfer will not somehow challenge the validity, scope or exclusivity of the first transfer.

3.3.5 NATIONALITY AND TERM OF PROTECTION OF THE WORK

Other aspects of the creator doctrine which may affect security in copyright commerce concern the work's nationality and the term of protection. In the creator doctrine, the term of protection is attached to the life of the author or, in case of a co-authored work, to the life of the longest surviving co-author.[60] If a work consists of more than one creative contribution, the producer must keep track of every possible author in order to find out when the longest surviving author dies and whether pre-existing material incorporated in the work is still protected.

The scope created in the Berne Convention for including provisions in the national copyright law to the effect that the term of protection for cinematographic works expires 50 years from first publication or creation, whichever term expires first (Article 7(2) BC), has not been adopted in American, Dutch and German copyright law.[61] The 1993 Duration Directive provides that the protection of cinematographic works expires 70 years after the death of the last surviving person in the group of the principal director, the author of the screenplay, the author of the dialogue and the composer of music specifically created for use in the film work, irrespective of whether they are considered (co-)authors.[62]

---

57. *See also infra* 6.4.
58. § 205(d) USCA: 'As between two conflicting transfers, the one executed first prevails if it is recorded, in the manner required to give constructive notice under subsection (c), within one month after its execution in the United States or within two months after its execution outside the United States, or at any time before recordation in such manner of the later transfer. Otherwise the later transfer prevails if recorded first in such manner, and if taken in good faith, for valuable consideration or on the basis of a binding promise to pay royalties, and without notice of the earlier transfer.' Geller, *Worldwide "Chain of Title"*, at 51-52, compares recordation under U.S. law with systems in other countries as well as with the WIPO Register for Audiovisual Works.
59. § 3:97(2) NBW: conveyance of future goods has no effect as against a person who has acquired the good in advance as a result of a prior conveyance. *See also* van Lingen, at 154; Spoor/Verkade, at 352-353. With respect to German law, see Judgment of May 21, 1992, BGH, Germany, 94 GRUR 605 (1992) ('Frau Luna'). *See also* Schricker, at 419; Ulmer, at 360.
60. Articles 7(1), 7bis BC; § 37 DCA; §§ 64, 65 GCA; § 302(a)-(b) USCA. *See also* Article 1(2) Duration Directive.
61. Instead, the American and Dutch Copyright Acts provide special duration rules in the event someone other than the creator is considered author. *See infra* 6.3.
62. Article 2(2) Duration Directive.

Protection under national copyright laws and international conventions is attached to the nationality of the author.[63] The uncertainty which may arise in this respect if a work is made by contributors of different nationalities, is mitigated by the increasing number of Berne ratifications and by the possibility of securing protection within the Berne Union by first publishing the work in a Berne country or by publishing it in a Berne country within 30 days of the first publication in a non-Berne country (Article 3(2)(b) BC).[64] For film producers from Berne countries, protection within the Berne Union is safeguarded by the provision that a cinematographic work is protected within the Berne Union if the producer is a domiciliary of a Berne country.[65]

3.3.6 LIMITATIONS TO THE SCOPE, TERM AND EXCLUSIVITY OF TRANSFERS

Other aspects of the creator doctrine which could affect security in copyright commerce are statutory and practical limitations to the scope, term and exclusivity of transfers. In order to prevent the creator from loosing all control over his works when contracting with a producer, a legislator may decide to designate certain rights as inalienable *per se*. Examples of rights which are generally considered to be inalienable are moral rights[66] and the right to terminate a transfer for either moral or economic reasons.[67] The existence of such inalienable rights, especially when they are unwaivable, implies that a transfer can never grant full title. There is always a chance that the author will exercise his inalienable right and, by doing so, interferes with the exploitation of the work or of works derived thereof.[68]

The actual threat which the exercise of inalienable rights may pose to the interests of exploitation should be put into the perspective, however, of statutory

---

63. Article 3(1)(a) BC; § 47(1) DCA; § 120 GCA; § 104(b) USCA. *But see supra* 2.16 note 340 discussing provisions in the American and German Copyright Acts extending protection to all authors in the case of unpublished works and moral rights.

64. *See also* Article II(1) UCC. Protection under the national copyright laws of Germany, the Netherlands and the United States may also be a result of first publication in these countries (§ 47(1) DCA; § 121(1) GCA; § 104(b) USCA). The original version of the Berne Convention provided that a 'publisher' would be entitled to protection within the Berne Union with respect to a work of a non-Berne author first published by him in a Berne country. This provision was amended in 1896. *See* Dietz, *The concept of author*, at 18-20.

65. Article 4(a) BC; § 47(6) DCA; § 121(4) GCA; § 104(4) USCA.

66. § 29 GCA provides that the author's right is only transferable upon death by will, bequest or intestate succession. § 106A(e)(1) USCA provides that the author's rights of attribution and integrity in respect of works of visual art are not transferable. For Dutch copyright law, see *supra* 2.15 notes 320-322 and accompanying text. *See also infra* 5.4-5.6.

67. The right of withdrawal in the event of non-use (§ 41 GCA) and the right of withdrawal in the event of changed convictions (§ 42 GCA) are inalienable parts of the author's right (§ 29 DCA). Under § 203(a) USCA, the right to terminate a transfer after 35 years may only be exercised by the author(s), or if the author is dead, by the author's widow and children.

68. Compare the statement of B.L. Linden on behalf of the American Textbook Publishers Institute, Hearings before Subcommittee No. 3 of the Committee on the Judiciary, H.R. Rep. 89th Cong., 1st Sess., 1458 (1965), CLR Part 5: 'Lacking such a concept [work made for hire], an encyclopaedia, for example, would be subject to 7,000 separate reversion negotiations if there were 7,000 contributors and the term of protection for each contribution would be governed by the life plus 50 years of each contributor.'

provisions which limit the applicability or the effects of these rights. Unreasonable and arbitrary exercise of moral rights is generally curbed by statutory provisions allowing contractual stipulations with respect to authorship credit or modifications to the work, or by provisions subjecting the entitlement to moral rights protection to a weighing up of interests.[69] With respect to the inalienable right of the author under the U.S. Copyright Act to terminate a grant after 35 years, the Act provides that termination does not affect the exploitation of derivative works created under the authority of the grant before termination (§ 203(b)(1) USCA).[70] Sound recordings of classic songs and screen adaptations of bestseller novels may therefore be continued to be exploited notwithstanding the termination of the grant under the authority of which they were made.[71]

Many copyright statutes provide rules for the interpretation of the scope of transfers, often designed to protect authors against unnecessarily far-reaching transfers. If these rules are open to misinterpretation or put in general terms, it may be difficult for a producer to assess which rights he has acquired and therefore may exercise. Which uses, for example, are 'not yet known' so that they cannot be validly transferred under German law in view of the provision that transfers of rights to unknown uses are void (§ 31(4) GCA)?[72] How specifically should a grant be defined in order to ensure that it includes all the rights necessary for exploitation, if the copyright statute provides that a grant only includes rights which have been specified in the agreement or which necessarily follow from the nature or purpose of the grant (§ 2(2) DCA; 31(5) GCA)?[73] In German

---

69. For case law, see *infra* 5.5; 5.6.

70. *See supra* 2.14 note 271 and accompanying text.

71. The 1976 Act does not regulate whether the termination of a grant of derivative work rights affects the exploitation of derivative works made by a *third party* on the basis of the grantee's authorization. Compare in this respect a case in which a composer granted the rights in his song to a publisher in return for a 50% share of the income from mechanical reproduction. In deciding on the effects of termination by the author's surviving relatives, the U.S. Supreme Court held in a 5 to 4 decision that the sound recordings of the song made with the publisher's authorization before termination could continue to be exploited and that the publisher would remain entitled to the compensation negotiated by him for the exploitation of the sound recordings, with an obligation to pass on 50% to the author. Mills Music v. Snyder, 105 S.Ct. 638 (1985).

72. *Cf. e.g.* Judgment of October, 11, 1990, BGH Germany, 93 GRUR 133 (1991) ('Videozweitauswertung I'): the video exploitation of motion pictures was still unknown in the sense of § 31(4) GCA at the time the motion picture was made, because it was not clear at that time (1968) that it would be technically and economically possible to exploit theatrical motion pictures on the market for use in private households.

73. German courts seem to take more notice of producer's interests in cases in which no express agreement whatsoever has been made up, than in cases in which there is doubt about the scope of a written grant. Compare Judgment of November 7, 1975, BGH, Germany, 78 UFITA 179 (1977) ('Kaviar'), dealing with a grant of worldwide motion picture and serial rights to a literary work, extending to all possible techniques, known or unknown, including television. Under the terms of the agreement, the grantee was prohibited from licensing television rights without the grantor's consent for a period of seven years from the date of contracting. The Bundesgerichtshof held that, since the grantee was in the business of producing theatrical motion pictures on the contracting date, the grant must be interpreted so as to include the right to broadcast the motion picture on television, but not the right to make an adaptation of the work for broadcasting purposes. In another case, a freelance photographer made a photoreport for a quality magazine pursuant to an oral agreement with the publisher. After the photographs had been made, the publisher notified the photographer that he would not be publishing the photographs in the quality magazine, but that he reserved the right to publish them in his other magazines. The appellate

law, there seems to be general agreement that § 31(5) GCA indeed requires every mode of exploitation to be specified in the agreement.[74] Dutch doctrine, on the other hand, remains divided on the question whether phrases such as 'assignment of the entire copyright' or 'full copyright assignment' are sufficiently specific under § 2(2) DCA to convey all rights included under the copyright.[75]

De facto limitations to the scope, term and exclusivity of transfers may result from collective agreements,[76] from an author's lack of cooperation in maintaining the work's exclusivity[77] and also from collective administration of rights. If the author has directly entrusted rights to a certain form of exploitation to a collecting society, the producer can only acquire non-exclusive rights to these forms of exploitation from the collecting society. This in particular affects producers who derive their primary income from these exploitations, such as phonogram producers with respect to the mechanical reproduction of musical works. But not only in this traditional case, the interests of producers may be affected if the creator entrusts rights to a collecting society. Investments in creative works are no longer based solely on the estimated revenues of the traditional modes of exploitation (theatrical exhibition in case of motion pictures, sale of copies in case of literary works), but also on secondary exploitations, of which an increasing part is subject to collective administration (rental, private

---

court held that the publisher had acquired a non-exclusive license for multiple publication of the photographs in his other quality magazines. Judgment of May 9, 1984, OLG Karlsruhe, Germany, 86 GRUR 522 (1984) ('Castles in Schleswig Holstein'). American courts seem to interpret transfers more restrictively if each use is defined separately under the reservation of 'all other rights and uses', than if the transfer is defined according to the set phrase 'all rights and uses, known or unknown, except for those specificly excluded'. See Bartsch v. M.G.M. Inc., 391 F.2d 150 (2d Cir. 1968); Rooney v. Columbia Pictures Industries, Inc., 538 F.Supp. 211 (S.D.N.Y. 1982) aff'd 714 F.2d 117 (2d Cir. 1982), cert.denied 460 U.S. 1084 (1983); Platinum Record Company, Inc. v. Lucasfilm, Ltd., 566 F.Supp. 226 (D.N.J. 1983); Cohen v. Paramount Pictures Corp., 845 F.2d 851 (9th Cir. 1988); Tele-Pac, Inc. v. Video Cinema Films, Inc., 79 N.Y. 2d 822; 588 N.E.2d 99; 580 N.Y.S.2d 201 (1991).

74. See Judgment of April 26, 1974, BGH, Germany, 76 GRUR 786 (1974) ('Anneliese Rothenberger'); Judgment of November 7, 1975, BGH, Germany, 78 UFITA 179 (1977) ('Kaviar'). See also Nordemann/Hertin, at 203; Schricker, at 473; Ulmer, at 365.

75. Affirmative: Spoor, Onzekere zekerheid, at 361. Van Lingen, at 153: 'full copyright assignment without any reservations' covers all rights including unknown exploitations, unless provided otherwise. In this sense also Gerbrandy (1988), at 31. Spoor/Verkade, at 358: the nature and purpose of an agreement may imply that a 'full copyright assignment' includes all rights. This reasoning was adhered to by the District Court of Maastricht in its Judgment of December 29, 1990, 7 IER 30 (1991) ('Anton Pieck'): the nature and purpose of the agreements between the artist and the publisher imply that the phrases 'assignment of the right of reproduction' and 'assignment of the author's right' include assignment of the right of communication to the public. See also Soetenhorst, at 62. But see Cohen Jehoram, Grenzen, at 524; the Netherlands, § 4[2][c], interpreting § 2(2) DCA so as to require specification of each individual right. See also Dietz (1984), at 56.

76. Compare the Memorandum to the proposal for a council directive on rental right, lending right, and on certain rights related to copyright, COM(90) 586 final - SYN 319, 24 January 1991, at 38, stating that the possibility cannot be excluded that in future strong unions of authors and performing artists will arise in the field of films, that they will cause the legal presumptions for assignment of rights to be restricted in their effect in practice and that therefore the film producers will have to rely on rights vesting directly in them more than up to now.

77. Authors of scientific works, for example, may refuse to exercise and enforce their remuneration rights for photocopying in libraries and educational institutions in order not to restrict the accessibility of their works. See Soetenhorst, at 218.

71

copying, photocopying, cable distribution). The tendency of authors to directly entrust rights in these secondary exploitations to a collecting society is likely to increase if the copyright statute provides that the right in question is inalienable or may be exercised by means of collective administration only.[78]

3.3.7 AUTHORIZATION TO EXPLOIT A WORK WITHOUT ACQUIRING COPYRIGHT OWNERSHIP

A final aspect of the creator doctrine which may affect security in copyright commerce concerns the situation in which an author retains copyright ownership while at the same time authorizing a producer to use his work. This could lead to uncertainty as to whether the producer has standing to sue, whether he can transfer his 'rights' to a third party and whether the authorization can be validated vis-à-vis subsequent rightholders. While the American and German Copyright Acts have clarified these issues to a considerable extent, the Dutch Copyright Act still leaves much uncertainty.

According to German copyright law, a grant of rights to use a work has priority over later grants of the same rights[79] and entitles the grantee to sue for infringement (§§ 31(3), 97 GCA).[80] The holder of an exclusive right to use a work must condone any non-exclusive rights which the author granted to third parties before the exclusive right was granted, unless the author and third party have agreed otherwise (§ 33 GCA). Exclusive rights-to-use are transferable on the condition that the author has authorized the transfer (§ 34(1) GCA). The agreement between the author and the holder of the right-to-use may provide that this authorization is not necessary (§ 34(4) GCA). The transfer of a right-to-use together with a business does not require the authorization of the author, unless stipulated otherwise (§ 34(3-4) GCA).[81]

Under the U.S. Copyright Act, an exclusive license is considered to be a transfer of copyright ownership,[82] which means that an exclusive licensee may sue for infringement of the license (§ 501(b) USCA), that the license may be transferred to third parties by written instrument (§§ 201(d)(1), 204(a) USCA) and that an exclusive license which was recorded first in good faith will have priority over later exclusive licenses and assignments (§ 205(d) USCA).[83] A non-exclusive license prevails in the case of a later transfer of copyright ownership, if the license is evidenced by a written instrument signed by the owner of

---

78. *See e.g.* § 16d DCA and § 54(6) GCA, providing that the remuneration right for private copying on audio and videotape can only be exercised through collective administration. *See also* Article 9(1) of the Satellite Directive, providing that the author's right of cable retransmission can only be exercised through collective administration. *See also infra* 6.4.

79. *See supra* 3.3.4.

80. § 9(2) of the 1901 Publishing Act allows publishers of literary, musical and dramatic works to sue for copyright infringement if this is necessary in order to exercise their 'publishing right'.

81. *See generally* Soetenhorst, 104-111.

82. § 101 (definition of 'transfer of copyright ownership').

83. *See supra* 3.3.4.

the rights licensed and if the license was granted before execution of the transfer or before recordation of the transfer without notice (§ 205(e) USCA).

Under Dutch law, the effects of exclusive licenses on third parties are less clear.[84] In a 1941 decision, the Hoge Raad suggested that it might be in the interest of international legal security to bind assignees to licenses issued by the assignor prior to the assignment, but it did not give a definite ruling to this effect.[85] The issue of conflicting licenses and assignments has not been much clarified since,[86] although the majority of the doctrine seems to agree that an assignee should be bound by a prior license if he is aware of its existence at the moment of assignment.[87]

Dutch copyright law furthermore does not regulate whether and how licenses may be transferred. If a copyright license is considered to be a contractual claim,[88] the general rules of civil law imply that a license may be transferred, unless this is precluded by law, by the nature of the right or by the licensing agreement (§ 3:83(1-2) BW).[89] As a contractual claim, a license would furthermore be transferable as part of the agreement of which it is part, if the author agrees (§ 6:159 BW). If a license is only valuable in relation to ownership of a particular good (e.g. the licensee's business), a transfer of that good may imply a transfer of the license.[90]

The owner of the copyright to a collective work may independently sue for infringement of the copyright to works which have been incorporated in the collective work on the basis of an exclusive or non-exclusive license (§ 5(2) DCA).[91] In all other cases, licensees can only sue for infringement if this has been stipulated in the agreement with the author (§ 27(a)(2) DCA).[92] In the absence of such a stipulation, the producer is dependent on the cooperation of the author or his heirs to bring an infringement action, with the risk that they may not be interested or even be untraceable. A proposal to confer standing to sue upon exclusive licensees was rejected by the Dutch legislator in 1989 with the

---

84. *See generally* Huydecoper; Van Lingen, at 155-157; Quaedvlieg, *Overdraagbaarheid*; Soeten-horst, at 70-76; Spoor/Verkade, at 361-368; Verkade, comment on Judgment of September 29, 1989, HR, Netherlands, NJ 1990, 307 (Van Spijk v. Beeldrecht).

85. Judgment of November 28, 1941, HR, Netherlands, NJ 1942, 204 ('Fire over England II').

86. *Cf.* Engels, 'Overeenkomst voor de verlening van verfilmingsrechten op een werk', in: *Uitgeef-overeenkomsten*, at 146: financiers of Dutch film productions generally do not accept an exclusive license to adapt a pre-existing work to screen, because an exclusive license does not fully ensure that the author of the pre-existing work does not assign screen adaptation rights to someone else.

87. *See* Van Lingen, at 155; van Oven, at 7; Verkade/Spoor, at 282. With a certain reservation also Huydecoper, at 69.

88. Affirmative, Huydecoper, at 67; Quaedvlieg, *Overdraagbaarheid*, at 494; Spoor/Verkade, at 362.

89. *See* Huydecoper, at 67; Quaedvlieg, *Overdraagbaarheid*, at 497; Spoor/Verkade, at 365.

90. § 6:251 BW. *See* Huydecoper, at 67. A similar result was achieved in Judgment of March 20, 1992, HR, Netherlands, NJ 1992, 563 note Verkade (Veld v. Suthormo), discussed *supra* 2.15 note 328.

91. § 5(2) DCA: 'The reproduction or communication to the public by someone other than the author or his successors in title of a work which is incorporated in a collective work and which is protected by author's right, is considered to infringe the author's right to the collective work as a whole.' [translation JS]

92. Act of July 3, 1989, S. 282.

argument that the copyright owner must be able to decide whether or not to retain the right to sue for infringement.[93]

A non-exclusive licensee does not have the right to sue under any of the three copyright laws. Producers who can only acquire a non-exclusive license as a result of a statutory license or industry practice are therefore dependent on the copyright owner to bring an action for copyright infringement.[94]

3.4 The impact of the creator doctrine on security in international copyright transactions

An important aspect of security in copyright commerce which I have not yet mentioned specifically, is the security in international copyright transactions. Aside from certain rules in the Berne Convention on copyright ownership of cinematographic works, to be discussed below, the international copyright treaties do not provide substantive rules on authorship, copyright ownership and copyright transfers or rules determining the law applicable to international copyright transactions. The validity and scope of a transfer must therefore be determined according to the law of the country that is applicable under the rules of international private law applied in the country where protection is being claimed.

Security about the validity, scope, exclusivity and duration of a transfer is greatest if the same law is applied in every country where the transfer is supposed to have effect. In determining the law applicable to the form in which a transfer must be executed, courts indeed attach to elements that are more or less predictable and fixed, such as the country where the transfer was executed or the transferor's or transferee's country of domicile.[95] When it comes to determining the scope of the rights which have been transferred, however, security in

---

93. *See* Memorandum to § 27a DCA, Parl.Gesch. 27a.4 (1989). The copyright owner may bring an infringement suit on behalf of the licensee, and the licensee may intervene in an infringement suit brought by the copyright owner in order to claim damages for himself (§ 27a(2) DCA). A licensee may bring an independent action to confiscate goods which infringe on rights to which he has an exclusive license (§ 28(1) DCA (1992 Amendment)). Compare in this respect Van Nispen, at 91, arguing that the status of licenses in Dutch copyright law is inconsistent.

94. *See infra* 6.4, discussing neighbouring rights as an alternative to ownership of exclusive rights in the work of authorship exploited.

95. *See* Judgment of February 24, 1992, Pres.Rb. Amsterdam, Netherlands, 16 Informatierecht/ AMI 112 (1992) ('Carmina Burana'): the validity of a transfer of ownership of moral rights upon the death of an author must be determined according to the law of the country where the transfer was executed. *See also* Article 9(1), 9(2) European Agreement on the Law Applicable to Contractual Obligations, providing that a contract is valid if it complies with the formalities required under (1) the law applicable to the contract pursuant to the European Agreement, (2) the law of the country where the contract was entered into or (3) if the parties are in different countries, the law of one of these countries. *See also* Schricker/Katzenberger, at 1256. *See also* De Boer, *Aanknoping*, at 708: a transfer is valid if it complies with the law of the country where the transfer was executed or the law of a country which is otherwise closely involved. Ulmer (1978), at 54: the law of the country where the transferee has its domicile. Meijers, NJ 1936, 443 at 783; Spoor/Verkade, at 544: the law of the country where the transfer is executed. *But see* Judgment of February 13, 1936, HR, Netherlands, NJ 1936, 443, note Meijers ('Das blaue Licht II'), applying the law of the country of protection. *Cf. also* Nimmer, § 17-11[C], arguing that the law of the protecting country should be followed both with respect to the form as well as to the substance of a transfer.

international copyright transactions seems to be less decisive for determining the choice of law. Many copyright statutes provide rules on the alienability of rights and on the scope of transfers (e.g. § 2(2) DCA; § 31(5) GCA), which may affect the actual scope of protection. The scope of protection, however, must be determined according to the law of the country where protection is claimed (Article 5(2) BC). If, then, such a rule exists under the law of the country where protection is being claimed, a court may be reluctant to apply any other law,[96] especially if the rule serves to protect the creator against unnecessarily broad transfers.[97] A producer must therefore be aware that he may not obtain the same bundle of rights in every country for which he seeks to acquire title.[98]

Additional security problems may occur if transfers do not have the same effects in the country where the transfer has been executed and the country for which protection is being claimed. The hazy status of licenses under Dutch law,[99] for example, may cause problems for foreign producers who expect their (worldwide) exclusive license to give full title and standing to sue within the Dutch territory. Security in international transactions will generally be greatest if the consequences of the transfer are determined according to the law of the country where the transfer has been executed or the law which the parties have designated as being applicable to the contract of which the transfer is part.[100] There is no guarantee, however, that courts will actually assess transfers in this way.[101]

---

96. *See* Corcovado Music Corp. v. Hollis Music, Inc., 981 F.2d 679 (2d Cir. 1993): the scope of a grant by a Brazilian composer to a Brazilian publisher must be interpreted according to U.S. law so as to determine whether the composer was entitled to grant the renewal term to another publisher. *See also* Judgment of February 13, 1936, HR, Netherlands, NJ 1936, 443 note Meijers ('Das blaue Licht II): question if and how a right can be transferred must be determined according to the law of the country where protection is claimed. *See also* Judgment of March 25, 1949, HR, Netherlands, NJ 1950, 643 note Veegens ('La belle et la bête'), in which the scope of a transfer by a French composer to a French producer was determined according to Dutch law.

97. *See* Judgment of October 15, 1987, BGH, Germany, 32 ZUM 214 (1988) ('Gema presumption'): a transfer of rights for German territory to a collecting society must comply with mandatory rules of German copyright contract law (§§ 31-44 GCA). *See also* De Boer, *Aanknoping*, at 707; Ulmer (1978) at 100. Schricker/Katzenberger, at 1255: the mandatory rules of German copyright contract law are applicable on German territory if it provides the author with better protection than the law of the contract, and if the contractual relationship has aspects which strongly link it with Germany.

98. Gerbrandy (1988), at 29, 30, suggests to apply the law of the country of the transferee in case of worldwide transfers. *But see* De Boer, *Aanknoping*, at 708: applying the law of the protecting country does not give rise to major concern in case of worldwide transfers.

99. *See supra* 3.3.7.

100. *See* Grosheide, *Juridische Typologie*, at 167: designating the applicable law by contract is generally considered to give more legal security in the case of international licensing contracts than formulating the license in conformity with internationally accepted customs or legislation.

101. *Cf. e.g.* Judgment of November 28, 1941, HR, Netherlands, NJ 1942, 205 ('Fire over England II'): agreement between English composer and English film production company stated that the company would hold all copyrights. HR: the assignment was invalid because it is impossible to assign rights to future works under Dutch law. The agreement must be interpreted so as to grant the company a license to do something which would otherwise constitute a copyright infringement. *See also* De Boer, *Aanknoping*, at 709, arguing that, in case of doubt, the question whether a license may be enforced against a third party must be determined according to the law of the country for which protection is being claimed.

Many copyright systems avoid the security problems discussed in the foregoing paragraphs (3.2, 3.3) by statutorily allocating rights to producers. The methods applied for allocating rights to the producer are anything but uniform, however. While one copyright law may consider a producer as 'author', the other copyright law allocates rights to the producer by means of a statutory presumption of transfer. Security for producers on a national level therefore does not necessarily imply security on the international level: if a producer is considered author and first copyright owner in his own country, will he also be regarded as such in countries which are more loyal to the creator doctrine?

With respect to *copyright ownership* of cinematographic works, the Berne Convention provides that ownership of copyright in cinematographic works is a matter for legislation in the country where protection is claimed (Article 14bis(2)(a) BC). Rather than to prescribe therefore in whom copyright ownership should vest (creator, producer), the Berne Convention provides a conflicts of laws rule for determining copyright ownership of cinematographic works.[102] Article 14bis(2)(a) BC does not regulate, however, which law must be applied to determine who the *author* of a cinematographic work is.[103] Although the creator doctrine is the basic rule of authorship in the Berne Convention,[104] the Convention does not define the term 'author', nor provide a conflicts of laws rule regarding authorship.[105] The identity of the author therefore probably must be determined according to the law applicable pursuant to the rules of international private law of the country where protection is claimed.[106] Security would be greatest if the author were determined according to the law of the country of origin of the work,[107] or the law applicable to the (employment) contract which

---

102. Ricketson, at 582: Article 14bis(2)(a) serves to make clear that each member state may decide for itself whether to vest ownership in the creators or the maker (producer) of the cinematographic work.

103. *See* De Boer, *Filmauteursrecht*, at 6; Dietz, *The concept of author*, at 31; Schack, *Der Vergütungsanspruch*, at 279; Seignette, *Subjectbepaling*, at 197. *But see* Boytha, *Some Private International Law Aspects*, at 409; Ginsburg, *Colors in Conflicts*, at 87; Ginsburg/Sirinelli, at 136; Ricketson, *People or Machines*, at 24, arguing that Article 14bis(2)(a) provides a conflicts of law rule for determining authorship of cinematographic works. Strowel, at 387: since Article 14bis(2)(a) does not concern the attribution of the status of 'author', but provides a special rule for the determination of copyright ownership, it may be argued *a contrario* from this rule that the Berne Convention is founded on the notion of the author as a physical person.

104. *See* Ricketson, at 159, 903; Strowel, at 381. Dietz, *The concept of author*, at 12, argues that, since the Berne Convention is founded on the concept of the author as the natural person who has created the work, the national legislators do not have discretion to define 'author' otherwise. *Cf. also* Ricketson, *People or Machines*, at 1-37, arguing that the basic notion of human authorship underlying the Berne Convention should not be undermined any further than it already has in the field of cinematographic works.

105. *See* Frey, at 66; Geller, *Worldwide 'Chain of Title'*, at 50; Grosheide, at 178; Larese, at 311; Seignette, *Subjectbepaling*, at 199; Verkade, *Het beste artikel 7*, at 11, 12. Ricketson, *People or Machines*, at 23-24, argues that authorship under the Berne Convention should be determined according to the law of the country where protection is claimed. It is not clear whether Ricketson refers to the substantive provisions or to the rules of private international law applicable in the country of protection.

106. *See* Ricketson, *People or Machines*, at 24.

107. *See* Judgment of August 27, 1969, Rb. Amsterdam, Netherlands, NJ 1969, 393 ('Emanuelle'); Judgment of March 31, 1983, Ger. Amsterdam, Netherlands, 7 Informatierecht/AMI 56 (1983) ('Pac Man'). *See also* Ginsburg, *Colors in Conflicts*, at 98, 99, with a possible exception for moral rights claims; Schack, *Der Vergütungsanspruch*, at 279, with the modification that the

governs the relationship between creator and producer.[108] In many cases, however, courts apply their own national law,[109] often without taking possible conflicts of laws into consideration,[110] and occasionally because specific creator interests, moral interests in particular, are given priority above the interests of security in international copyright transactions.[111]

In view of the differences between the national copyright laws and the fact that it is difficult to predict which law will be applied in a particular situation, security in international copyright transactions would be best served by a harmonization of the rules on authorship, copyright ownership and transfers,[112] or at least adoption of conflicts of laws rules regarding international copyright transactions.[113] The fact that hundred years of Berne Convention have not produced any substantive rules, indicates however that consensus will not be easy to achieve.[114]

---

country of origin of an audiovisual work is the country where the producer has its actual domicile; Spoor/Verkade, at 45. *But see* Ulmer (1978), at 36, favouring application of the law of the country for which protection is being sought, with special rules for employment works.

108. With regard to employment works: Judgment of June 30, 1950, HR, Netherlands, NJ 1952, 36. *See also* De Boer, *Aanknoping*, at 692; De Boer, *Filmauteursrecht*, at 5; Gerbrandy, at 49; Schack, at 279; Seignette, *Subjectbepaling*, at 200; Spoor/Verkade, at 543.

109. *See* Judgment of November 28, 1940, Ger. Amsterdam, Netherlands, NJ 1941, 773, *aff'd on other grounds* Judgment of November 28, 1941, HR Netherlands, NJ 1942, 205 ('Fire over England II'); Dae Han Video Productions, Inc. v. Kuk Dong Oriental Food, Inc., 19 U.S.P.Q. 2d (BNA) 1294 (D.Mar., 1990). *See also* Geller, *Worldwide "Chain of Title"*, at 51: as a rule of thumb, judges will apply the law of the country where protection is being sought, but this rule of thumb is not a rule of law.

110. *See* Judgment of November 30, 1936, Ger. 's-Gravenhage, Netherlands, NJ 1937, 282 ('Das Blaue Licht II'); Judgment of January 30, 1986, Pres.Rb. Amsterdam, Netherlands, 55 BIE 149 (1987) (Belga-Stone v. Blokker); Judgment of February 28, 1991, Ger. Amsterdam, Netherlands, 60 BIE 128 (1992) (Chanel v. Maxis).

111. *See* Judgment of May 28, 1991, Cass.civ. 1re, France, 149 RIDA 197 (1991) (Huston v. La Cinq). In this case, the widow and children of American film director John Huston brought a moral right infringement suit in France to prevent the telecasting of a colorized version of the black-and- white film 'The Asphalt Jungle', made by Huston in the course of his employment at an American film studio. The French broadcasting company had acquired a license from an American company which had purchased the copyrights to the film and colorized it. The appellate court dismissed the claim, *inter alia*, because the studio was 'author' under the American law based on the employment agreement. The Cour de Cassation reversed this decision, stating that § 6 FCA and Article 1(2) of Law No. 64-689 of 8 July 1964 are of 'imperative application' in France, with the effect that in France actual creators are always entitled to invoke the right of integrity, regardless of the country where the work was first published. *See* Strowel, at 59-70. *See also infra* 6.3. If, as has been argued, Article 14bis(2)(a) BC refers to both the copyright owner *and* the author, the court might have applied this rule in order to acknowledge that the actual creator is entitled to the protection of his moral rights in France. Ginsburg/Sirinelli, at 142, suggest that the court may have wanted to solve the issue for every category of work and therefore chose not to apply Article 14bis(2)(a) BC.

112. *See also* Frey, at 67.

113. *See also* Ricketson, at 905.

114. Efforts to reach a consensus on the definition of 'author' within the Committee of Experts on Model Provisions for Legislation in the Field of Copyright have been fruitless up till now. *See* Report of the Committee of Experts on Model Provisions for Legislation in the Field of Copyright, Third Session, Geneva, 2-13 July 1990, 26 Copyright 282, 290 (1990). The 1994 Agreement on Trade-related Aspects of Intellectual Property Rights (TRIPS), obliges Members of TRIPS to accord national treatment to nationals of Members, 'nationals' to be understood as the *natural or legal persons* who or which would meet the criteria for eligibility of protection under the Berne Convention (Article 1(3)). Ricketson, at 905, argues that the adoption of common rules for dealing with conflicts of laws is a more fruitful approach than including substantive rules on employment relationships, publishing contracts and other agreements for the

With respect to harmonization within the European Union, the European Commission has taken the position that 'the issues of ownership and subject matter are best harmonized not in relation to particular rights but in a uniform way which means in relation to all national copyright provisions'.[115] Sofar, harmonization has however been restricted to *ad hoc* provisions in Council Directives harmonizing other aspects of copyright law, such as the provision in the Software Directive that, unless agreed otherwise, the employer is exclusively entitled to exercise all economic rights in a computer program created by an employee in the execution of his duties or following the employer's instructions (Article 2(3) Software Directive), and the provision in the Rental Directive that Member States may provide for a presumption of transfer of the rental right to the film producer (Article 2(6) Rental Directive).[116] The Software and Duration Directives specifically recognize the attribution, under the national copyright law, of authorship to a legal entity or, in the case of a collective work, to the person designated as its author.[117] A proposal to define the author of an audiovisual work as the natural person who has made a creative contribution to the work, was not adopted.[118] The definition of the 'author' in respect of audiovisual works has however been harmonized to the extent that the principal director of an audiovisual work is considered to be its author,[119] thereby disqualifying the attribution of authorship to the film producer with respect to the director's contribution to the film.[120]

In the absence of international harmonization or adoption of common choice of law rules, securing title in the countries of exploitation requires producers to conclude written agreements with every possible (co-)author of the work, using

---

exploitation of rights in the Berne Convention.

115. Memorandum to the EC proposal for a directive on rental right, lending right, and on certain rights related to copyright, COM(90) 586 final - SYN 319, 24 January 1991, at 38. The Memorandum defines 'author' as '[t]he creator of the work within the meaning of Article 2 BC. To the extent that the national laws of the Member States are in conformity with the Conventions, this reference to the law of the Conventions therefore is equivalent to a reference to national law.' *Id.* at 37. Since the Conventions do not define 'author' as being the creator of the work, the meaning of this definition is unclear.

116. A presumption of transfer will not affect an author's unwaivable right to an equitable remuneration for rental of copies of his works, as guaranteed under Article 4 of the Directive. Compare Cohen Jehoram, *Bescherming van de auteur*, at 110-112, regarding the remuneration guarantee as an expression that the European Commission has moved towards a more creator-oriented approach.

117. Article 2(1) Software Directive; Article 1(3) Duration Directive.

118. *See supra* 3.2.2 note 20 and accompanying text.

119. Article 2(2) Rental Directive; Article 1(5) Satellite Directive; Article 2(1) Duration Directive. See *supra* 3.2.2 note 20 and accompanying text.

120. Compare § 9 BCA, designating as author of a film the person by whom the arrangements necessary for the making of the film are undertaken. Compare also § 45a DCA, recognizing the possibility that a person acquires the status of 'author' of a film work on the basis of §§ 7 and 8 DCA. *See supra* 3.2.2 note 21 and accompanying text.

unambiguous language on the scope, duration, territory and exclusivity of the rights to be transferred.[121]

3.5 The impact of the creator doctrine on the efficiency in the process of acquiring and establishing title to works of authorship

If a producer organizes the process of acquiring title efficiently, he is able to invest maximum organizational and financial effort in the work's production, promotion and distribution. Efficiency could be improved at every point at which a producer is required to invest time, effort and money to acquire the necessary rights and to establish these rights vis-à-vis financiers and buyers of his product as well as infringers. This could include negotiations with creative contributors to the work, drafting agreements in compliance with statutory rules on copyright contracts, establishing priority over possibly conflicting transfers, acquiring licenses from collecting societies for collectively-administered modes of exploitation, tracking down authors or successors in title, preventing the author from exercising inalienable rights, etc. The costs incurred by these activities increase if the producer is required to acquire rights from multiple contributors, if the work is distributed internationally, if the work needs regular updating and if the producer's business requires that the process of acquiring title must be repeated with great frequency, as is the case with newspapers, periodicals, television news programs, etc.

Since it is likely that a producer will try to deduct the estimated costs of acquiring and establishing title from the compensation paid to the creators and the budget available for the work's promotion and distribution, cutting these costs is not necessarily only in the producer's interests. It is not possible within the context of this study to assess the actual consequences of the creator doctrine on the exploitation and dissemination of creative works. Over the years, several studies have been conducted on the economic importance of copyright,[122] but none addresses the specific issue of copyright ownership.[123] Advocates of the

---

121. Ginsburg in: Kernochan, *Works-Made-For-Hire*, at 554, 555, remarks that if employers and parties commissioning 'works made for hire' have to expressly stipulate exploitation rights to ensure that they acquire full title outside the United States according to the applicable law there, they may as well bear the burden of requesting those same rights for U.S. exploitations as well.

122. *See* United States Copyright Office, *Size of the Copyright Industries in the United States*, Report to the Subcommittee on Patents, Copyrights and Trademarks, Washington D.C. (1984); Stichting voor Economisch Onderzoek der Universiteit van Amsterdam, *De economische betekenis van het auteursrecht* 2, Report to the Stichting Auteursrechtbelangen, supported by the Dutch Ministry of Economic Affairs, Amsterdam (1989); M. Hummel, *Die volkswirtschaftliche Bedeutung des Urheberrechts*, Report to the Federal Secretary of Justice. Schriftenreihe des Ifo-Instituts Für Wirtschaftsforschung Nr. 125, Berlin/Munich (1989). *See also* Cohen Jehoram, *Critical Reflections*, at 485.

123. The *economic analysis of law* as developed in American legal doctrine has been applied to analyze whether intellectual property rights serve as an incentive to creation and innovation. *See e.g.* Breyer, at 281. Traditionally, however, this analysis only concerns the expediency of intellectual property rights. How these rights must be allocated once their expediency has been established often remains unanswered, either because efficiency considerations are not allowed

economic analysis of law[124] do seem to recognize, however, that the relationship between creators and producers may incur costs.[125] It has been argued that inalienable rights, such as moral rights, the right to terminate a transfer and resale rights may reduce the incentive to create new works, because they withhold the creator from shifting the risk to the producer: 'A publisher (say) who must share any future speculative gains with the author will pay the author less for the work, so the risky component of the author's expected remuneration will increase relative to the certain component. If the author is risk averse, he will be worse off as a result.'[126] This suggests that inalienable rights are only fruitful for an author if his economic situation at the moment of transfer allows him to accept a remuneration in which the producer has deducted the estimated costs involved in the exercise of these inalienable rights by the author.

It is furthermore argued that an increase in costs may follow from the accumulation of rightholders in a marketable unit: owners or co-owners of rights in original, collective or derivative works, holders of neighbouring rights, etc.[127] The process of collecting all the rights necessary to exploit the unit and the occurrence of conflicts and competition between the various rightholders, *inter alia*, about the distribution of collectively administered uses, could increase transaction costs.

3.6 Conclusions

In this Chapter, I have discussed the impact of the creator doctrine on the exploitation of creative works and, in particular, on the producer's ability to acquire and establish title to works of authorship. We have seen that the principle that copyright vests in the creator of the work may complicate proof of title for the producer if there is uncertainty about the validity, scope, term and exclusivity of a transfer, about the work's nationality and term of protection, about the exercise of inalienable rights and, in Dutch law in particular, about the effects on third parties of a license to use a work. Problems in respect of security and efficiency accumulate if the producer seeks to acquire title in a work which involves multiple creative contributions, if the author(s) of the work are difficult

---

to be taken into account when it comes to attributing rights (in this sense Spector, at 273), or because the relationship between creators and producers is expected to complicate the analysis in such a manner that researchers rather prefer to ignore it. *See* Landes/Posner, at 327: 'To simplify the analysis, we ignore any distinction between costs incurred by authors and publishers, and therefore use the term "author" (or "creator") to mean both author and publisher. In doing this we elide a number of interesting questions involving the relation between author and publisher.'

124. For a discussion of this theory, see generally Grosheide, at 134-136; Landes/Posner, at 325-363; Lehmann, at 1-36; Quaedvlieg, *The Economic Analysis*, 379-393.

125. *See* Breyer, at 316; Hardy, at 191; Holzhauer/Teijl, at 45, 73; Landes/Posner, at 327.

126. Landes/Posner, at 327.

127. *See* Holzhauer/Teijl, at 76, 77, 88. *See also* Katzman, at 879, n. 71, arguing that it is more efficient to concentrate ownership in one person in the case of the nine categories of commissioned works which may be deemed to be 'works made for hire' in a written instrument (§ 101(2) USCA) and that, since the marketable unit is the whole and not the parts, the commissioning party is the most obvious choice.

to identify, if the legal status of the creative contributions to the work is unclear (joint work, collective work, derivative work, etc.), if the work has not yet been created at the moment of contracting, if the work is distributed internationally, if the work needs regular updating and, finally, if the nature of the business entails that the producer must repeat the process of acquiring title with great frequency.

A producer may seek to secure his position by means of contractual guarantees, such as waivers, indemnities, power of suit, etc. Not every contractual stipulation is valid under the law, however,[128] and there is no absolute certainty that the creator will abide by the agreement with the producer or that the agreement binds the creator vis-à-vis third parties to whom the producer transfers his rights.[129]

To enhance security, most copyright laws provide for tailor-made statutory measures, such as presumptions of authorship, provisions conferring the right to sue upon exclusive licensees or provisions allowing contractual waivers in specific agreements between creators and producers. In certain cases, however, legislators revert to the more drastic measure of allocating exclusive rights to producers. In the next Chapter, I will analyze in what situations the American, Dutch and German Copyright Act allocate exclusive rights to producers. This survey may give an idea of the type of creator-producer relationships in which the creator doctrine is challenged most.

---

128. Compare e.g. § 203(a)(5) USCA, providing that the termination of a grant may be effected notwithstanding any agreement to the contrary, including an agreement to make a will or to make any future grant.

129. About the effects of contractual stipulations between the creator and the producer on the party to whom the producer transfers his rights, see Huydecoper, at 67; Quaedvlieg, *Overdraag-baarheid*, at 485.

Chapter 4

Allocation of rights according to the division of risks between creator and producer

4.1 Division of risks between creator and producer

In Chapter 3, we have seen that a producer may have problems acquiring and proving title if the work involves numerous creative contributions, if the author has transferred the same rights to a third party, if the scope of the transfer is disputed, etc. As the risks of defective title weigh on the budget available for compensating the creators and for the work's promotion and distribution, it may be in the common interest of creators, producers and the public to facilitate the acquisition of title by the producer, especially in those cases in which the creator, by contracting with the producer, has transferred the major risks involved in the creation and publication of the work to the producer, i.e. if:

1. before commencement of the creation process, the producer has undertaken to pay for the costs of creation and, as such, has assumed responsibility for the risk that the income from the exploitation of the work will not be sufficient to cover the costs of creation (*production risk*);
2. the producer has made considerable organizational investments in order to transform the creator's contribution into a marketable product (*organizational risk*);
3. the work is presented to or perceived by the public as originating in the producer rather than the creator (*associative risk*).[1]

If the title to exclusive rights is allocated between the creator and producer according to the division of these risks, security and efficiency are improved where this is needed most and where it will least affect the creator's ability to lay down conditions for the use of his work. The more a creator transfers the risks involved in the creation and publication of a work to a producer, the smaller his opportunities will be to retain rights in the work and, consequently, to negotiate

---

1. For a similar distinction between risks, *see* Hösly, at 121. Hösly's definition of organizational risk differs from mine in that he regards the right to control the creative process as an element of organizational risk. In my definition, organizational risk refers to the actual investment necessary to transform a work into a marketable product.

separate remunerations for additional uses.[2] Similarly, the compensation which a creator can maximally negotiate in relation to the estimated revenues will be influenced by the extent to which he shifts the risks to the producer.[3]

Allocating rights according to the division of risks between creator and producer cannot in itself provide sufficient security, however, because the division of risks differs from case to case and is not always predictable in advance. In order to improve predictability for both the creator and the producer, the statute must somehow define the situations in which rights are allocated to producers, e.g. by defining the category of work, the type of producer or the type of relationship between the creator and the producer. In this Chapter, I will analyze how American, Dutch and German copyright legislation have defined the situations in which they allocate rights to producers, and examine to which extent the division of risks between creator and producer is reflected in these definitions. This analysis serves to compare the *situations* in which American, Dutch and German copyright legislation allocate rights to producers, not the *methods* according to which this is done. The various methods applied for allocating rights to producers will be discussed in more detail in Chapters 5 and 6.

4.2 Factor 1: production risk

The creator doctrine is unchallenged in situations in which the creator creates a work at his own initiative and expense without knowing whether he will be able

---

2. Other factors which can effect the outcome of negotiations are the parties' respective positions on the market, the bargaining method (individual or collective) and the extent to which the parties are aware of the markets for the work and the legal ramifications of their agreement. *Cf.* Mona Mangan, Executive Director, Writers Guild of America, East, Inc., in: Kernochan, *Work-Made-For-Hire*, at 519, 520, discussing the effects of copyright ownership on collective bargaining agreements between film producers and screenwriters in the United States. In order to be able to enter into binding collective agreements, the Writers Guild has an interest in classifying screenwriters as 'employees', even if this implies that the film production companies are considered authors under the work-for-hire provisions: '[W]e believe that the companies are not interested in giving up copyright if we change our definition and say we are no longer employees....Our problem is not that we've failed to negotiate for additional uses. Copyright wouldn't help us with that. In many cases we've done better than copyright necessarily does for a writer who is unrepresented. Our problem is the problem of having our work butchered, of having work rewritten and being absolutely unable to protect the integrity of the script....At any international conference, writers who retain copyright tell stories about preserving their scripts from rewrites by, for example, threatening to pull them from a production. Our members are invariably saddened by their own inability to protect their work. At the same time, I might add, many foreign writers are eager to give up their copyright in exchange for money.'

3. Compare Judgment of June 27, 1991, BGH, Germany, 93 GRUR 901 (1991) ('horoscope calendar'). In this case, the plaintiff claimed judicial reformation of his publishing agreement alleging gross disproportionality between the compensation negotiated and the actual revenues from exploitation (§ 36 GCA). BGH: if the compensation negotiated strongly deviates from what is generally considered within the line of business as a fair minimum compensation in relation to the actual revenues, there is a presumption that a reasonable co-contractor could not have refused a higher compensation if the actual revenues had been taken into consideration on the contracting date. This means that the defendant/publisher must establish why the compensation was not grossly disproportionate or unfairly low under the circumstances. Relevant in this respect are the circumstances in which the work was made, such as the involvement of entrepreneurial risks and the extent to which the defendant's contribution to the end product determined its commercial success.

to sell the work.[4] Many works, however, are created in fulfilment of a contractual obligation which the creator entered into before commencing the creative process in exchange for the producer's undertaking to pay the costs of creation in whole or in part. The extent to which the producer assumes financial responsibility in these situations varies from case to case. An independent contractor who is commissioned to create one, particular work for a fixed compensation upon delivery of the work, still runs the risk that he will fail to deliver according to the agreed conditions and that he may not be given any new commissions. An employee, on the other hand, who is hired to create works on a more or less permanent basis in return for payment of a regular salary, enjoys a secure income throughout the employment relationship and independent from the delivery of one, particular work.

There is a whole range of relationships in between these two examples, in which the producer more or less secures the creator's financial position. A freelance photographer, for example, who regularly works for a particular magazine publisher at an hourly rate knows that at least part of his income is secure as a result of the fact that the magazine publisher will hire him for future projects. It follows that, from the perspective of financial risk, there is no inherent justification in drawing a sharp line dividing the works made by employees and the works made on commission by independent contractors.[5] Most copyright legislators nevertheless prefer to distinguish between employment works and works made on commission in allocating copyright ownership. During the revision of the copyright law resulting in the 1912 Act, the Dutch government rejected a proposal to consider both employers *and* commissioning parties as 'authors', stating that while an employer has a right to the fruits of his employees' labour and should therefore be considered author unless agreed otherwise,[6] vesting copyright ownership in the commissioning party merely because he pays for the work would be contrary to the basic principle that copyright vests in the person who made the work.[7]

---

4. *But see* §§ 1, 9 German Publishing Act of 1901 and §§ 38, 88 GCA, in which exclusive rights are allocated to the publisher and producer of a film work irrespective of whom took the initiative for the creation and who paid the costs. *See infra* 4.3.

5. *See* Barta, at 86; Hösly, at 167; Varmer, at 142. The duties of confidentiality and non-competition are characteristic of employment relationships, but an independent contractor's ability to retain rights to additional uses may also be restricted by the commissioning party's interest in confidentiality and non-competition. *See e.g.* Judgment of May 9, 1985, BGH, Germany, 87 GRUR 1041 (1985) ('non-competition'): contract for the exclusive development of a computer program implies an obligation for the commissioned party not to exploit the program in a more or less identical form.

6. Memorandum to § 7 DCA, Parl.Gesch. 7.4 (1912).

7. Comment of the Minister of Justice on a proposal of 18 June 1912 by representative Van Doorn, Parl.Gesch. 7.5 (1912). Parl.Gesch. 7.7; 7.10 (1912). A somewhat curious exception to the principle that a commissioning party cannot acquire copyright ownership simply by paying for the work, is the provision in the Benelux Designs and Models Act (Trb. 1966, 292) that, unless agreed otherwise, the employer or the party who has commissioned a design for commercial purposes is deemed the 'designer' and as such is considered to own the copyright in the design (§ 23 BDMA). *See also infra* 7.5. Although assumption of production, organizational and associative risks (factors 1, 2 and 3) by the producer is likely in the industrial design field, there are many industrial design works that bear the personal imprint of and are presented to the public as the work of a particular designer.

The distinction between employment works and works made on commission is also visible in the Software Directive. Whereas, throughout the legislative process, the proposal allocated exclusive exploitation rights to both employers and commissioning parties,[8] the version which was finally adopted allocates exclusive exploitation rights to the employer only.[9] And also in the United States, where the distinction between employment works and commissioned works had been eroded away in lower case law,[10] the U.S. Supreme Court sharpened the distinction in stating that, beyond the nine categories of commissioned works which may be deemed 'works made for hire' in a written instrument (§ 101(2) USCA), there is no legal basis for attributing authorship and copyright ownership to a commissioning party, unless of course the commissioning party (co-)created the work.[11]

In German copyright law, the distinction between employment works and works made on commission by independent contractors is less clear, probably because the absence of a writing requirement for grants of rights-to-use and the 'purpose transfer' rule of § 31(5) GCA allow courts to look at the allocation of risks when determining the validity, scope and exclusivity of a grant.[12] As a rule of thumb, however, one could probably say that the scope and exclusivity of an implied grant is interpreted more restrictively under German law in the case of works made by independent contractors than in the case of works made by employees in the couse of their employment contract.[13]

The special treatment of works made by employees may probably be explained from the fact that the marketability of these works often depends on the organizational investments made by the employee's organization as a whole (factor 2). Employment works are furthermore often associated with the employer rather than with the employee (factor 3).[14] Independent contractors differ from

---

8. Article 2(3), (4) Proposal for a Council Directive on the legal protection of computer programs, COM [88] 816 fin. - SYN 183.

9. Article 2(3) Software Directive.

10. *See* 2.14; 7.2.

11. Community for Creative Non-Violence v. Reid, 109 S.Ct. 2166, 2172 (1989). *See also infra* 7.2.

12. *See e.g.* Judgment of May 9, 1984, OLG Karlsruhe, Germany, 86 GRUR 522, 529 (1984) ('Castles in Schleswig Holstein'): since the freelance photographer had made the photographs after the publisher had agreed to pay him, the publisher took a risk. The purpose of the agreement between the photographer and publisher must therefore be interpreted in such a way that the scope of the transfer balances the publisher's risks.

13. Compare German case law presuming a comprehensive an exclusive grant of territorially and temporarily unrestricted rights to use computer programs made by the employee in the course of employment. *See* Judgment of May 27, 1987, OLG Karlsruhe, Germany ('computer program'). *See also* Judgment of September 13, 1983, BAG, Germany, 86 GRUR 429 (1984) note Ulmer ('statistical programs'): the circumstances of the case implied a grant of rights to use computer program without additional remuneration, even though the work was not a part of the employee's immediate duties.

14. Assumption of organizational and associative risk by the employer may enhance the legitimacy of attribution of authorship to the employer. Compare Spoor/Verkade, at 34, suggesting that authorship of the employer is most defendable in the case of '[c]reations made in the course of employment in a close vertical and/or horizontal collaboration, and/or presented as the employer's intellectual product.' [translation JS]

employees in this respect in that they are not an integral part of the hiring party's organization and therefore will not necessarily make use of the hiring party's technical and human resources and name. In the next paragraphs, I will examine whether the American, Dutch and German coyright laws provide for special ownership rules in those situations in which the hiring party assumes responsibility for the organizational and/or associative risks other than as employer.

4.3 Factor 2: organizational risk

The second factor may come into play if the creator is dependent on the producer in order to make his work ready for consumption, i.e. if his contribution is only a component of the product which the producer sells to the consumer. Here, the producer complements the creator's contribution with other components of a creative and/or technical nature and ensures that all components meet the specifications required for achieving the final, marketable product.[15] In this way, the producer relieves the creator of the necessity of adding whatever creative, organizational and financial investments which may be necessary to transform his contribution into a marketable product.[16] Examples are illustrations for a book, the set design for a television talk show, a manual for a computer program, the package design for a food product, etc.

In all these situations in which the creator is dependent on the organizational investments of a producer to transform his work into a marketable product, statutory allocation of exclusive rights to the producer is most necessary for the producer and least damaging for the creator, if:

- the producer assumes the production risk (concurrence of factors 1 and 2);[17]
- the producer rather than the creator is associated with the work (concurrence of factors 2 and 3);
- the creator's contribution constitutes only a minor component of the final marketable product;
- the creator's contribution is not technically or economically exploitable standing alone;
- the work's additional uses compete with the producer's business.

It is clear from a comparison of the three countries covered by the study that the American and German copyright legislators have taken the producer's organizing and coordinating role into consideration most explicitly in allocating exclusive

---

15. *See* Varmer, at 141, emphasizing the producer's role in the case of collaborative works such as motion pictures, periodicals, directories, encyclopaedies and catalogues: assembling the group, furnishing the facilities and directing the project.

16. In relation to the creator, it is not relevant whether the producer pays the costs out of his own pocket or obtains funds from a third party (bank, distribution company, commissioning party, etc.). *See infra* 7.6.

17. *See* Hösly, at 144, 168, arguing that copyright ownership should be assigned to the producer by operation of law if he has assumed responsibility for the production risk and has general supervision over the creative process.

rights in works of authorship. Apart from provisions allocating exclusive rights to film producers, which is also done under the Dutch copyright law (§ 45d DCA), German and American copyright legislation also provide special rules for allocating rights to publishers.

In American copyright law, statutory allocation of exclusive rights to producers (other than as employers) occurs with respect to nine categories of specially ordered or commissioned works (§ 101(2) USCA), all of which require additional organizational investments in order for the work to become a marketable product: contributions to a collective work, contributions to an audiovisual work, compilations, translations, supplementary works, instructional texts, tests, answer material for tests and atlases.[18] If these works are deemed a 'work made for hire' in a written instrument signed by the parties, the commissioning party is considered to be the author and, unless agreed otherwise, owns all the rights comprised in the copyright (§ 201(b) USCA).

In Dutch copyright law, exclusive rights are allocated to producers (other than as employers or legal entities) with respect to contributions of a creative nature which have been specifically designed for a film work (§§ 45a, 45d DCA). Except for the authors of the film music, the authors of these contributions are presumed to have assigned certain exclusive exploitation rights to the producer (§ 45d DCA).[19]

Although not explicitly, both § 45d DCA and § 101(2) USCA suggest that these provisions are applicable only if the producer undertakes to assume the production risk in whole or in part before the commencement of the creative process (concurrence of factors 1 and 2).[20] In this respect, American and Dutch copyright legislation differs from German copyright law, which allocates exclusive rights to publishers and film producers with respect to certain, specified works even if these works already exist at the moment of contracting and, therefore, may have been made at the creator's own initiative and expense.

The German Publishing Act of 1901 provides that, if an author has expressly or implicitly agreed to submit his literary, dramatic or musical work to a publisher for reproduction and distribution at the publisher's expense,[21] and the publisher has undertaken to publish the work, the publisher acquires a territorially unrestricted exclusive right to reproduce and distribute at least one edition of

---

18. A 'supplementary work' is a work prepared for publication as a secondary adjunct to a work by another author for the purpose of introducing, concluding, illustrating, explaining, revising, commenting upon, or assisting in the use of the other work, such as forewords, afterwords, pictorial illustrations, maps, charts, tables, editorial notes, musical arrangements, answer material for tests, bibliographies, appendixes, and indexes. An 'instructional text' is a literary, pictorial, or graphic work prepared for publication and with the purpose of use in systematic instructional activities (§ 101(2) USCA).

19. *See* Dommering, *De sportprestatie*, at 14 ('group work'); Grosheide, *De Auteurswet*, at 122-123. *See also* 3.2.2; 6.2.

20. *See* Memorandum to § 45 DCA, Parl.Gesch. 45a.10 (1985): the essential task of the film producer is to supply capital, to run financial risk and to hire the creative contributors to the film. *See also infra* 7.6. *See also* CCNV v. Reid, 109 S.Ct. 2166, 2173 (1989): 'The unifying feature of these works is that they are usually prepared at the instance, direction and risk of a publisher or producer.'

21. 'At the publisher's expense' refers to the costs of reproduction and distribution, not of creation. *See* Ulmer, at 433.

the work upon delivery of the manuscript ('publishing right').[22] If the work is commissioned according to a plan in which the commissioning party has prescribed the content as well as the treatment in considerable detail,[23] or if the work is commissioned as a contribution to an encyclopaedic project or as an ancillary or supplementary contribution to another auhor's work or to a collective work (concurrence of factors 1 and 2), the commissioning party ('Besteller') is not obliged to publish the work (§ 47 Publishing Act 1901). The purpose of the agreement and the circumstances of the case furthermore determine whether the commissioning party is entitled to publish more than one edition in the absence of an express agreement.[24]

Another situation in which German law allocates exclusive rights to a publisher with respect to existing works is if an author authorizes the publication of his work in a periodical collection other than a newspaper (e.g. magazine, calendar, almanac). In case of doubt, such an authorization must be interpreted as granting the publisher or editor an exclusive right to reproduce and distribute the work, which converts into a non-exclusive license one year after publication (§ 38(1) GCA).[25]

The 1965 Act furthermore provides that if an author authorizes another person to make a screen adaptation of his work, this authorization must be interpreted in case of doubt so as to grant an exclusive right to screen adaptation, to broadcast the screen adaptation in case of a television film and to publicly perform it in the case of a theatrical motion picture, as well as to make translations and other technical adaptations (§ 88 GCA).[26] For contributions which are specifically commissioned as part of a film (concurrence of factors 1 and 2), the 1965 Act provides that the film producer is presumed to have acquired exclusive rights to *all* known modes of exploitation (§ 89(1) GCA).[27]

---

22. § 1, 8, 9(1) Publishing Act 1901. Unless agreed otherwise, a publisher does not acquire broadcasting rights, public performance rights, translation rights, sound or audiovisual recording rights, dramatization rights, novelization rights in the case of dramatic works and adaptation rights in the case of musical works (§ 2(2) Publishing Act 1901). In practice, most works are published pursuant to a written publishing agreement involving extensive transfers of rights for additional uses. *See* Ulmer, at 448.

23. *See* Judgment of March 15, 1984, BGH, Germany, 86 GRUR 528 (1984) ('contract of commission'): determinative is the extent to which the commissioned party is bound by the limits set by the commissioning party.

24. *Id.*

25. Memorandum to § 38, 45 UFITA 274 (1965): publishers generally want to acquire excluse rights, which seems justified. Nordemann/Hertin, at 223: beneficiary of § 38 GCA is the owner of the enterprise which founds the newspaper or periodical, invents the title, hires the contributors, runs the financial risks and has a right to control lay-out, title and presentation of the periodical or newspaper. Schricker, at 520: beneficiary is the person authorized by the author to use the contribution in the collection.

26. Compare the Memorandum to § 88 GCA, 45 UFITA 317 (1965): § 88 GCA serves to recognize producers' widespread practice of stipulating exclusive rights to pre-existing works, facilitating legal transactions and avoiding conflicts on the scope of the grant. *But see* Judgment of February 6, 1985, BGH, Germany, 87 GRUR 529 (1985) ('Happening'): professor developed and directed theatrical performance during guest-lectureship and allowed the university to videotape the performance. BGH: the presumption of § 88 GCA was inapplicable, because the professor had authorized the videotaping in order to be able to use the tape as an aid for his university lectures, not for commercial exploitation.

27. *See also* 3.2.2; 6.2.3.

4.4 Factor 3: associative risk

The third factor which may influence the allocation of rights between a creator and a producer is the extent to which the creator is associated with the work.[28] If the creator has expressed his *persona* in the work, he has a personal interest to control its use. If the relation between the creator and the work is not obvious from the work itself but from the fact that his name is mentioned on it, he may still have a personal interest in controlling the work's use. If, on the other hand, the work is only or predominantly associated with the producer and the producer is the only person held responsible for the work, the latter may have a greater interest to control the use of the work than the creator, especially if he has assumed responsibility for the production risk (factor 1) and has made a considerable investment in transforming the work into a marketable product (factor 2).[29] A work is more likely to be associated with the producer than the creator if:

(A) the work is meant to reflect the identity of the producer or a third party rather than the creator's *persona* and therefore is presented to the public as originating in the producer or third party rather than in the creator: press releases, trademark designs, corporate logos, business cards, package designs, annual reports, etc. The nature of these works implies that a producer hired to deliver such a work has a special interest in acquiring all rights from the employees and freelancers involved in the creative process, because the commissioning party may require that all rights are transferred to him.[30]

(B) the nature or purpose of the work or the circumstances in which the work was created do not allow the creator to fully express his *persona* in the work. This typically concerns works with significant technical aspects, works of an informational nature, works involving multiple contributors, and works made within a budget and according to the more or less detailed and functionally inspired specifications of a commissioning party.[31] Creative freedom is generally

---

28. *See also* Auf der Maur, at 48; Hösly, at 140; Larese, at 308.
29. *See* Hösly, at 141; Larese, *Fragen*, at 195; Spoor/Verkade, at 34. Quaedvlieg, *Het belang van de werkgever*, at 85, distinguishes between associating the employer with the work as its producer, and associating the employer with the work as the person or entity who or which is held responsible for it 'almost as if he were the author'. Quaedvlieg argues that, in the latter case, the employer may have an interest to protection of his reputation, but that this interest should be protected outside copyright law. *See also infra* 5.5.3.
30. *See e.g.* Judgment of April 12, 1960, BGH, Germany, 62 GRUR 609 (1960) ('advertisement work'): if a film producer has undertaken to make a film for advertising purposes for payment of a fixed sum covering the costs of production, including compensation of creative contributors, he is obliged to transfer all the exploitation rights to the commissioning party. *See also* Article 11(1) Model Agreement of the (Dutch) Association of Advertisers, requiring the advertising agency to transfer all copyrights to the advertiser on the date on which the invoice is paid.
31. *See* Ginsburg, *Moral Rights*, at 127; Larese, *Fragen*, at 192; Schuijt, *Schrap artikel 7*, at 22-23; Thole, at 70. *See also* statement of H. Johnston, Time Magazine, in: *Round Table Moral Rights*, at 30: 'So in the news magazine field change is the name of the game. It is constant. It occurs to every player in the game and it all rises up to the top where there is the managing editor, the one who puts the unitary viewpoint on it. So I think it is fair to say that the individual contributors, who by the way include staffers and freelancers as well, frequently will

related to the allocation of production and organizational risks (factors 1 and 2). If, for example, a producer insists on selecting the assistants, the creator may well demand that they are directly paid by the producer. If the creator stipulates absolute creative freedom, the producer may want to negotiate a fixed price. If the creation of the work and its transformation into a marketable product requires a substantial financial and organizational investment from the producer, the latter will most likely have a right to control the creation process. Etc., etc. This correlation between production and organizational risks on the one hand and creative freedom on the other is characteristic of the commercial production of creative works. Only if a particular person's contribution is considered to be crucial for the product's commercial succes will that person be able to stipulate large budgets, creative freedom and broad integrity rights. These stipulations often go hand-in-hand with a compensation based on a percentage of the gross proceeds or net profits which, indeed burdens the creator with the production risk.

If a work does not reveal the individual contributor's personal imprint, associative risk will be restricted.[32] If at all, associative risk may result from the fact that the contributor's name is mentioned on or in relation to the work. The contributor's ability to stipulate authorship credit (or to uphold his waivable right to authorship credit), will depend on the commercial value of his name, on trade practice and on the extent to which he is dependent on the producer for financing the creative process (factor 1) and for transforming his contribution into a marketable product (factor 2).[33]

In the three countries covered by the study, the ownership provision which is most clearly based on the element of presentation, is the Dutch provision that a legal person is considered to be the author of a work if that work was published as originating from that legal person without identifying a natural person as author, unless such publication was unlawful (§ 8 DCA). The legislative history refers to works made on commission for the legal entity, such as reports, memos or announcements.[34] The provision is, indeed, mostly invoked by parties commissioning works of the A-category, either to refute an infringement claim by the actual creator or his employer (advertising agency, design studio),[35] or to

---

not recognize what emerges from what they submitted.'

32. *See* Ginsburg, *Moral Rights*, at 127, with respect to the right of integrity; Hösly, at 140-142; Larese, *Fragen*, at 194; Quaedvlieg (1992), at 31; Schuijt, *Schrap artikel 7*, at 22-23; Spoor/Verkade, at 305.
33. *See infra* 5.5.2.
34. Parl.Gesch. 8.3 (1912).
35. *See* Judgment of June 4, 1980, Ger. Amsterdam, Netherlands, 49 BIE 239 (1981) (Van den Biggelaar v. Katholieke Universiteit Nijmegen): if a work serves to give the commissioning party a personal identity, the latter is entitled to use the work, even after the relationship with the commissioned party has ended. In that case, the commissioning party may invoke § 8 DCA to prove title. *See also* Judgment of February 21, 1992, Pres.Rb. 's-Gravenhage, Netherlands, 60 BIE 393 (1992) ('brochures'). *See also infra* 7.5.

prevent competing uses of the work.[36] However, since the language of § 8 DCA does not limit the scope of the provision to works which are, by their nature, associated with the legal person for whom the work is made, courts have permitted producers to also invoke § 8 DCA in other cases, thus treating § 8 DCA as a general presumption of title for producers vis-à-vis third parties who imitate or otherwise use their products.[37] This understandable extension of the scope of § 8 DCA does not fully comply with the statement by the Minister of Justice in 1912 that paying for the creation of the work is insufficient in order for the commissioning party to qualify as author.[38]

Although works in the A or B-category qualifying as 'writings' are protected under the Dutch Copyright Act even if they do not meet the regular standard of authorship,[39] the 1912 Act does not provide special ownership rules with respect to 'impersonal writings'. While, in most cases, the producer will be considered author pursuant to § 7 or § 8 DCA, there is no consensus in legal doctrine as to who should become first owner in the event these provisions do not apply.[40] If the producer assumes production risk, he should arguably become the first owner irrespective of whose name is identified on the work. Support for this proposition may perhaps be found in the statement of the Hoge Raad that the applicability of the individual provisions in the Copyright Act to 'impersonal writings' must be determined according to the purpose of these provisions.[41]

Except for certain provisions designed to limit the moral rights protection in the case of works in the A or B-categories,[42] the German and American Copyright

---

36. *See* Judgment of March 31, 1987, Pres.Rb. Haarlem, Netherlands, 55 BIE 300 (1987) ('Videofilmer'): since the plaintiff/magazine publisher published the sample brochure for a new magazine without identifying the name of the freelancer who wrote the text of the brochure, the plaintiff is the author on the basis of § 8 DCA. The publication by the defendant, a former employee of plaintiff, of parts of the brochure in a competing magazine therefore constitutes an infringement on plaintiff's copyrights.
37. Judgment of October 20, 1982, Ger. 's-Hertogenbosch, Netherlands, NJ 1983, 503 (Vlisco v. Dessina): fabric designs; Judgment of January 9, 1991, Ger. 's-Hertogenbosch, Netherlands, 61 BIE 225 (1993) ('shoe design'); Judgment of April 5, 1991, Pres.Rb. Amsterdam, Netherlands, 60 BIE 203 (1992) ('christmas cards').
38. *See supra* 4.2, note 7. *See also* Spoor/Verkade, at 41.
39. *See supra* 2.15 notes 300-305 and accompanying text.
40. Hugenholtz, at 47: the person who fixes the writing. *But see* Van Engelen, *Geschriftenbescherming*, at 250, arguing that the first owner should be the person who made the writing financially possible. Van Engelen defines the subject matter of protection as the financial activities related to the production and publication of an impersonal writing. The object of an intellectual property right, however, can never be a financial activity: a pirate does not copy financial activities.
41. Judgment of June 25, 1965, HR, Netherlands, NJ 1966, 116 note Hirsch Ballin ('radio program listings').
42. Section 44 of the German Publishing Act of 1901 entitles the publisher to alter works which have been incorporated in a collective work which does not mention the creator's name, provided that this is usual for the type of collective work at issue. Compare also § 93 GCA, providing that the authors of a film work can only invoke the right of integrity of § 14 GCA in the event of *gross* mutilations or other *grossly* derogatory treatment of the film work. *See also* § 101 USCA, providing a list of works that do not qualify as a 'work of visual art' and of which the authors therefore are excluded from the protection of the right of integrity and attribution provided by § 106A USCA. *See supra* 2.14 note 246 and accompanying text. The list covers virtually every work in the A and B-category.

Acts do not contain any provisions which are specifically designed to allocate rights to producers because the producer rather than the creator is presented and viewed as the originator of the work. In determining the scope of a grant to a commissioning party, however, German courts generally look at the degree of authorship, the purpose of the work and the circumstances under which the work was created.[43]

In American copyright law, ownership of copyrights to works of the A and B category will only be allocated to the producer if these works are made by an employee within the scope of his employment or if they are included in one of the nine categories of section 101(2) USCA and the parties have signed a written instrument in which the work is deemed a 'work made for hire'.[44] For commissioned advertisements, computer programs and sound recordings which cannot somehow be qualified under one of these nine categories,[45] the ownership can therefore only be statutorily allocated to the producer in the case of true employment works.[46]

4.5 Conclusions

In Chapter 3, I discussed the problems producers may encounter when they seek to acquire and establish title to works of authorship. Not in all cases in which producers encounter problems of this kind, however, legislators decide to allocate rights to the producer directly. One might perhaps expect that the actual decision whether to allocate rights to producers depends on what they are supposed to achieve with the exploitation of creative works: a reward for creators, the

---

43. *See e.g.* Judgment of March 20, 1986, BGH, Germany, 88 GRUR 885 (1986) ('Metaxa'): an implied grant to a commissioning party must be considered to include the right to mass reproduction and distribution of the work if practice in the same line of business indicates that a commissioning party regularly acquires these rights in a comparable situation (i.e. the same level of remuneration, the same degree of authorship, work made according to the instructions of the commissioning party).

44. § 201b USCA. CCNV v. Reid, 109 S.Ct. 2166 (1989).

45. Computer programs may arguably be deemed a 'work made for hire' as a contribution to a collective or audiovisual work, as a compilation, translation, supplementary work or as an instructional text. *See* Beck, at 40. Sound recordings may arguably be 'works made for hire' as a contribution to a collective work, as a supplementary work, or as a compilation. There is no evidence that the sound recording industry has ever pursued the inclusion of sound recordings in the list of § 101(2) USCA. Sound tracks, however, are specifically mentioned in the House Report as a contribution to an audiovisual work. H.R.Rep. 92-487, 92d Cong., 1st Sess., 6 (1971).

46. CCNV v. Reid, 109 S.Ct. 2166 (1989); MacLean Assoc., Inc. v. Wm.M. Mercer-Meidinger Hansen, 952 F.2d 769 (3d Cir. 1991). *See* Sher, at 75, for a critical comment on the consequences of *CCNV v. Reid* in the computer software field. Before *CCNV v. Reid*, courts applied extensive interpretations to bring works of the A or B category under the 'work for hire' provisions. *See e.g.* Paul Peregrine v. Lauren Corp., 601 F.Supp. 828 (D.Colo. 1985): photographs made by professional photographer on commission for advertising agency are works made for hire, because the advertising agency had the right to supervise the work of the photographer and to veto any course the project might take. *See also* Evans Newton, Inc. v. Chicago Systems Software, 793 F.2d 889 (7th Cir.), *cert. denied*, 479 U.S. 949 (1986): software and manual made by defendant for use in educational institutions are works made for hire, because the plaintiff sufficiently controlled and supervised the creation of the program and manual.

dissemination of culture, or merely a profitable business? The latter would probably be guided by considerations of efficiency and would require that ownership be allocated in such a way that the need for an express transfer arises infrequently. A reward for creators, on the other hand, would require ownership to be allocated to the creator so that the burden of contracting is on the producer. Dissemination of culture would require that ownership be allocated in such a way which optimizes the public availability of both old and new works.

This Chapter has indicated, however, that in spite of their different underlying rationales for copyright protection, the American, Dutch and German copyright laws are quite similar in the situations in which they allocate ownership of exclusive rights to producers. All three copyright systems to some extent take into account how the production, organizational and associative risks are allocated between creator and producer, i.e. whether the producer has undertaken to pay for the costs of creation before commencement of the creative process (factor 1), whether the marketability of the work is due to the producer's organizational investments (factor 2) and whether the work is presented and/or viewed as the work of the creator or the producer (factor 3).

In employment relationships, in which assumption by the producer of production as well as organizational and associative risks is most likely to occur, all three copyright laws allocate rights to the producer/employer. In the case of works made by independent contractors, the producer's assumption of production risk (factor 1) may lead to the statutory allocation of rights to producers if combined with factors 2 and/or 3. All three copyright systems allocate exclusive rights to producers in case of commissioned contributions to film works and in American and German copyright law also in case of certain commissioned contributions to larger publishing projects, such as contributions to periodicals, works ancillary or supplementary to literary works and in American copyright law also contributions to educational publications. This corresponds with the situations discussed in Chapter 3 in which the application of the creator doctrine leads to the most problems: multiple creative contributions, the author(s) are difficult to identify, the legal status of the various creative contributions is unclear, the work has not yet been created at the moment of contracting, international distribution of the work, the work needs regular updating or revising, the nature of the business requires the producer to repeat the process of acquiring title with great frequency.

In comparison with American and German copyright legislation, Dutch copyright law provides no specific support to publishers beyond the general allocation rules of §§ 7 and § 8 DCA. This may explain why Dutch publishers, more than their American and German counterparts, advocate protection for their own contributions under a neighbouring rights regime.[47] In Chapter 6, I will briefly discuss to what extent the introduction of such a neighbouring right can solve the problems which publishers encounter when they seek to exploit works of

---

47. *See e.g.* Alberdingk Thijm, at 75; Asscher, *Viewpoint from the Netherlands*, at 307; Grosheide/Obertop, at 163. Sceptical about the need of a neighbouring right for publications which include works of authorship: Resius, 67-69; Soetenhorst, at 98-100; Spoor/Verkade, at 377.

authorship and, consequently, whether such a right may serve as an alternative to statutory allocation of exclusive rights in the work of authorship to the publisher.

Rather than in the situations in which they allocate rights to producers, the different rationales behind the American, Dutch and German copyright laws are manifest in the means by and the extent to which they allocate rights to producers. In the following Chapter, I will discuss the admissibility of attributing authorship and copyright ownership as a method for allocating rights to producers, followed in Chapter 6 by a discussion of the practical consequences of presumptions of transfers and attribution of authorship as the two most important means of allocating rights in works of authorship to producers.

Chapter 5

Attributing authorship and initial copyright ownership to producers: a discussion

5.1 Introduction

I ended Chapter 4 by pointing out that there are more differences between the ways in which the American, Dutch and German copyright systems allocate rights to producers than in the situations in which they have chosen to do so. Aside from practical factors such as political feasibility or the economic importance and lobbying power of a particular industry, the options available for allocating rights to producers are indeed determined by the rationale underlying copyright protection and the resulting views on whether or not the creator doctrine is imperative. While the monistic concept of author's rights underlying the German copyright system precludes the attribution of authorship and copyright ownership as a method for allocating rights to producers,[1] both the American and Dutch copyright systems vest authorship in the producer in certain cases. This method for allocating rights to producers is not entirely uncontroversial, however. Dutch commentators have often questioned the compatibility of this method with the moral rights protection afforded to 'authors' under section 25 of the 1912 Copyright Act.[2] To date, the majority of the lower Dutch courts have treated the employer or legal entity who is considered to be the 'author' under sections 7 and 8 DCA to also be the 'author' for the purposes of section 25 DCA, with the effect of denying protection to the creator in the case of claims directed against an employer[3] or a third party-infringer,[4] and also with the effect

---

1. Memorandum to § 43 GCA, 45 UFITA 277 (1965): the attribution of the author's right to an employer would be contrary to the 'creator' doctrine codified in § 7 GCA. Memorandum to § 89 GCA, 45 UFITA 318 (1965): the proposal to vest copyright ownership in the producer of a film work in view of the fact that the authors of a film are often difficult to identify, has not been adopted. Since film works are not the only collaborative works of which the authors are difficult to identify, such a deviation from the creator doctrine might create a precedent the consequences of which are unforeseeable.

2. *See supra* 2.15 note 298. In an English translation of the 1989 Amendment of the Dutch Copyright Act drafted by the Ministry of Justice, the word 'maker' has been translated as 'creator' and the word 'rechtverkrijgende' as 'the person in whom his rights are vested'. The word 'vested' is somewhat confusing in view of the fact that 'rechtverkrijgende' refers to a person who acquired ownership as a result of inheritance or assignment. *See* Copyright, text 1-01, at 1 (1991).

3. Judgment of May 24, 1978, Ger. 's-Hertogenbosch, Netherlands, 53 BIE 99 (1985) (van Gunsteren v. Lips); Judgment of May 27, 1992, Rb. 's-Gravenhage, Netherlands, 17 Informatie-recht/AMI 94 (1993) note Quaedvlieg (Gorter v. PTT).

of protecting the reputation of the employer or legal entity against mutilations of the work by third parties.[5]

And also in the United States, where the traditionally economic nature of copyright has always ensured a certain degree of legislative discretion in allocating copyright ownership,[6] the issue of authorship and works made for hire has become the focus of attention in the light of the ratification of the Berne Convention and the debate on the possible introduction of moral rights protection at a federal level.[7] With respect to the moral rights protection granted to authors of works of visual arts by the 1991 Amendment, this problem was however circumvented by excluding protection for authors of works made for hire.[8]

In this Chapter, I will discuss the admissibility of the statutory attribution of authorship and initial copyright ownership as a means of allocating rights to producers. I will commence with a brief discussion of a number of modern continental-European theories which allow the creator doctrine to be 'overruled' by another rule of attribution in certain cases, as well as a theory which advocates an alternative system for attributing authorship and copyright ownership in all cases (5.2). In the subsequent paragraphs, I will discuss the 'imperativeness' of the creator doctrine in the light of the creator's economic and moral interests in his work (5.3-5.6). On the basis of a discussion of the nature and scope of the moral rights of publication (5.4), integrity (5.5) and attribution (5.6), I will try to examine how these rights relate to the rights of exploitation and how they affect the allocation of authorship and copyright ownership.

5.2 The advocates in continental-European doctrine

If an employee creates a work within the scope of his employment, he is generally considered to have a contractual obligation to allow the employer to use the

---

4. *See* Judgment of August 20, 1987, Pres.Rb. Amsterdam, Netherlands, 12 Informatierecht/AMI 18 (1988) note Cohen Jehoram ('Zeinstra v. Van den Hoek').

5. *See* Judgment of July 12, 1988, Pres.Rb. Leeuwarden, Netherlands, 13 Informatierecht/AMI 17 (1989) note Cohen Jehoram (Bonnema v. Gemeente Tietjerksteradeel); Judgment of February 28, 1991, Ger. Amsterdam, Netherlands, 60 BIE 128 (1992) (Chanel v. Maxis). *But see* Judgment of February 10, 1970, Ger. Amsterdam, Netherlands, NJ 1971, 130 ('the Forgers'): a statutory author on the grounds of § 8 DCA cannot invoke § 25 DCA.

6. *See supra* 2.8 note 100 and accompanying text.

7. *See* Statement by Ralph Oman, U.S. Register of Copyrights, before the Subcommittee on Patents, Trademarks and Copyrights of the Senate Committee on the Judiciary, 101st Cong., 1st Sess. (Sept. 20, 1989). *See also* Hearings on H.R. 2690 before the Subcommittee on Courts, Intellectual Property, and the Administration of Justice of the House Committee on the Judiciary, 101st Cong., 2nd Sess. (Jan. 9, 1990), reported in: 39 PTCJ (BNA) 206 (1989). *See also* Kernochan, *After U.S. Adherence*, at 164: not only producers but also directors, screenwriters and cinematographers felt that they should be entitled to moral rights as 'authors'. *See also* Kastenmaier, at 21: 'The major copyright battles of the next decade may be fought between creators and their successors in interest over artists' rights and works for hire. The congressional role will be a difficult one. We may need to re-examine the definition of the term "author".'

8. Compare the definition of a 'work of visual art' in § 101 USCA, providing that a 'work of visual art' does not include any work made for hire. *See also supra* 2.14 note 246 and accompanying text.

work for business purposes. It would however require a derogation from the creator doctrine to apply the principle that the results of an employee's labour *automatically belong* to the employer. Several commentators have argued that this principle should nevertheless be applied unrestrictedly to works of authorship, albeit by means of an express statutory provision vesting the copyright in the employer.[9] Rehbinder and Frey have based this on the theory that the fruits of an employee's labour are attributed ('zugeordnet') to the employer as a result of the dependency created upon the employee's employment within the employer's labour organization.[10] Other Swiss commentators have also emphasized an employer's right to the fruits of an employee's creative labour, but have argued that it is unnecessary to derogate from the principle that copyright vests in the creator of the work, if the copyright is assigned to the employer by operation of law (*cessio legis*),[11] or if the employee is presumed to have agreed to assign the copyright before commencement of the creative process, so that it automatically passes to the employer at the point at which the author's right arises.[12]

In Dutch doctrine, Maeijer has argued that a natural person's activities may be attributed to a legal entity for the purposes of legal efficiency and that the designation of the employer and legal entity as 'author' in § 7 and § 8 DCA therefore does not mean that they are fictitiously deemed to be author, but that they are actually considered authors for reasons of legal efficiency.[13] This reasoning is supported by Spoor and Verkade with respect to works which are generally attributed to the employer and for which the employer is held responsible, e.g. works which are the result of a close vertical or horizontal collaboration between the employees and/or which are presented as the employer's intellectual product.[14]

Maeijer however does not accept the full consequences of granting employers and legal entities authorship. In order to protect the creator's interest in deciding if and when to disclose his work, the author's right can not be seized if it is held by the 'author' (§ 2(3) DCA) or if it is part of an author's bankrupt estate (§ 21 Bankruptcy Act). According to the present formulation, these provisions seem to apply regardless of whether the author actually has a justifiable interest in preventing the disclosure of his work. In order to prevent anomalies in those

---

9. *See* Frey, at 68; Rehbinder, *Recht am Arbeitsergebnis*, 1-23; Rehbinder, *Recht am Arbeitsergebnis und Urheberrecht*, at 484. Critical comments on this theory, in particular from Dietz, *Entwickelt*, 112-119; Dietz, *Transformation of authors rights*, at 35-47.

10. Frey, at 55; Rehbinder, *Recht am Arbeitsergebnis*, at 7.

11. *See* Hösly, at 139, 168, 169, proposing a *cessio legis* in those cases in which the producer assumes the major financial, organizational and moral risks, unless the parties have made a contractual stipulation to the contrary before the creation of the work. Recher, at 341, also proposes a *cessio legis* to the employer, but only in respect of the exploitation rights and in return for the right to additional remuneration and the reversion of rights to the employee/creator in the event of non-exploitation.

12. Hunziker, *Urheberrecht*, at 54, 73.

13. Maeijer, at 352. De Beaufort (1932), at 57, and Vermeijden, at 146 also accepted authorship of a legal entity.

14. Spoor/Verkade, at 34. *See also* Verkade, *Het beste artikel 7*, at 18; Hösly, at 141. Spoor and Verkade do not venture an opinion on the validity of Maeijer's argument in respect of § 8 DCA.

cases in which a legal entity or employer is considered to be 'author',[15] Maeijer proposes to exclude employers and legal entities from the applicability of § 2(3) DCA by treating their designation as author in § 7 and § 8 DCA as an assignment by the operation of law.[16] Maeijer thus interprets 'author' in these provisions as the person to whom the author's right as a whole, including the moral rights of § 25 DCA, has been assigned by the operation of law, thereby adding one more confusing theory to the ever-growing list of 'author' theories.

The element of public responsibility and public association with the work discussed in the foregoing chapter,[17] has been presented by Larese as the basis for an alternative system for attributing copyright ownership.[18] To avoid the problem of having to identify the actual creator, in particular of works involving numerous contributors and works which lack an identifiable personal expression,[19] the creator doctrine is overruled in favour of the person who presents a work as his ('wer zeichnet gilt als Urheber').[20] This person or entity then becomes the author, and his status of author cannot be invalidated by proving that he did not create the work.[21] According to this system, Larese seeks to achieve what he sees as the purpose of copyright protection: allowing the person who the public sees as the originator of the work and whose personality is therefore associated with it, to exercise control over the use of the work.[22] The idea of vesting authorship in the person who presents a work as his should therefore not be regarded as some kind of playful deviation from an unshakeable principle, but rather as a serious attempt to preserve the meaning of the principle under changing circumstances.[23]

To however prevent just anyone claiming authorship regardless of his connection with the work, Larese is forced to fall back on the creator, albeit that he prefers the term 'Hersteller' (author, maker) to prevent what he describes as the irrational connotation of the word creator.[24] The 'Hersteller' of the work has a right to claim authorship.[25] If there are two or more 'Herstellers', they can

---

15. *See* Hugenholtz/Spoor, at 43; Spoor, *Onzekere zekerheid*, at 362.
16. Maeijer, at 354. I would argue that § 2(3) DCA should be inapplicable if there are no moral interests at stake, both in cases in which the creator is the 'author' as well as in cases in which the employer or legal entity is considered the 'author'. *See also* Spoor/Verkade, at 309.
17. *See supra* 4.4.
18. Larese, at 304; Larese, *Fragen*, at 194-195. Larese elaborates on the French author Savatier, who has argued that in the case of works made by multiple contributors, the author is the person or persons under whose name the work is published with the authorization of the actual creators. *See* Larese, at 296; Savatier, at 1.
19. Larese, at 314.
20. Larese, at 308. *See also* Auf der Maur, at 70. In this attribution theory, Larese elaborates on Kummer's theory that a visually or audibly perceptible expression may be protected under copyright law if it is statistically unique and presented as an artistic or literary work. Kummer, at 75, 80.
21. *Id.* at 311.
22. *Id.* at 206, 308. *See also supra* 4.4.
23. *Id.* at 311.
24. *Id.* at 312.
25. *Id.* at 313.

decide amongst themselves who can claim authorship: collectively, one of them, the hiring party, etc.[26] For employment works, Larese proposes introducing a special provision which grants the employer the right to claim authorship.[27] The 'Hersteller' or the employer may authorize someone else to claim authorship. Claiming authorship without the holder's express authorization to claim authorship merely constitutes a presumption of authorship.[28]

While this system may help a producer to prove title vis-à-vis third parties, he may still be confronted with evidence that the actual creators of the work did not authorize him to claim authorship. This means that in order to secure title, the producer must still identify the actual creators of the work in order to obtain their authorization. Larese's system therefore cannot solve all the identification problems which it is designed to resolve.[29]

All the above-mentioned authors deny that attributing initial copyright ownership to the creator is imperative in all cases because of the continuing nexus between the creator and his work, partly by arguing that the circumstances in which works are created do not always allow personal expression,[30] partly by denying that the rights conferred on authors by the copyright statute are personal to the creator of the work,[31] and partly by arguing that creators' moral interests are also protected outside copyright law.[32] In the coming paragraphs, I will discuss these arguments within the framework of a larger discussion on the imperativeness of the creator doctrine.

5.3 The imperativeness of the creator doctrine in view of the creator's moral and economic interests in the work

Recent literature on authorship and copyright ownership has emphasized the imperativeness of the creator doctrine as a necessary consequence of copyright as the creator's natural or human right.[33] In relation to the economic element of

---

26. *Id.* at 314.
27. *Id.* at 313. *See also* Auf der Maur, at 88, favouring a presumption of transfer of the right to claim authorship at the point at which the employment contract is signed which he believes will prevent employees from transferring future rights to a collecting society. The collecting society can however still acquire rights if the employee transfers his future rights to claim authorship to the collecting society before he enters into an employment relationship.
28. *Id.* at 313.
29. In this sense also Hösly, at 108. Hösly does agree with Larese and Kummer, however, that initial ownership should extend to persons who disclose a perceptible expression as a work of authorship. He therefore proposes to drop the term 'creator' and replace it by 'first author' ('Ersturheber'). *Id.* at 111.
30. Frey, at 59-60; Hösly, at 137-143; Larese, at 307; Larese, *Fragen*, at 192.
31. *See* Auf der Maur, at 35-38; Hösly, at 88-102; Hunziker, *Monismus*, at 131; Hunziker, *Urheberrecht*, at 54; Rehbinder, *Recht am Arbeitsergebnis und Urheberrecht*, at 499-502; Vermeijden, at 147. *See also* Spoor/Verkade, at 301, arguing that Dutch doctrine assumes, perhaps too easily, that moral rights are inalienable under Dutch copyright law.
32. *See* Auf der Maur, at 72; Maeijer, at 353; Rehbinder, *Recht am Arbeitsergebnis und Urheberrecht*, at 503; Spoor/Verkade, at 307.
33. Most prominently, Dietz, *The concept of author*, 2-57; Ricketson, *People or Machines*, 1-37.

copyright protection, this reference to natural and human rights would seem to be of a predominantly persuasive nature: creators' claims to economic protection have found recognition in international human rights conventions[34] and national constitutions,[35] but these conventions and constitutions do not seem to automatically disqualify statutory provisions which allocate the ownership of exploitation rights to someone other than the creator.[36] Lacking a definition of the 'author' as the work's actual creator,[37] the Berne Convention furthermore does not seem to provide a direct legal basis for economically protecting creators who are not considered authors under the applicable law.

While the concept of copyright as a human right and the recognition of the economic protection of creators under international human rights conventions may constitute arguments in favour of allocating exploitation rights to creators,[38] the final legislative decision will involve a weighing up of the interests of creators, producers and the public. The foregoing chapter has indicated that, in view of the diverging allocation of production, organizational and associative risks between creators and producers, there is no single answer to the question whether exploitation rights should vest in the creator *per se*.

Creators' moral interests are more universally protected than their economic interests. In countries such as Germany and France, with a predominantly natural right approach to author's rights, authors are guaranteed certain moral interests regardless of their nationality or the country in which the work is first published.[39] In countries where foreign authors can only invoke moral rights protection under copyright law if they meet the general criteria for applicability (e.g. § 47 DCA), foreign authors may nevertheless enjoy protection of their moral interests under other theories.[40] More in general, creators may enjoy protection of their moral interests outside the copyright law, e.g. under the law of contracts or

---

34. *See supra* 2.8 note 103.
35. *See supra* 2.9, note 122 and accompanying text, discussing the property guarantee of Article 14 of the German Constitution.
36. *See e.g.* Judgment of December 23, 1988, Pres.Rb. Rotterdam, Netherlands, Computerrecht 149 (1989) ('NavalConsult'): the Berne Convention and legislation on human rights do not preclude the employer in whose service, at whose expense and with whose infrastructure the work was made, from being designated author for purposes of the copyright law. *See also supra* 3.4 note 101. *See also supra* 2.14, notes 247-251 and accompanying text, discussing the compatibility of the 'work made for hire' provisions in the U.S. Copyright Act with the clause in the U.S. Constitution that Congress has the power to grant authors the exclusive right to their writings. *Cf. also* Judgment of October 25, 1978, BVerfG, Germany, 84 UFITA 317 (1979) ('church music'): subjecting a certain use to a remuneration right instead of an exclusive right in order to guarantee public access does not necessarily violate the property guarantee of Article 14 of the Constitution.
37. *See supra* 3.4 note 100 and accompanying text.
38. Larese at 148, and Verkade, *Rechtsbeginselen*, at 147, deny the existence of a creator's fundamental right to claim economic protection.
39. *See supra* 2.16 note 340.
40. *Id.*

torts.[41] Reference is increasingly being made to constitutional rights and international conventions guaranteeing the right of privacy and the freedom of expression.[42]

This apparently broad legal basis for protecting creators' moral interests merits further discussion of the relationship between the protection of these moral interests and the attribution of copyright ownership. It is often argued that the protection of moral interests is a result of the special bond between the creator and his intellectual creation, and that copyright ownership, or at least the moral rights which constitute a part of that ownership, should therefore vest in the creator.[43] In Chapter 2 we have seen that the German legislature has declared author's rights to be completely inalienable for this reason (§ 29 GCA).[44]

This reference to the continuing bond between the creator and his work raises questions in the context of this study about the nature of the moral rights protection afforded by copyright law. Are moral rights personal to the creator and how do they relate to exploitation rights? Can creators successfully invoke moral rights in every situation? Does the protection of the creator's moral interests require that copyright ownership vests in the creator as a whole? Etc., etc. In the following sections, I will try to answer these questions with respect to those interests of creators which are most broadly protected under national copyright legislation: the creator's interest in deciding if, when and how his work will be dis-closed to the public (the right of first publication), the creator's interest in being recognized as the author of the work (the right of attribution) and the

---

41. See e.g. Judgment of March 21, 1975, HR, Netherlands, NJ 1975, 410 (Miletic v. Gemeente Amsterdam I): the destruction by the municipality of Amsterdam of paintings in its possession was unlawful vis-à-vis the artist. See also Judgment of June 22, 1973, HR, Netherlands, NJ 1974, 61 note Wachter (Patrimonium v. Reijers): placing a different statuette on a building than the statuette which had been agreed by the sculptor and the defendant constitutes a breach of contract. See also Judgment of June 1, 1985, HR, Netherlands, NJ 1986, 692 note Brunner (Frenkel v. KRO), discussed infra 5.4.

42. See Articles 8-10 European Convention for the Human Rights; Articles 17-19 of the International Covenant on Civil and Political Rights. See also Judgment of May 25, 1954, BGH, Germany, 53 GRUR 197 (1955) ('publication letter'): on the basis of the protection of the personality guaranteed under Articles 1 and 2 of the Constitution, private letters may not be published without the author's permission, even if they do not meet the standard of authorship required by copyright law. Judgment of August 8, 1990, Pres.Rb. Arnhem, Netherlands, KG 1991, 14 ('diary'): a father violated his daughter's right to privacy by reading and distributing parts of her diary with the object of establishing his wife's misconduct in divorce proceedings. See also Article 27(2) of the Universal Declaration on Human Rights and Article 15(1)(c) of the International Covenant on Economic, Social and Cultural Rights, guaranteeing protection of the moral interests arising from the creation of works of authorship. See also Verkade, Rechtsbeginselen, at 863, recognizing a legal principle based on the freedom of expression, according to which authors have certain claims in respect of the disclosure of their works, recognition of authorship and preservation of the integrity of their works.

43. See e.g. Judgment of October 26, 1951, BGH, Germany, 54 GRUR 257 (1952) ('patient card index'): the personal nature of author's rights means it is impossible to attribute initial ownership to an employer, unless the employee has only made a minor contribution in an assistant and dependent capacity. See also Nordemann/Hertin, at 114; Schricker/Dietz, at 232, referring to the 'Urheberpersönlichkeitsrecht' ('droit moral') as the elaboration of the indissoluble personal, intellectual bond between a creator and his work. See also Judgment of February 10, 1970, Ger. Amsterdam, NJ 1971, 130 at 369 ('the Forgers'): attributing moral rights to a legal entity which is considered the 'author' under § 8 DCA is irreconcilable with the highly personal bond between the creator and his work. See also Gerbrandy, at 290; Kuypers, at 11; Quaedvlieg, Het belang, at 83. See also supra 2.8. note 110.

44. See supra 2.13.

creator's interest in preventing his work from being mutilated (the right of integrity).

5.4 The right of first publication

The author's right to decide if, when and how his work will be disclosed to the public is explicitly guaranteed under German law as part of the inalienable 'Urheberpersönlichkeitsrecht' (§ 12 GCA). Under the Dutch Copyright Act, the right of first publication arises from the exclusive right of communication to the public (§ 1 DCA) and, under the U.S. Copyright Act, from the exclusive right of distribution (§ 106(3) USCA).

First ownership of the exclusive rights of distribution and communication to the public necessarily implies an exclusive right of first publication. Ownership of the exclusive rights of reproduction and adaptation furthermore provide a means to control the manner in which a work is communicated to the public. Vesting ownership of these rights in the creator is therefore obvious in view of his interest in deciding if and how his work is published.[45] Not every creator will however be equally able to effectuate control by determining the moment and scope of the grant to the producer. Employment, production and publishing contracts entered into before commencement of the creative process will generally include an express or implied authorization to distribute the work.[46] With respect to film works, section § 45d DCA specifically provides that the film producer decides when a film is ready to be performed, unless the parties agree otherwise in a written instrument. Absent such an agreement, the film author cannot, at least not on the basis of his position as initial (co-)owner of the copyright, refuse exploitation of a version he does not approve of. If he does not wish to be associated with the film, the 1912 Act merely allows him to demand that his name is not mentioned in connection with the film, unless such demand were to be unreasonable (§ 45e(c) DCA).[47]

For creators who contract with a producer before creation of the work, maintaining control over the manner and time of publication will therefore more

---

45. *See* Rey v. Lafferty, 990 F.2d 1379 (1st Cir. 1993): the plaintiff, surviving co-author of the 'Curious George' childrens' book character, does not unreasonably invoke his position as licensor of merchandising rights in refusing its approval to certain merchandising products, because it concerns ancillary products of which it may be expected that they are made in conformity with the aesthetic image which the author envisions for her artistic creation, especially since, in this case, such product conformity would neither set unreasonably high levels of commercial practicality nor foreclose all prospects of profitability on which the contract was predicated. Exploitation of the products without the author's approval therefore constitutes copyright infringement.

46. *See* Schricker/Rojahn, at 586: to the extent that an employee is obliged to grant rights to an employer, he must also allow the employer to exercise the right of first publication. There is however dispute as to whether an express or implied grant of rights to a future work requires an additional statement by its creator that the work is ready for publication in order for the grantee to be able to exploit the work. Affirmative: Nordemann/Hertin, at 175; Schricker/Dietz, at 246, with the exception of employment works. Schricker/Rojahn, at 586: an employer has the right to decide when the work will be published.

47. 1985 Amendment.

often be a matter of contract than of copyright law.[48] Protecting the creator's interest in ensuring that his work is actually exploited after he has granted rights to a producer, is also primarily a matter of contract law. The German Copyright Act provides additional support in this respect by allowing the author to withdraw an exclusive right-to-use in the event of non-use, provided the right is not withdrawn within a period of two years of being granted, and provided the owner of the exclusive right is indemnified (§ 41 GCA).[49] Although such a provision does not exist in Dutch law, the courts seem to reach adequate solutions in the case of conflicts about non-exploitation by interpreting the duties of the parties under the contract. In the 1985 case of *Frenkel v. KRO*, the Dutch Hoge Raad specifically recognized a creator's interest in publication of his works by stating that the defendant broadcasting organization, in exercising its contractually stipulated right to decide whether or not to broadcast a documentary, must take into account the 'author's justified interests and moral rights'.[50] According to the court, the programming director's promise after the documentary had been made that it would be broadcast, must be interpreted in the light of the agreement, the purpose of which was to broadcast the documentary.[51]

5.5 The right of integrity

5.5.1 STATUTORY PROVISIONS

If the creator has expressed his *persona* in his work, he has a legitimate interest in preventing others from distorting the work. The most direct legal basis for protecting this interest is ownership of the exploitation rights and, in particular,

---

48. *See e.g.* Judgment of May 14, 1964, Ger. Amsterdam, Netherlands, NJ 1964, 453 (Geesink v. Terra Nostra): a publisher published illustrations eighteen years after the illustrator had granted it the right to publish them. The publication is prejudicial to the illustrator's reputation because the illustrations are out-dated for the purpose for which they were being used. The publication with the illustrator's name was in breach of good faith, unless his name was accompanied by the year in which he made the illustrations.

49. Withdrawal is possible three months after the grant in the case of contributions to a newspaper, six months in the case of contributions to a periodical which is published at least once a month, and a year in the case of contributions to other periodicals (§ 41(3) GCA). *See e.g.* Judgment of March 6, 1986, BGH, Germany, 30 ZUM 534 (1986) (Ligäa): under § 41 GCA, the plaintiff was not entitled to withdraw the right to publish her musical composition 'Ligäa' when the defendant notified her that he did not intend to publish 'Ligäa' separately, but as part of another composition 77% of which coincided with 'Ligäa', indicating the parts which would be left out in order to be able to perform 'Ligäa'. Instead of withdrawing the right-to-use, the plaintiff should have cooperated in solving the conflict, not in the last place because she had made it seem as if the two compositions were different works.

50. Judgment of June 1, 1985, HR, Netherlands, NJ 1986, 692 note Brunner. Compare also Judgment of May 20, 1994, HR, Netherlands, RvdW 1994, 112 ('Negende van Oma'), in which the court recognized the plaintiff's interest in publication of his work, but also that his interest must be weighed against the interests of third parties in non-publication.

51. On remand, the court ordered the broadcasting organization to broadcast the documentary. Judgment of June 4, 1986, Ger. 's-Gravenhage, Netherlands, NJ 1987, 472. For German law, see §§ 1, 47 VerlG, discussed *supra* 4.3.

ownership of the right to adapt the work.[52] If an author has granted a producer exclusive exploitation rights, subsection 1 of Article 6bis of the Berne Convention provides that the author nevertheless has the right to object to any mutilation of his work or any other derogatory action in relation to his work which would prejudice his honour or reputation.

Section 25(1)(d) of the Dutch Copyright Act is formulated similarly to Article 6bis BC. On top of this protection, the Dutch Copyright Act grants authors the right to object to changes to their works, unless such objection were unreasonable (§ 25(1)(c) DCA). The author may waive the latter right (§ 25(3) DCA), and it is indeed presumed to have been waived by the (co)author of a film work, unless the author and producer agree otherwise in a written instrument (§ 45f DCA).

Under the German Copyright Act, an author has a right to oppose mutilations or other distortions of his work which may endanger his justified personal or intellectual interests (§ 14 GCA). 'Justified personal or intellectual interests' is meant to reflect the fact that § 14 GCA not only protects the author's personal interests in safeguarding his honour and reputation, but also his intellectual interest in the status of the work, i.e. his interest in deciding how his 'brainchild' will be presented to the public.[53] The German Copyright Act furthermore provides that the owner of a right-to-use is not entitled to make changes to the work, unless the parties have agreed otherwise (§ 39(1) GCA) and unless the author cannot refuse his authorization for a particular alteration in good faith (§ 39(2) GCA). The authors of a film work can only object to gross mutilations to the film work or other grossly derogatory actions (§ 93 GCA).

Under the U.S. Copyright Act, the authors of works of visual art have the right to prevent any intentional distortion, mutilation or other modification to their works which would be prejudicial to their honour or reputation, as well as the right to prevent the destruction of a work of recognized stature (§ 106A(a)(3) USCA). These rights may be waived in a written instrument signed by the author and identifying the work and the uses to which the waiver applies (§ 106A(e) USCA). Authors of other categories of works must seek protection against distortion under state statutes, trademark law or theories of contract or tort.[54]

5.5.2 THE SCOPE OF PROTECTION

The protection which authors enjoy under these provisions is not absolute. In assessing claims based on these provisions and in determining whether the

---

52. *See e.g.* Gilliam v. American Broadcasting Companies, Inc., 538 F.2d 14 (1976): the broadcast of edited versions of Monty Python's Flying Circus interrupted by commercials and omitting several scenes exceeds the license, as the Monty Python writers and performers had specifically reserved the right to make changes to the programs after they had been recorded. *See also* Rey v. Lafferty, 990 F.2d 1379 (1st Cir. 1993), discussed *supra* 5.4 note 45.

53. Schricker/Dietz, at 261; Ulmer, at 216.

54. *See e.g.* Gilliam v. American Broadcasting Companies, Inc., 538 F.2d 14 (1976): the broadcast constituted a misrepresentation of the Lanham Act in the sense of § 43(a), because the version broadcast was presented to the public as the plaintiffs' product, whereas it was actually a mere caricature of their talents. *See also* Ginsburg, *Moral Rights*, at 124; Kernochan, IV, at 163-188, discussing case law.

modification is covered by a contractual stipulation between the creator and the alleged infringer, courts generally weigh up the creator's interest in preserving the integrity of the work against the interests of the alleged infringer. Under German copyright law, the respective interests are always presumed to be balanced.[55] According to Dutch copyright law, the author's right to object to modifications must be examined in the light of the principles of reason and fairness (§ 25(1)(c) DCA) and, as such, also requires a weighing up of the respective interests. The author's right to object to mutilations (§ 25(1)(d) DCA) is not dependent on a test based on the principles of reason, but courts generally find ways of somehow taking the user's interests into consideration.[56]

Case law indicates that the following factors may affect the creator's ability to successfully oppose alterations of his work:[57]

1. the authorization to adapt a work implies a certain discretion to make changes;[58]
2. the envisaged medium in which the work is to be exploited may require certain modifications, which must be endorsed even in the absence of an express authorization to adapt the work;[59]

---

55. *See* Schricker/Dietz, at 237, 526: relevant factors are: the nature and purpose of the work, the degree of authorship, commercial practice and, particularly in employment relationships, the purpose of the agreement. *See e.g.* Judgment of August 1, 1985, OLG Munich, Germany, 88 GRUR 460 (1986): although the final scene of the film adaptation of the plaintiff's novel 'The Endless Story' constituted a 'gross mutilation' of the novel in the sense of § 93 GCA, the infringement action was dismissed on the basis of a weighing up of the respective interests: the plaintiff had authorized a two-part film adaptation based on his novel without making any reservations as to the final scene of the first part, which still had to be written at the moment of contracting; the plaintiff contractually waived the right to oppose other similarly severe mutilations; he publicly dissociated himself from the film; the defendant would have suffered serious damage if the exploitation of the film were discontinued.

56. *See* Quaedvlieg (1992), at 40-41 n. 90; Seignette, *Inkleuring*, at 1628. Courts have applied different methods for taking account of the user's interests: (1) by weighing up the user's interest in deciding whether the alteration constituted a mutilation which could harm the author's reputation. *See e.g.* Judgment of October 10, 1993, Pres.Rb. Groningen, Netherlands, 18 Informatierecht/AMI 102 (1994) ('wall painting'); (2) by deciding that the alteration did not constitute a mutilation which prejudiced the author's reputation (§ 25(1)(d) DCA), thereby necessarily subjecting the action to the test of reason and fairness of § 25(1)(c) DCA. *See e.g.* Judgment of December 15, 1989, Pres.Rb. Amsterdam, Netherlands, 14 Informatierecht/AMI 95 (1990) note Schuijt (Lieshout v. VPRO); (3) by deciding on the moral rights claim as a matter of contract law. *See e.g.* Judgment of July 13, 1989, Rb. Arnhem, Netherlands, 14 Informatierecht/AMI 33 (1990) note Verkade ('tapestry').

57. *In extenso* Quaedvlieg (1992), at 28-37.

58. *See e.g.* Judgment of November 28, 1985, BGH, Germany, 88 GRUR 458 (1986): alterations to scenery used for the annual performance of the Oberammergau passion play must be evaluated in the light of the author's implied grant of the right to develop and adapt the scenery so as to ensure that the passion play would continue to be performed from generation to generation. Taking into account the purpose of the scenery, which is to serve the performance, the implied grant allows relatively far-reaching modifications to the scenery to fit in with the views of the new director and set designer.

59. *See e.g.* Judgment of April 29, 1988, Pres.Rb. Haarlem, Netherlands, NJ 1989, 644 ('Waiting for Godot'): stage director must be considered to have a certain interpretational freedom in the play's mise en scène to the extent permitted by the script. Compare also Linnemann, *Tegen het viertje*, at 116, arguing that an assignment of television performance rights to the producer of a film work implies that the author, barring extreme situations, cannot object to commercial breaks.

3. the work was made by multiple contributors;[60]
4. the functional purpose of the work;[61]
5. the work reflects little personal character;[62]
6. high costs involved in preventing the alteration or financial risks in the event of an injunction.[63]

These factors may coincide if the producer has assumed responsibility for the production risk and if the creator has largely relied on the producer's efforts to transform his work or contribution into a marketable product (organizational risk), as this tends to limit creative freedom during the creative process (nos. 3, 4 and 5),[64] as it extends the modes of exploitation for which the producer will stipulate rights as security for the production costs (nos. 1 and 2), and as it increases the financial risks in the case of an injunction (no. 6).

While a completely independent creator is therefore more likely to succeed in an infringement action than a creator who has shifted the production and organizational risks to a producer, even the latter type of creator cannot be denied protection against an extreme distortion of the work by a producer or third party if the work reflects on him as its originator.[65]

5.5.3 THE LEGAL NATURE OF THE RIGHT OF INTEGRITY

Although a creator may enjoy protection against mutilations as first owner of the exclusive rights of reproduction and adaptation, the nature of the protection guaranteed by Article 6bis BC differs from the protection offered under these

---

60. Compare § 93 GCA, providing that film authors must take the interests of the producer and the other authors into consideration when seeking an injunction on the grounds of gross mutilation of the film.

61. *See e.g.* Judgment of March 2, 1988, Pres.Rb. Zwolle, Netherlands, 12 Informatierecht/AMI 128 (1988) note Cohen Jehoram ('Meerpaal'): the mutilation of an architectural work is only actionable if the building's essence and appearance have changed unrecognizably, without it being necessitated by a change in the building's function.

62. *See* Quaedvlieg (1992), at 32, discussing cases in which the architect of a series of private homes for the elderly was unable to prevent the installation of dormitories designed by another architect, and was therefore less fortunate than the architect of a town hall with a shining black glass edifice, who was able to prevent the installation of external sun-blinds. *See* Judgment of October 18, 1977, Pres.Rb. Utrecht, Netherlands, 3 Auteursrecht 16 (1979) note Wichers Hoeth ('dormitories'); Judgment of July 12, 1988, Pres.Rb. Leeuwarden, Netherlands, 13 Informatierecht/AMI 17 (1989) note Cohen Jehoram (Bonnema v. Gemeente Tietjerksteradeel). *See also* Ginsburg, *Moral Rights*, at 127, referring to databases and directories; Schuijt, *Schrap artikel 7*, at 23, referring to press releases, memos written by civil servants and minor journalistic pieces; Spoor/Verkade, at 305, referring to documentaries, technical drawings, architectural works and computer programs.

63. *See* Judgment of August 1, 1985, OLG Munich, Germany, 88 GRU 460 (1986) ('The Endless Story'), discussed *supra* note 55.

64. *See supra* 4.4. *See also* with respect to employment works: Hunziker, p. 66-67; Quaedvlieg (1992), at 27; Schuijt, *Schrap artikel 7*, at 27. *See also* Ginsburg, *Moral Rights*, at 127; Quaedvlieg (1992), at 25 n. 53, referring to works made by multiple contributors under the supervision of a co-ordinating entity.

65. *See also* Schricker/Dietz, at 271: the creation of a work in a situation of dependency (e.g. an employment contract) implies that the producer has a far-reaching, but not unlimited discretion to alter the work in accordance with the purpose of the agreement.

exclusive exploitation rights. The right of integrity is not a property interest in the work, but the right of the person who expressed his *persona* in a work of authorship[66] to object to derogatory actions in relation to that work which could be prejudicial to his honour or reputation.[67] This person may allow others to modify the work in a certain way, e.g. by granting a producer adaptation rights, but he can not waive or alienate the right to protect his honour or reputation.[68] As such, the right of integrity as guaranteed by Article 6bis BC is a recognition of every person's interest in protection of his personal integrity, which can be and is indeed often afforded outside copyright law.[69] The nature of this right implies that a person may invoke this right even after he has transferred the exploitation rights to a producer or even if he never owned these rights in the first place.[70]

The Berne Convention does not oblige Union members to guarantee the author's integrity rights under copyright law.[71] There is no objection to it either, as long as the nature of the protection is borne in mind: protecting the person whose *persona* is reflected in a work of authorship against derogatory actions in relation to that work which could be prejudicial to his honour or reputation. If the term 'author' in respect of the right of integrity of Article 6bis BC is regarded in this sense, the right of integrity may be invoked by any person who meets this criteria, whether this is a natural or a legal person. It is quite possible that a work will reflect the identity of the legal entity for which the work is made rather than the *persona* of the individual contributor(s) and that a mutilation of the work will therefore affect the reputation of the legal entity more than it affects the contributor's reputation.[72] Whether this is the case, must be determined on a case-by-case basis.

---

66. Compare the terminology used by Ginsburg, *Moral Rights*, at 127: the 'persona found' in the work'; 'emanation of its author's vision'; 'a sort of extension of the author herself'; 'subjective authorial characteristics'.

67. *See* De Beaufort (1932), at 25; Hösly, at 84, 85; Quaedvlieg (1992), at 42; Troller, *Bedenken*, at 292, 298. *See also* Maeijer, at 353; Spoor/Verkade, at 299, both emphasizing that the moral rights under copyright law are designed to protect the author, not the work.

68. Compare in this respect § 25 DCA. While an author is allowed to assign the right to make changes to the work (§ 2 DCA) and to waive the right to object to changes to his work (§ 25(1)(c); § 25(3) DCA), he cannot waive the right to object to mutilations which may prejudice his honour, reputation or dignity as an author (§ 25(1)(d) DCA). The right of integrity under the U.S. Copyright Act is waivable, but only in a written instrument signed by the author and only in respect of the uses specified in the written instrument (§ 106A(e) USCA).

69. *See supra* 5.3 notes 41-42. *See also* De Beaufort (1932), at 25; Grosheide, at 301; Hösly, at 85; Kabel, at 68; Quaedvlieg (1992), at 42; Spoor/Verkade, at 299, 303.

70. Van Lingen, *Morele rechten*, at 198; Maeijer, at 353; Quaedvlieg (1992), at 52 and Spoor/Verkade, at 307, all argue that the protection of moral rights in general, i.e. not only the right of integrity, should be available to creators under the law of contract or tort law if they are not considered 'author' under copyright law.

71. *See* Ricketson, at 475.

72. *See* Larese, *Fragen*, at 194-195; Maeijer, at 353; Verkade, *Het beste artikel 7*, at 17-18. *See also* Quaedvlieg, *Het belang*, at 85-86. Quaedvlieg nevertheless argues that the protection of the right of integrity under the Copyright Act is reserved for flesh-and-blood authors and that an employer or legal entity should therefore seek to protect their reputation under § 6:162 NBW (tort).

Similarly, if, for the purposes of the right of integrity of Article 6bis BC, an 'author' is considered to be the person who expressed his *persona* in a work of authorship, it should not be decisive who is designated as 'author' for the purposes of copyright ownership.[73] Most Dutch courts, however, interpret 'author' in § 25(1)(d) DCA as a reference to the person who is designated as the 'author' for the purposes of copyright ownership, irrespective of whether this is the work's creator or the employer or legal entity pursuant to § 7 and § 8 DCA.[74] The person who expressed his *persona* in a work of authorship should however not be denied the right to protect his honour or reputation for the mere reason that he is not considered to be the 'author' under the terms of the copyright statute.

5.6 The right of attribution

5.6.1 STATUTORY PROVISIONS

The other moral right guaranteed by Article 6bis of the Berne Convention is the author's independent right to claim authorship of the work, even after he has transferred the exploitation rights to the work. This right, also designated as the right of attribution, is elaborated in the German Copyright Act by the provision that the author has the right to claim authorship as well as the right to decide whether the work will include an authorship credit and how this credit should be formulated (§ 13 GCA). Stipulations on authorship credits in agreements with producers are permitted (§ 39(1) GCA).

The Dutch Copyright Act grants authors a waivable right to object to the publication of their works without the inclusion of their name or any other reference as author, unless this objection were to be unreasonable (§ 25(1)(a) DCA).[75] The author furthermore has the right to oppose the publication of his work under another person's name (§ 25(1)(b) DCA). The author of a film work has the right to claim an authorship credit specifying his contribution on the usual place in the film work as well as the right to object to the use of his name, unless this objection were to be unreasonable (§ 45e DCA).

Under the U.S. Copyright Act, the author of a work of visual art has the right to claim authorship (§ 106A(a)(1)(A) USCA), the right to prevent the use of his name as the author of a work he did not create (§ 106A(a)(1)(b) USCA), and the right to prevent the use of his name as author of the work in the event of a

---

73. This autonomous interpretation of 'author' for the purposes of the right of integrity formulated in Article 6bis of the Berne Convention may also be applied for determining whether a foreign creator is entitled to protection of its integrity, even if he is not considered 'author' under the applicable law. *See supra* 3.4.

74. *See supra* 5.1 notes 3-5. *Cf. also* Schuijt, *Schrap artikel 7*, at 26: there is no support in legal history for the suggestion that the word 'author' in § 25 DCA has a different meaning than 'author' in §§ 7, 8 DCA. *But see* Gerbrandy (1988), at 290, arguing that the 'author' referred to in § 25 DCA is the person who performed the creative labour to which the work owes its existence.

75. 1989 Amendment. § 25(3) DCA (waivability).

distortion, mutilation or other modification which could be prejudicial to his honour or reputation (§ 106A(a)(2) USCA). These rights are inalienable, but the author may waive them in a written instrument specifying the work and the uses to which the waiver applies (§ 106A(e) USCA). Authors of other categories of works must stipulate authorship credit in their agreements with producers.[76] False attribution of authorship or a credit for the authorship of mutilated versions of the work may be actionable under the system of contract law, unfair competition or as an invasion of privacy.[77]

5.6.2 SCOPE OF PROTECTION

In assessing a claim for authorship credit, courts examine the parties' respective interests, the public's interest in not being inundated with unnecessary information or being misled on the origin of the work, commercial practice and, if the claim is directed against the producer, the agreement between the creator and producer.[78] In general, claims for authorship credit are more likely to be upheld in the case of works made at the creator's own initiative and expense rather than in the case of (contributions to) works which are primarily associated with the person or entity for whom and at whose initiative and expense they were made, such as government documents, advertisements, press releases, package designs or trivial works made within the scope of employment.[79]

5.6.3 THE RIGHT OF ATTRIBUTION AND THE STATUTORY ATTRIBUTION OF AUTHORSHIP TO PRODUCERS

If a claim for authorship credit is upheld, remedies such as damages, rectifications, inserts, etc. will not seriously inhibit the work's continued exploitation.[80] The right to claim authorship therefore does not necessarily pose insurmountable problems for the interests of exploitation.[81] This raises the question of whether

---

76. *But see* Community for Creative Non-Violence v. Reid, 846 F.2d 1485, 1498 *aff'd on other grounds* 109 S.Ct. 2166 (1989): CCNV could be obliged to credit Reid as creator of the sculpture without regard to the ownership of the sculpture's copyright.

77. *See e.g.* Smith v. Montoro, 648 F.2d 602 (9th Cir. 1981): a film distributor had substituted the plaintiff's name with the name of another actor, despite the fact that in his agreement with the film producer the plaintiff had stipulated star billing in the screen credits and in advertising. The distributor's actions were considered in breach of § 43a of the Lanham Act as 'express reverse passing off'.

78. *See* Van Lingen, at 96; Rehbinder, *Das Namennennungsrecht*, at 225; Schricker/Dietz, at 256, with the exception of trade practices which merely result from the unequal position of creators and producers; Ulmer, at 214.

79. *See supra* 4.4 (the adoption of the production, organizational and associative risks by the commissioning party or employer). *See also* Judgment of July 3, 1967, OLG Munich, Germany, 71 GRUR 146 (1969) ('credit'): an employer may prevent authorship credit on graphic designs made by an employee if the credit threatens to affect the advertising nature of the work. *See also* Rehbinder, *Das Namennennungsrecht*, at 225-227; Schricker/Rojahn, at. 589.

80. *See* Spoor/Verkade, at 327.

81. *See also* Ginsburg, *Moral Rights*, at 130.

it is possible to guarantee creators a right to claim authorship while allocating the ownership of exploitation rights to the producer. Vesting initial ownership of exploitation rights in the producer does not necessarily require the latter to be designated as the 'author': 'first owner' will do.[82] Nor does vesting the right to claim authorship in the creator require the latter to be considered the 'author', as 'creator', 'designer', 'director', etc. will do.[83] Copyright law may furthermore exclude 'authors' who did not create the work from the statutory right of attribution.[84] This implies that the copyright legislator has several options for making an explicit distinction between initial ownership of exploitation rights and initial ownership of the right to claim authorship.

The Dutch legislator has not made use of any of these options: employers and legal entities are considered to be authors under § 7 and § 8 DCA (in Dutch: 'maker'), while the author may invoke the right to claim authorship (in Dutch: 'maker') (§ 25(1)(a) DCA). It could be argued that § 8 DCA is indeed designed to designate the legal entity as the author towards the outside world.[85] This is not necessarily the case for § 7 DCA, because the presumption that the employer is considered to be author is not invalidated if the employee's name is identified on the work.[86] It is therefore possible for the employer to credit the employee without forfeiting its legal status of 'author' under § 7 DCA.[87] One might use this fact to argue that the right to claim authorship does not necessarily vest in the employer who is designated 'author' under § 7 DCA,[88] but there is however no conclusive evidence to this effect in legislative history.[89]

The fact that the statutory authors of § 7 and § 8 DCA are entitled to claim authorship under § 25(1)(a) DCA has been described as absurd in view of the

---

82. *See e.g.* § 11(2) BCA: 'Where a literary, dramatic, musical or artistic work is made by an employee in the course of his employment, his employer is the first owner of any copyright in the work subject to any agreement to the contrary.' Section 77(1) BCA grants authors of literary, dramatic, musical and artistic works a right of attribution, even if they made their works in the course of their employment. The author/employee cannot however enforce his right of attribution against his employer (§ 79(3)(a) BCA).

83. *See e.g.* § 77(1) BCA, granting film directors the right to be identified as director of the film. This right cannot be enforced, however, against the statutory author of a film, *i.e.* the person who assumed responsibility for the arrangements necessary for making the film (§ 79(3)(b) BCA).

84. *See* § 101 USCA (1991 Amendment), excluding 'works made for hire' from the definition of 'works of visual art', thereby excluding authors of works made for hire from the right of attribution accorded to authors of works of visual arts under § 106A(a)(1) USCA.

85. *See* Maeijer, at 352. *See also supra* 4.4.

86. Statement by the Dutch Minister of Justice, Parl.Gesch. 7.8 (1912). *See also* Judgment of October 14, 1987, Ger. 's-Gravenhage, Netherlands, NJ 1989, 220 (Rooijakkers v. Rijksuniversiteit Leiden).

87. *See* Judgment of August 20, 1987, Pres.Rb. Amsterdam, Netherlands, 12 Informatierecht/AMI 18 (1988) note Cohen Jehoram (Zeinstra v. van den Hoek).

88. *See* Ginsburg, *Copyright in the 101st Congress*, at 484: the American work-for-hire doctrine is not a labelling law, despite the fact that the employer is statutorily deemed to be 'author'; the introduction of an employee's right to claim authorship therefore does not necessarily change the employer's status as owner of the exploitation rights under the work-for-hire doctrine.

89. *But see* statement by the Dutch Minister of Justice, November 21, 1991, reprinted in: *Werkgeversauteursrecht*, at 6, in which the Minister of Justice subscribes to the arguments advanced by the 1912 legislature in favour of the introduction of § 7 DCA, but also states that the EC Software Directive, which allocates exploitation rights to employers and moral rights to employees, is more in keeping with the classical approach to author's rights.

personal bond between the creator and his work.[90] The chance that the work will refer to someone other than the creator as its author is not entirely unrealistic, however. Creators may prefer to publish a work as an anonymous or pseudonymous work or allow others to publish a work under their name in exchange for a consideration (ghostwriting). This indicates that the right to claim authorship is also an exclusive right to decide whether to include an authorship credit on a particular work and, if so, to decide which person should be credited on the work.[91] This is most clearly reflected in the German provision that an author has a right to decide whether the work includes an authorship credit and how this credit should be formulated (§ 13 GCA). The interest in exercising this right arguably shifts from the creator to the producer in those situations in which the major production, organizational and associative risks are allocated to the producer.[92] Especially when it is impossible to specify for which creative element of the work each one of a number of contributors is responsible, it may be more realistic to allow the producer to claim authorship or to exploit the work without an authorship credit.[93]

The exclusive right to decide who must be identified as author on the work must be distinguished from the right to use the creator's name.[94] Creators may have a considerable interest in having their names mentioned in connection with their works. Authorship credit may give an unknown creator recognition and the prospect of future work, while a famous creator may be able to capitalize on the value of his name when negotiating a fee for the use of his work. In this sense, ownership of an exclusive right to decide who should be identified on the work as author gives creators a direct legal basis for realizing these interests.[95] An

---

90. Quaedvlieg, *Het belang*, at 83. *See also* Cohen Jehoram, 12 Informatierecht/AMI 18 (1988); Van Lingen, *Morele rechten*, at 195. All three commentators criticize but acknowledge that, under the present law, the authorship status of employers and legal entities under § 7 and § 8 DCA implies that they are entitled to invoke moral rights. *But see* Gerbrandy (1988), at 290, and Kuypers, at 11, stating that the statutory authors of § 7 and § 8 DCA are not entitled to invoke the moral rights of § 25 DCA.

91. *See also* Larese, at 91.

92. *See supra* 4.1-4.4.

93. *See* Ginsburg, *Moral Rights*, at 127: '[T]oday, so many works are created by a multiplicity of authors, with tens or scores or even hundreds of contributors, revisers and re-revisers of individual components, that any one contributor's or reviser's identity as an author may become very attenuated. In these cases, it may make more sense to ascribe creative responsibility to a single co-ordinating entity, often a corporation.' *See also* Quaedvlieg, *Het belang*, at 84, with respect to works made by a team of employees according to the product or business philosophy developed by the employer; Verkade, *Het beste artikel 7*, at 18, with respect to the more or less anonymous contributions made by employees in a tightly organized horizontal or vertical collaboration.

94. *See* Larese, at 91.

95. Dutch copyright law has never considered financial motivations for claiming authorship credit to be improper. Compare the Memorandum to § 25(1)(a) DCA (1989), referring to the arguments advanced by a Dutch photographers' organization in favour of introducing a right to authorship credit: it facilitates the enforcement of copyright and the collection of royalties, it prevents infringement and it makes the author better-known amongst the public, including future commissioning parties. Parl.Gesch. 25.22 (1989). The conclusion that the reason for invoking § 25(1)(d) DCA is irrelevant, supports my view that this provision regulates an exclusive right to the work, rather than a personal claim to protection of a non-economic interest. *Cf. also* Ricketson, at 465: the formulation of the right to claim authorship in Article 6bis BC does not necessarily imply that this right is inalienable.

authorization by the creator or a legal duty to identify the creator's name can however never extend to a work the creator did not make or to a mutilated version of his work to which he never agreed and which could prejudice his honour or reputation. The creator's interest in not using his name in these situations may be protected under contract law or theories of misrepresentation, defamation, passing off, fraud, invasion of privacy or, as in Germany, under the general right of personality.[96] A legislator may decide to protect this interest under the copyright statute, as does the U.S. Copyright Act with respect to authors of works of visual art,[97] but the nature of the protection is however not the same as the exclusive rights to the work.

5.7 Conclusions

Although the economic protection of creators is rooted in a sense of justice and recognized under national constitutions and international conventions, the attribution of exploitation rights to creators is not an imperative, automatic result of their claims to economic protection, but the most obvious instrument for realizing this protection. Attributing exploitation rights to someone other than the creator is therefore not impossible *per se*, but may be considered undesirable if the economic and moral protection of creators is considered as the primary purpose of copyright protection.

In those situations in which first ownership of exploitation rights is only minimally effective for the creator for achieving participation and ensuring continued control over the use of the work as a result of the fact that he has shifted the major production, organizational and associative risks involved in the creation and publication of the work to the producer, the copyright legislator may take interests other than the creator's into consideration in allocating ownership of exploitation rights, such as the public's interest in a broad dissemination of works, the interest of security in copyright commerce and the economic interests of producers. In these situations, statutory provisions on copyright contracts may well be a more effective means for creators to secure adequate participation than ownership of exploitation rights.

Departures from the creator doctrine are often rejected on the basis of the argument that authorship and copyright ownership can only vest in the human being in whose mind the work originated and that attributing copyright ownership to anyone else would negate the continuing bond between the originator and his work and the moral interests which flow from it. In this Chapter, I have examined this argument on the basis of a discussion of the nature and scope of the

---

96. *See supra* 5.3. Compare § 326bis of the Dutch Criminal Code, qualifying as a criminal act the publication of a work under a false name with the object of passing the work off as a work made by the person whose name was on the work. The violation of this provision may constitute a 'tort' under Dutch law vis-à-vis the person whose name is on the work. *See* Spoor/Verkade, at 325, arguing that this protection is regulated outside the Copyright Act for evident reasons.

97. § 106A(a)(1)(b) USCA.

moral rights of first publication, attribution and integrity. We have seen that protection against undesired publication or mutilations of a work may be based on first ownership of the exclusive rights of distribution, communication to the public and adaptation. We have however also seen that the creator cannot always retain these rights if he contracts with a producer before commencing the creative process. In that case, the creator must rely on the moral rights of integrity or on the general principles of contract law or tort law.

With respect to an author's right to object to any mutilation of his work or any other derogatory action in relation to his work which would be prejudicial to his honour or reputation (right of integrity), I have argued that this right is a recognition of every person's interest in protection of his personal integrity in the specific situation in which he has expressed his *persona* in a work of authorship. As such, this protection is not dependent on the allocation of ownership or exploitation rights to the work. It is therefore not the person who is designated 'author' for the purposes of ownership of exploitation rights who is determinative, but whether the work reflects the *persona* of the person invoking the integrity right. The nature of the protection furthermore implies that it may be invoked by a legal entity if the works expresses that entity's identity rather than the *persona* of the contributors to the work.

With respect to the moral right of attribution, I have argued that although this right may be considered to be an exclusive right to the work, it is possible to distinguish between ownership of the right of attribution and ownership of the other exclusive rights to the work. However, by designating the employer and legal entity as 'authors' (§§ 7, 8 DCA) instead of, for example, the 'first owner of the exclusive rights of reproduction and communication to the public', the Dutch legislator has apparently chosen to allocate not only the exclusive rights of reproduction and communication to the public but also to allocate the right of attribution to the employer and legal entity.

It follows from the above that the nature of the exclusive rights of exploitation and the moral rights of integrity and attribution do not necessarily imply that each of these rights should vest in the creator of the work *per se*. In those situations in which the creator has transferred the major financial, organizational and associative risks involved in the creation and publication of the work to the producer, attribution of initial ownership of the exploitation rights may therefore be taken into consideration in allocating rights to producers.

Chapter 6

The practical implications of the various methods for allocating rights to producers: statutory presumption of transfer, attribution of authorship and neighbouring rights

6.1 Introduction

After having discussed the theoretical ramifications of attributing authorship and copyright ownership to producers, I will now examine the practical implications of the various methods by which rights are allocated to producers in the United States, Germany and the Netherlands. In the first paragraph (6.2), I will discuss statutory and judicial presumptions of transfer in Dutch and German copyright law and attempt to establish whether these presumptions are sufficiently clear in terms of the moment at which the transfer is executed as well as the scope, territory, term, exclusivity and transferability of the rights transferred. In the second paragraph (6.3), I will examine the various methods used in the American and Dutch Copyright Acts for vesting authorship and copyright ownership in producers and will discuss the consequences for the term of the protection and for the creators' scope for reserving rights to their works.

Since neighbouring rights for producers are being increasingly promoted as an alternative for or as a complement to statutory allocation of copyright ownership to producers, I will also devote a paragraph to discussing these neighbouring rights and their impact on the relationship between creators and producers and on the exploitation of creative works in general (6.4).

6.2 The presumption of transfer

6.2.1 INTRODUCTION

According to the creator doctrine, producers can only acquire rights to works of authorship from the actual creator(s). The least radical way for a copyright legislator to allocate rights to a producer is therefore to presume that he has been granted certain rights by the creator(s). Examples are the provision under Dutch law that the authors of a film work are presumed to have assigned certain exploitation rights to the producer (§ 45d DCA),[1] and the German provision that in case of doubt, the authors of a film work are considered to have granted the

---

1. *See also supra* 2.15; 3.2.2; 4.3.

producer the exclusive right to exploit the work in every way known (§ 89(1) GCA).[2] If courts consistently treat a particular kind of relationship between creators and producers so as to give rise to an implied grant of rights to the producer, the existence of such a relationship may also have the effect of a presumption of title for the producer, as is the case in German law with respect to works made in the course of employment.[3]

Under American and Dutch copyright law, where producers can only acquire exclusive, transferable and independently enforceable rights to works of authorship by means of a written transfer or statutory attribution, judicial presumptions are generally restricted to the presumption that, in the absence of an express transfer, a commissioning party has acquired a non-exclusive right to use the work in the manner for which he commissioned the creation of the work.[4] The U.S. Copyright Act codifies this minimum presumption with respect to collective works by providing that, in the absence of an express transfer, the owner of the copyright to a collective work only acquires a privilege to reproduce and distribute the contribution as part of the collective work, any revision of that collective work or as part of any later collective work in the same series (§ 201(c) USCA).[5]

Statutory or judge-made presumptions generally serve as a minimum safety net in the event that the producer should fail to stipulate a written agreement. Presumptions may also serve as an alternative to a written grant and, as such, serve as an instrument for improving efficiency. A presumption will however only be seen as an adequate alternative to a written grant if it is clear to the producer what the ownership situation will be if he does not stipulate an express grant, i.e. if it is clear to the producer:

1. in which situation the presumption is applicable and to whom the rights are presumed to have been granted;
2. at which point the rights are presumed to have been granted and how the presumption can be rebutted;
3. what the scope of the presumed grant will be in terms of rights, territory, term, exclusivity and transferability.

How do the Dutch and German presumptions of transfer in the case of film works and the German presumption in the case of employment works score on

---

2. *See also supra* 2.13; 3.2.2; 4.3.
3. *See supra* 2.13 note 192 and accompanying text.
4. *See e.g.* Effects Associates v. Cohen, 908 F.2d 555 (9th Cir. 1990), *cert. denied* 111 S.Ct. 1003 (1991): the defendant hired plaintiffs to provide special effects footage for a film. In the absence of a written agreement, the defendant has only obtained a non-exclusive license to incorporate the footage in the film. *See also* Judgment of January 4, 1989, Ktg. Amsterdam, Netherlands, 14 Informatierecht/AMI 29 (1990) note Spoor (De Jong v. Courant-Nieuws van de Dag): in the absence of an express assignment, a newspaper publisher needed an additional authorization to reprint photographs made on commission by a freelance photographer in the course of a former relationship with the newspaper publisher.
5. *See e.g.* Oddo v. Ries, 743 F.2d 630 (9th Cir. 1984).

these points? The applicability of a presumption (factor 1) may be difficult to assess if the statute does not clearly define the type of works for which the presumption is applicable,[6] or if it is unclear who the grantee is presumed to be in the case of more or less complex contractor-subcontractor relations (e.g. A hires B and C, B hires D, and C and D create the work). This problem of definition, which is inherent to the attribution of rights in general (who is the author?), shall be discussed in more detail in Chapter 7.

6.2.2 THE MOMENT OF THE GRANT AND THE MANNER IN WHICH THE PRESUMPTION CAN BE REBUTTED

The moment at which the right is granted and the manner in which the presumption can be rebutted determine whether a creator can validly grant rights to third parties, e.g. to a collecting society. Since the 1985 amendment, the Dutch Copyright Act provides that the authors of a film work, with the exception of the authors of the film music, are presumed to have assigned certain exploitation rights to the producer at the point at which the film work is completed, unless the authors and producer agree otherwise in a written instrument (§ 45d DCA). A film work is 'completed' at the point at which the film is ready for public screening, which is determined by the producer, unless the parties have agreed otherwise in writing (§ 45c DCA).

Since it is possible to assign rights to specified, future works under the new Netherlands Civil Code,[7] the question arises how the statutorily-presumed assignment to the producer relates to an assignment to a third party prior to the completion of the work. Does the *nemo plus* principle imply that the assignment to the third party has priority, or is the *nemo plus* principle set aside by the provision that the assignment to the producer takes place 'unless the authors and the producer agree otherwise in a written instrument' (§ 45d DCA)?[8] It is

---

6. *See e.g.* Judgment of February 6, 1985, BGH, Germany, 87 GRUR 529 (1985) ('Happening'): the presumption that an authorization by the author of an existing work to use his work for making a film includes certain exclusive rights (§ 88 GCA), is inapplicable since the video producer had not made the video for commercial distribution. *See also* Judgment of December 15, 1989, Pres.Rb. Amsterdam, Netherlands, 14 Informatierecht/AMI 95 (1990) note Schuijt (Lieshout v. VPRO): the presumption that the authors of a film have waived the right to object to the producer making changes to the work (§ 45f DCA) does not apply to film works made by one person. This decision seems to be wrong, as § 45f DCA is applicable to film works irrespective of the number of contributors involved.

7. *See supra* 3.3.4.

8. Since the assignment of rights to future works was not considered possible under the old Netherlands Civil Code, collecting societies contractually obliged authors to assign their rights to them upon completion of the work. Compare in this respect the Judgment of January 11, 1990, Ger. Amsterdam, Netherlands, 14 Informatierecht/AMI 164 (1990) note Grosheide (Vevam v. NOS I): a contract between a broadcasting organization and freelance contributors obliging the latter to ignore their contractual obligation in respect of a collecting society to assign cable distribution rights at the point at which these arose, was not 'tortious' under Dutch law vis-à-vis the collecting society because the result was in keeping with § 45d DCA's presumption of assignment. This ruling was confirmed by the District Court of Amsterdam in ordinary proceedings on the same case. Judgment of March 25, 1992, Rb. Amsterdam, 17 Informatierecht/AMI 34 (1993) (Vevam v. NOS II), discussed *supra* 3.3.4 note 48. Grosheide, 14 Informatierecht/ AMI 166 (1990), argues that § 45d DCA does not imply that producers are free to simply ignore

unclear in this respect how the provision that the presumption does not apply to film music (§ 45d DCA) - introduced in 1985 to enable the authors of film music to exploit their rights directly through a collecting society[9] - must be construed in view of the possibility of assigning rights to future works.

Section 89 GCA, the German counterpart of § 45d DCA, does not specify at which moment the presumed grant to the film producer takes place. Instead, § 89(2) provides that, if an author has granted rights to a future film work to a third party, he remains entitled to grant those same rights to the film producer. This rule, which serves to protect producers against the risk of prior commitments and allows authors to commit themselves to film productions without having to obtain their collecting society's prior permission,[10] does not apply to the authors of novels, screenplays and film music, which are subject to the more limited presumption of § 88 GCA.[11]

In 1974, the Bundesgerichtshof held in respect of works made by an employee within the scope of an employment relationship, that an employee is presumed to grant certain rights to the employer upon handing over the original copy of the work.[12] The majority of the doctrine seems to agree, however, that the implied grant to the employer may also take place prior to the completion of the work and, in particular, at the moment the parties enter into the employment relationship.[13] The German Copyright Act, in the meantime, merely provides that employment works are subject to the general rules on authors' contracts, unless the import and essence of the employment relationship determine otherwise (§ 43 GCA).[14]

All the presumptions in the German Copyright Act (§§ 37, 38, 88, 89)[15] are applicable 'in case of doubt'. According to the Bundesgerichtshof, the phrase 'in case of doubt' in section 88 GCA means that the presumption is only applicable if the purpose of the agreement is in keeping with the rationale underlying the statutory presumption.[16] The purpose of the individual agreement therefore determines whether the scope of the grant must be determined according to the statutory presumption or according to the general purpose transfer rule of § 31(5)

---

author's prior contractual commitments.

9. Although co-authors can only assign rights to the co-authored work collectively (*see supra* 3.3.2), it would seem to be generally accepted that the co-author of a film may assign rights to a collecting society individually, unless these rights have already been assigned to the producer.

10. Memorandum to § 89 GCA, 45 UFITA 319 (1966).

11. *See supra* 3.3.2; 4.3.

12. Judgment of February 22, 1974, BGH, Germany, 76 GRUR 480 (1974) ('Hummelrechte').

13. Schricker/Rojahn, at 575; Ulmer, at 404. *See also* Vinck, at 86, with respect to works made by multiple contributors. Schricker/Rojahn, at 576: § 40 GCA (discussed *supra* 2.13; 3.3.4) is not applicable to employees who have been specifically hired to create works of authorship.

14. *See supra* 2.13 note 193 and accompanying text.

15. *See also supra* 2.13; 4.3.

16. Judgment of February 6, 1985, BGH, Germany, 87 GRUR 529 (1985) ('Happening'), discussed *supra* note 6.

GCA.[17] A statutory presumption which applies 'unless the author and the producer agree otherwise in a written instrument' (§ 45d DCA) provides more security in this respect.[18] But even this clause may leave uncertainty about the ownership of rights which are covered by the statutory presumption, but which have not been referred to specifically in the agreement as signed by the parties. In other words: does the existence of a written agreement on ownership invalidate the presumption as a whole, or only in respect of those rights which the author has expressly reserved? The latter view, which seems to be visible in case law on § 45d DCA,[19] provides most security for the producer, but places a heavy burden on the creator who wishes to retain rights.

6.2.3 THE SCOPE AND EXCLUSIVITY OF THE RIGHTS TRANSFERRED

The scope and exclusivity of the rights which are subject to the presumptions of § 45d DCA and § 89 GCA are relatively clear, although there is some uncertainty in respect of the ownership of statutory remuneration rights and the extent to which a film producer is entitled to make post-production changes to the work.

According to § 45d DCA, a film producer is presumed to have acquired ownership of the exclusive right of communication to the public, the exclusive

---

17. *See e.g.* Judgment of July 8, 1993, BGH, Germany, 96 GRUR 41 (1994) note Poll ('Videozweit-auswertung II'): the presumption of § 88 GCA merely concerns the rights which the author of the pre-existing work is presumed to have granted upon his authorization to use his work for the making of a film. The question whether video exploitation rights have been granted must be determined according to § 31(5). For interpretation according to § 31(5) GCA instead of § 37(1) GCA, see Judgment of November 28, 1985, BGH, Germany, 88 GRUR 458 (1986): the authorization by a former director to use his stage sets used in performances of the Oberammergau Passion Play in the 1930-1970 period must be considered to imply an authorization to adapt the sets for the next performance in 1980. For interpretation according to § 31(5) GCA instead of § 38 GCA: Judgment of May 9, 1984, OLG, Karlsruhe, Germany, 86 GRUR 522 (1984) ('Castles in Schleswig Holstein'). *See also* Schricker, at 509, favouring § 31(5) GCA over §§ 37 and 38 GCA. Schricker/Katzenberger, at 1046: § 31(5) GCA must have priority over § 88 GCA, but not over § 89 GCA. Nordemann/Hertin, at 205: §§ 37 and 38 GCA must have priority over § 31(5) GCA.
18. Note that § 45d DCA specifically requires that the agreement be made between author and producer. *See* Judgment of December 24, 1993, Pres.Rb. Amsterdam, Netherlands, KG 1994, 42 (1994) ('Hoffman's Honger'). In this case, a film producer commissioned a casting company to hire actors. In their agreement with the casting company, the actors licensed a one-time performance of the film upon payment, which license would become effective upon payment by the producer. According to the court, this agreement could not rebut the presumption of § 45d DCA (applicable to film actors pursuant to § 4 WNR), because this presumption can only be rebutted in a written agreement between the actors and the producer. *See also infra* 7.6 note 112.
19. Judgment of March 25, 1992, Rb. Amsterdam, Netherlands, 17 Informatierecht/AMI 34 (1993) (Vevam v. NOS II): the fact that the business terms used by the Dutch broadcasting corporation NOS for contracts with freelance contributors refer to broadcasts via a transmitter or wire, but not cable, does not reflect the intention to exclude cable distribution rights from the assignment presumed by § 45d DCA. The fact that the terms were amended in 1987 so as to include 'cable', does not mean that the parties 'agreed otherwise' in the sense of § 45d DCA before the amendment. Judgment of January 29, 1993, Arbitration Committee for the Dutch Film and Movie Theatre Industry, 17 Informatierecht/AMI 115 (1993) note Kabel (Scheffer v. Pauwels): the model agreement applicable to the parties' relationship, although drafted before the adoption of § 45d DCA, does not reflect the parties' intention to depart from § 45d DCA, because the director has a duty under this agreement to assign the rights to his contribution to the producer upon completion of the film.

right of reproduction in the sense of § 14 DCA, and the right to subtitle the film and to dub its dialogue. The assignment includes modes of exploitation which are unforeseeable at the moment the film work is ready for public screening (§ 45d jo 45c DCA). Reproduction in the sense of § 14 DCA refers to reproduction on an audibly or visually perceptible device. Although copying on videocassettes is covered by this qualification, the Minister of Justice has stated that the statutory remuneration right for private copying (§ 16c DCA) does not fall within the presumption of § 45d DCA because allocation of this statutory remuneration right to the producer is not considered necessary in order to facilitate the circulation of film works.[20]

By limiting the reproduction right to reproduction in the sense of § 14 DCA, § 45d DCA implicitly excludes the right to reproduce a modified version of the work (§ 13 DCA) from the presumption. The author is however presumed to have waived the right to object to alterations in the sense of § 25c DCA (§ 45f DCA).[21] It is unclear in this respect to which extent the producer is entitled to adapt the film work for a particular medium or audience other than by dubbing or subtitling, e.g. by including logos or commercial breaks.[22]

The Memorandum to the Dutch bill implementing the EC Rental Directive states that, as a form of communication to the public, rental is included in the presumption of assignment to the film producer.[23] While the rental right is thus allocated to the producer, the film authors are guaranteed an unwaivable right to claim remuneration in the case of rental.[24]

Section 89(1) GCA provides that, in case of doubt, the author grants the film producer the exclusive right to use the film work and adaptations of the film work in every way known. Contrary to § 45d DCA, the presumption of § 89 GCA therefore includes the right to adapt the film work, but not the right to make use of unknown modes of exploitation.[25] This implies that under German

---

20. EK 1992-1993, 21244, no. 15b. The Bill introducing neighbouring rights for film producers also includes a remuneration right for private copying. *See also infra* 6.4 notes 61-62 and accompanying text.

21. *See also supra* 5.5.1.

22. Gerbrandy (1988), at 398, suggests that § 45f DCA implies that the adaptations necessary to screen a film according to local practice, such as cuts, intervals etc., may be admissible. Linnemann, at 116: since it is clear from §§ 45a-g DCA that the producer is entitled to exploit the film on television - barring extreme situations - the author cannot object to commercial breaks or the insertion of a logo if he had not made any provisions in advance with respect to the manner in which the film may be shown on television. Seignette, *Inkleuring*, at 1626: the colorization of black-and-white films is reproduction in modified form in the sense of § 13 DCA and, as such, does not fall within the presumption of § 45d DCA.

23. TK 1992-1993, 23247, no. 3, at 23. Article 2(6) of the Rental Directive recognizes the scope for a statutory presumption of transfer of the rental right to the film producer. *See also supra* 3.4.

24. Article II E of the bill on the implementation of the EC directive on rental and lending, TK 1992-1993, 23247, nos. 2, at 4.

25. A certain use is considered 'known' if it concerns a technically and economically independent mode of exploitation. Judgment of June 5, 1985, BGH, Germany, 88 GRUR 62 (1986) (Gema presumption I). *See also* Judgment of October, 11, 1990, BGH, Germany, 93 GRUR 133 (1991) ('Videozweitauswertung I'): in 1968 video exploitation was not known as a mode of exploitation with a commercial importance similar to theatrical exhibition. The compensation which the plaintiff negotiated for his contribution to the film would have been higher if he had been aware of the future economic importance of video exploitation.

law, a producer is entitled to adapt the film work for a particular medium or audience, unless the adaptation constitutes an unknown use or a gross mutilation in the sense of § 93 GCA.[26]

Whether the presumption of § 89 GCA includes the right to claim remuneration for private copying on video cassettes (§ 54(1) GCA), is disputed.[27] It is furthermore disputed whether the explicit reference in § 89(1) GCA to all known modes of exploitation ('alle bekannten Nutzungsarten') actually refers to *all* modes of exploitation, irrespective of the type of contribution made by the author and irrespective of the mode of exploitation for which the film work was made (motion picture, television show, etc.).[28]

The Bundesgerichtshof has held in respect of works made by an employee within the scope of employment that the employer is presumed to have acquired the right to use the work in conformity with the purpose of the agreement.[29] In doctrine, this presumption is generally construed as a modified application of the purpose transfer rule (§ 31(5) GCA) in the sense that in case of doubt, the scope and exclusivity of the grant are determined according to the purpose of the employer's business or, in the case of government employees, according to the objectives of the government agency.[30] While apparently in line with the principle that the creator should retain as many rights as possible,[31] the reference to the purpose of the employer's business does not provide much security on the scope and exclusivity of the implied grant.[32] Uncertainty may, in particular, arise about adaptation rights and rights to additional uses which are of commercial interest to the employer, but which are not part of the core of his business activities. The only guideline the Bundesgerichtshof has issued in this respect is that employment relationships are not, in general, exempted from the provision that grants of rights to unknown uses are void (§ 31(4) GCA).[33]

This type of presumption, which relates the scope and exclusivity of a grant to the circumstances of the individual case or to general criteria such as trade

---

26. *See* Dreier/von Lewinsky, at 645.

27. Affirmative: Schack, *Der Vergütungsanspruch*, at 270. Negatively: Nordemann/Hertin, at 367; President German Patent Office, 33 ZUM 507 (1989); Schricker/Katzenberger, at 1053.

28. *See* Schricker/Katzenberger, at 1049, interpreting the scope of § 89(1) GCA so as to refer only to the rights which are necessary for the usual modes in which film works are exploited, i.e. no video rights in the case of a television production and, in general, no rebroadcasting and cable distribution rights. *Cf. also* Ulmer, at 496: the presumption encompasses all known uses, but not with respect to the director.

29. *See* Judgment of February 22, 1974, BGH, Germany, 76 GRUR 480 (1974) ('Hummelrechte'); Judgment of March, 7, 1984, BAG, Germany, 86 GRUR 429 (1984) ('statistical programs').

30. Nordemann/Vinck, at 250; Rehbinder, *Recht am Arbeitsergebnis*, at 492, 494; Schricker/Rojahn, at 577; Ulmer, at 405. *See also* Judgment of November 29, 1974, KG Berlin, Germany, 78 GRUR 264 (1976) ('Gesicherte Spuren').

31. *See supra* 2.13 note 183 and accompanying text.

32. *See* Rehbinder, *Recht am Arbeitsergebnis*, at 492; Schricker/Rojahn, at 578; Ullmann, at 11; Verkade, *Het beste artikel 7*, at 16. Dietz, *The Relation Employer-Employee*, at 44, argues that the Copyright Act should be amended so that uses outside the employer's normal activities are not covered by the presumption; this would prevent courts using the present interpretation rules to achieve a similar result as would be the case if the employer were initial copyright owner.

33. Judgment of October 11, 1990, BGH, Germany, 93 GRUR 133 (1991) ('Videozweitauswertung I').

practice or the principles of reason and fairness allows courts to reach equitable decisions in individual cases. The downside of these flexible criteria, however, is that neither the producer nor the creator can fully assess their negotiating position when dealing with each other or with third parties.

6.3 Attribution of authorship to producers

Uncertainty about the moment, scope, transferability and exclusivity of the rights transferred may be avoided by initially vesting the copyright in the producer.[34] Uncertainties connected with authorship, such as the nationality and term of protection of the work[35] and the exercise of rights which are reserved for the 'author',[36] may be avoided by providing that the producer is considered the 'author'.

The least radical way for a legislature to attribute authorship to the producer is to allow the creator and producer to designate the 'author' in writing. This method is applied with respect to the nine categories of commissioned works listed in § 101(2) USCA.[37] If both the commissioning and the commissioned party *agree in a written instrument that the work is a 'work made for hire'*, the commissioning party is considered the 'author' and, unless agreed otherwise in a written instrument signed by the parties, owns all the rights comprised in the copyright (§§ 101(2); 201(b) USCA). The creator doctrine is therefore applicable unless there is a written work-for-hire agreement.[38]

Although the requirement of a work-for-hire agreement seems to ensure maximum predictability of copyright ownership, independent contractors are often asked to sign a work-for-hire agreement after the creative process has commenced and, consequently, when they have already spent too much time, effort and money to withdraw from the project.[39] A legislative proposal to amend § 101(2) USCA so as to require that the work-for-hire agreement be signed prior to the creation of the work, has not been adopted.[40] However, in the 1992 case of *Schiller & Schmidt, Inc. v. Nordisco Corporation*,[41] the Seventh Circuit explicitly required that the work-for-hire agreement be signed prior to the

---

34. The risk of conflicting transfers can also be avoided by providing that the copyright is assigned to the producer by operation of law (*cessio legis* or legal assignment). Although copyright ownership still vests in the creator of the work according to this method, the consequences are similar to the situation in which copyright ownership initially vests in the producer. If the legal assignment cannot be overruled in an agreement between the creator and producer, the consequences are even more drastic than if the producer is considered first owner, subject to an agreement to the contrary.
35. *See supra* 3.3.5.
36. *See supra* 3.3.6.
37. *See supra* 2.14; 4.3.
38. *See* Community v. Creative Non-Violence v. Reid, 109 S.Ct. 2166, 2180 (1989).
39. *See* Ginsburg, *Developments*, at 155; Hamilton, at 1310.
40. S. 1253, 101st Cong., 1st Sess. (1989).
41. 969 F.2d 410 (7th Cir. 1992).

creation of the work in order to serve its purpose of unequivocally identifying the copyright owner.

By making authorship dependent on the existence of a written work-for-hire agreement, § 101(2) USCA cannot serve as a safety net for commissioning parties who have failed to stipulate a written transfer.[42] This is in contrast to the Dutch rules on employment works (§ 7 DCA) and works published by legal entities without identification of a natural person as the author (§ 8 DCA). According to § 7 DCA, an employer is designated the 'author' of works made by an employee, *unless the parties have agreed otherwise*.[43] The circumstances may imply an agreement to the contrary, but this does not arise from the fact that the employee is identified on the work as its author.[44] Section 8 DCA provides that the legal entity under whose auspices a work is published which does not identify a natural person as author, is designated the author *unless it has been established that publication under these circumstances was unlawful*. Case law indicates that a creator who authorizes a legal entity to publish his work, can only become the 'author' by claiming authorship credit or by reserving the status of 'author' in another explicit manner.[45]

The most radical attribution rule is the American rule for employment works. According to § 201(b) USCA, an employer is considered the author of a work made for hire and, unless agreed otherwise in a written instrument, owns all the rights comprised in the copyright. While the parties are thus free to designate the employee as first owner of the copyright, they cannot change the employer's status of 'author'.[46] In the absence of any overriding security interest, this rule can probably be explained by American producers' somewhat irrational fear of moral rights claims outside the United States. To the extent that such fear is real, the French case of *Huston v. La Cinq*[47] has demonstrated that a moral rights claim cannot simply be refuted by arguing that the creator was not an 'author' under the law of the country of origin of the work. In this case, the widow and children of American film director John Huston brought an infringement action in France in order to prevent the telecast of a colorized version of 'The Asphalt

---

42. *See e.g.* Effects Associates v. Cohen, 908 F.2d 555 (9th Cir. 1990), *cert.denied* 111 S.Ct. 1003 (1991): in the absence of an express transfer or work-for-hire agreement, the film producer who commissioned the plaintiff to provide special effects for his film, has only acquired a non-exclusive license to use the special effects footage in the film.

43. *See infra* 7.4.2 for the additional requirement that the employee's labour must constitute specific works.

44. *See* Statement by the Dutch Minister of Justice, Parl.Gesch. 7.8 (1912). *See also* Judgment of August 20, 1987, Pres.Rb. Amsterdam, Netherlands, 12 Informatierecht/AMI 18 (1988) (Zeinstra v. van den Hoek); Judgment of October 14, 1987, Ger. 's-Gravenhage, Netherlands, NJ 1989, 220 (Rooijakkers v. Rijksuniversiteit Leiden). *See also supra* 5.6.3.

45. *See e.g.* Judgment of February 21, 1992, Pres.Rb. 's-Gravenhage, Netherlands, 60 BIE 393 (1992) ('brochures'): in view of the fact that there is no agreement about copyright, the defendant must be considered to be the author of brochures made by the plaintiff on the defendant's commission. The plaintiff has not disputed that the defendant published the work as coming from her, while the plaintiff's name was not mentioned in the brochures. *See also infra* 7.5.

46. *See supra* 2.14 notes 247-251 and accompanying text on the constitutionality of this rule.

47. Judgment of May 28, 1991, Cass. Civ. 1re, France, 149 RIDA 197 (1991). *See also supra* 3.4 note 111.

Jungle'. The defendant argued that U.S. law was applicable to the question of authorship and that, as a result, Huston was not the 'author' of the film because he had directed the film in the course of his employment at the studio. The Cour de Cassation dismissed this argument, stating that the integrity of a work may be protected in France regardless of the country of origin of the work (Article 2(1) Law No. 64-689 of 8 July 1964) and that the author, by virtue of the work's creation, is entitled to this protection under § 6 of the French Copyright Act. According to the court, both provisions are of 'imperative application'.[48]

If the producer is considered the 'author', there is no inherent logic in making the term of protection dependent on the life of the 'author'. Both the American and Dutch Copyright Acts therefore provide special rules for the term of protection if the producer should be considered the author. The protection of works made for hire under the U.S. Copyright Act expires 75 years after first publication or 100 years after creation, whichever term expires first (§ 302(c) USCA). The protection of works of which a public institution or legal entity has been designated as the author pursuant to § 7 or § 8 DCA, expires 50 years after the work's first, lawful publication (§ 38(2) DCA).[49] The term of protection in the specific situation in which an employer is a natural person, has not been regulated and therefore must probably follow the general rule, i.e. expiry 50 years after the author's (employer's) death.

It has been argued that if a copyright vests in a producer, he should not enjoy protection any longer than is necessary to recoup his investments and that if the work belongs to the traditional categories of literature, music, art and film, the remaining period of protection should benefit the creator through a reversion of rights.[50] The developments would seem to indicate in a different direction, however. We have already seen in Chapter 2 that, while authors are given an opportunity under American copyright law to reclaim their rights by terminating a transfer 35 years after its execution, such reversion of rights does not take place with respect to works of which the employer or commissioning party is considered to be the 'author' under the work-for-hire provisions.[51] With respect to copyright protection in the European Union, the 1993 Duration Directive has lifted the protection of all categories of original works to 70 years after the author's death. In the event a legal person is considered to be rightholder, the term of protection is 70 years from the first lawful publication, unless the natural persons who have created the work are identified on the work as such, in which

---

48. *Id. See also supra* 3.4 note 111.
49. Implementation of Article 1(3) of the Duration Directive requires the term of 50 years to be amended into 70 years before July 1, 1995. *See infra* note 52 and accompanying text.
50. *See* Dietz, *Entwickelt*, at 111; *The Relation Employer - Employee*, at 44. Dietz, *Transformation of authors rights*, at 61: 'If copyright in the film and television market is no longer realized other than in connection with film package deals, it may admittedly be possible to reduce considerably the necessary period of protection according to the extent of investment interest.' Aside from the author's right, Dietz proposes to introduce related rights for producers with a limited term of protection. In areas other than literature, music, visual arts and cinematography, this related right should replace the author's right completely. Dietz, *Entwickelt*, at 116.
51. H.R.Rep. No. 94-1476, 94th Cong., 2d Sess., 125 (1976). Picture Music, Inc. v. Bourne, Inc., 457 F.2d 1213, 1216 (2d Cir. 1972). *See also supra* 2.14 note 272 and accompanying text.

case the term of protection is calculated from the death of the last surviving author.[52] The term of protection of the related rights for film producers, producers of phonograms and broadcasting organizations has furthermore been harmonized to a period of 50 years from the first lawful publication of the film or phonogram or the first transmission of the broadcast.[53]

6.4 Neighbouring rights

So far, I have discussed how producers obtain title from the author. As we have seen in Chapter 3, however, producers can not always acquire the rights they would like to have, e.g. because the copyright is not completely alienable, or because the author has entrusted rights to a collecting society. Although there is a legislative tendency to accommodate producers in this respect, the methods discussed in the previous paragraphs are being increasingly rejected as undermining the scope for creators to retain rights and to entrust rights to a collecting society.[54] Instead, alternative instruments are applied which do not affect the allocation of copyright ownership directly, varying from tailor-made measures within copyright legislation to the introduction of new intellectual property rights which vest in the producer (neighbouring, related or *sui generis* rights).

In this study, I have already discussed several tailor-made measures, such as special rules for the work's nationality and term of protection,[55] limitations to the moral rights protection in certain cases,[56] and provisions conferring the right to sue on exclusive licensees.[57] In those cases in which copyright legislation does not confer the right to sue on exclusive licensees, or in which the producer is only a non-exclusive licensee (e.g. a phonogram producer with respect to the music recorded on his phonograms), additional protection against unauthorized uses of a producer's products has been sought under theories of unfair competition, with varying success.[58]

Producers' interests in additional protection go beyond the need to have effective instruments to redress piracy, however. The increasing number of rights which authors entrust to a collecting society limit the modes of exploitation to which the producer can acquire rights. Occasionally, the collecting society's distribution regulations guarantee producers a share of the income from collectively-administered uses. The government-endorsed regulations adhered to by the

---

52. Articles 1(1), 1(3), 1(4) Duration Directive.
53. Article 3 EC Duration Directive. If publication of the film or phonogram does not take place within 50 years from their fixation, the protection expires 50 years after the fixation is made.
54. *See* Dietz, *Transformation of authors rights*, 23-75; Dietz, *Entwickelt*, 111-119.
55. *See supra* 3.3.5; 6.3.
56. *See supra* 5.5.1; 5.6.1.
57. *See supra* 3.3.7.
58. *See e.g.* Judgment of April 2, 1993, HR, Netherlands, NJ 1993, 573 note Verkade (NVPI v. Snelleman): unauthorized reproductions of sound recordings and unauthorized recordings of live performances are, in principle, 'tortious' under Dutch law vis-à-vis the producer who had acquired the exclusive recording rights from the performing artists, as well as vis-à-vis his exclusive licensees.

Dutch collecting society Stichting Reprorecht, for example, provide that the fees collected for photocopying in libraries, educational institutions and government bodies are transferred to the work's publisher, with a duty to pass on 50% to the author.[59] The publisher is thus guaranteed a share of the fees, irrespective of whether the author has assigned the remuneration right to him.[60]

Aside from this *de facto* publisher's protection, there is a legislative tendency to secure producers a share of the income from collectively-administered uses by introducing special producers' rights (copyrights, neighbouring rights, related rights). By extending these producers' rights to collectively-administered uses, the producer may obtain income from these uses, even if the author has directly entrusted his rights to a collecting society. The Dutch bill implementing the Rental Directive, for example, proposes to introduce a neighbouring right in the first fixation of the film, including the right to remuneration in the case of private copying,[61] thus securing film producers a share of the income from levies on blank video tapes, even if the authors have assigned their remuneration rights (§ 16c DCA) to a collecting society.[62]

The advantages of neighbouring rights for producers seem clear: they provide a legal basis to sue for infringement as well as to negotiate a remuneration for the use of their products by others. Neighbouring rights are not equally beneficial to every category of producers, however. The actual benefits depend on the creator's contribution to the final marketable product and the concomitant need for the exclusivity of the work of authorship incorporated in it.[63] The smaller the producer's contribution as compared with the creator's contribution, the greater his need will be to acquire and maintain exclusive rights to the creator's contribution. Not only because the marketability of his product will be more dependent on the creator's contribution, but also because the reproduction of the work of authorship will only constitute an infringement of the producer's neighbouring rights if the producer's contribution has also been reproduced.

In this respect it is fair to say that neighbouring rights offer phonogram producers greater benefits than film producers and publishers.[64] A phonogram

---

59. *See* Article 5(3) Distribution Regulations of the Dutch Stichting Reprorecht, endorsed by the Minister of Justice in the Memorandum to § 7 of the Decree of June 20, 1974, S. 351, concerning copying of works protected by copyright law, as amended by Royal Decree of August 23, 1985, No. 103, S. 1985, 471. *See also* bill to amend provisions on reprography TK 1992-1993, 22600.

60. Whereas distribution of royalties irrespective of the individual contractual situation works out in favour of the producer in this example, there is a tendency, especially in Germany, to treat distribution of royalties without regard as to the individual contractual situation as an instrument for securing participation by the creators. *See* Dietz, *Transformation of authors rights*, at 55.

61. TK 1992-1993, 23247, no. 2, at 5, proposing to introduce a new section 7a in the Dutch Act on Neighbouring Rights.

62. *See also supra* 6.2.3 note 20 and accompanying text.

63. *See also supra* 4.3, discussing the creator's contribution in relation to the end product marketed by the producer.

64. In Dutch literature, the protection of phonogram producers under the Act on Neighbouring Rights has often been advanced as an argument in favour of - and as a blueprint for - neighbouring rights for film producers and publishers. *See* Asscher, *Viewpoint from the Netherlands*, at 307-308; Frequin/Grosheide, at 46; Grosheide, *Auteurswet*, at 125; Grosheide/Obertop, at 163. *But*

producer who has secured exclusivity in the performance of certain musical works through a recording agreement with the artist, is not necessarily commercially dependent on the exclusivity of the music he records. If the ownership of a copyright or neighbouring right to the performance and/or recording[65] enables him to redress piracy, he can successfully exploit the recording, despite the fact that he has acquired no more than a non-exclusive license to the music from a mechanical rights society.[66]

Strictly speaking, a film producer who has been granted a neighbouring right to the first fixation of a film[67] can exploit the film on an exclusive basis, even if he has only acquired a non-exclusive license to use the creative contributions to the film work. In practice, however, producers generally insist on exclusivity in the creative contributions to the film, both in respect of the use of these contributions as part of the film as well as for other uses (remakes, serials, merchandising, novelization of the film script, etc.).

Similarly, the fact that a neighbouring right would allow a publisher to exploit his publications on an exclusive basis does not mean that he can do without exclusive rights to the work published. Especially in those cases in which it is commercially worthwhile for competitors to publish the same work in a competing edition, the first publisher needs exclusivity to the work of authorship. This will in particular be the case if the work's commercial success is dependent on the contribution of one, particular creator (novel, memoirs, etc). But even if the success is largely dependent on the publisher's coordinating efforts in moulding a number of more or less creative contributions into a marketable product (data bases, encyclopeadias, educational works), he may still want exclusivity to the contributions to prevent competition and to exploit additional uses.

In all those cases in which publishers are commercially dependent on the exclusivity of the works they publish, they remain prone to the problems of security and efficiency which the acquisition of rights to works of authorship may entail (Chapter 3). A neighbouring right in the 'edition' can only make up for the fact that, under Dutch law, an exclusive licensee cannot sue for infringement if he has not stipulated the right to do so[68], and only in those cases in which the work is actually copied in that 'edition'. If the work is copied in a different edition, the publisher is better off with a statutory provision conferring the right to sue on exclusive licensees.[69]

Since neighbouring rights do not always eliminate the producer's need to acquire exclusive rights in the work(s) of authorship they exploit, the benefits of such

---

see Resius, at 68: the fact that phonogram producers can only acquire a non-exclusive license justifies a neighbouring right and distinguishes phonogram producers from publishers.

65. See § 102(a)(7) USCA: copyright in sound recording. § 2 WNR, § 74-77 GCA: neighbouring rights to performance. § 6 WNR; § 85 GCA: neighbouring rights to phonograms.

66. But even here, the ownership of copyrights or neighbouring rights in sound recordings (phonograms) has not prevented producers from increasingly seeking copyright ownership of the musical works they record.

67. See Article 2 Rental Directive.

68. See supra 3.3.7.

69. See also Soetenhorst, at 98-100.

rights for producers should not be over-estimated. For the same reason, the fact that the producer has a neighbouring right of his own does not necessarily mean that it will be easier for the creator to retain rights to his work.

It cannot be denied, however, that neighbouring rights have important repercussions on the exploitation of creative works. We have seen that neighbouring rights may serve as an instrument for ensuring producers income from modes of exploitation which the author has entrusted to a collecting society (rental, private copying) or which the author refuses to exploit on a commercial basis (public lending, readers). By introducing such neighbouring rights, it is easier for legislators to subject certain uses to collective administration,[70] to guarantee authors an unwaivable share in the income from these collectively-administered uses,[71] to make the author's rights to these uses inalienable,[72] or to exclude these uses from the statutory presumption of transfer to the producer.[73] The existence of neighbouring rights for producers may furthermore stimulate collecting societies to distribute the royalties they have collected irrespective of the individual contracts between creators and producers. The ultimate consequence of this development is that more and more uses are subjected to collective administration and that the income obtained from these uses is increasingly being allocated in negotiations between representatives of creators, performers and producers on the distribution of the royalties collected, rather than in individual negotiations between creators and producers. One can only speculate about the impact of this almost irreversible process of collectivization[74] and accumulation of claims on the exploitation and dissemination of creative works.

6.5 Conclusions

In this Chapter, I have discussed the two major methods used in the American, Dutch and German copyright systems to allocate rights to producers: presumption of transfer and attribution of authorship. Under German copyright law, the grant of exclusive, enforceable rights-of-use may be implied by the circumstances,

---

70. Compare Article 9(1) of the Satellite Directive, providing that Member States ensure that the rights of copyright owners and the holders of related rights to grant or refuse a cable operator the authorization for cable retransmission rights may be exercised only via a collecting society.

71. Compare Article 4 of the Rental Directive, guaranteeing authors an unwaivable right to remuneration in the case of rental, while at the same time recognizing related rights for film and phonogram producers, including rental rights.

72. The German Copyright Act grants authors an inalienable right to remuneration in the case of private copying on audio or videotapes, which may be exercised through a collecting society only (§ 54 GCA). The related rights of phonogram and film producers also include a right to remuneration in the event of private copying (§ 85(3) GCA; § 94(4) GCA). Each rightholder is entitled to a fair share of the fees collected (§ 54(6) GCA).

73. See e.g. Statement by the Dutch Minister of Justice during a parliamentary debate on the Act on Neighbouring Rights, EK 1992-1993, 21244, no. 15b, that the right to remuneration in the event of private copying on audio or videotape does not fall within the statutory presumption of assignment to the film producer (§ 45d DCA). See also supra 6.2.3 note 20 and accompanying text.

74. See also Grosheide, at 182.

allowing courts to allocate rights on a case-by-case basis. The need for statutory allocation of rights to producers is therefore less pressing than in American and Dutch copyright law, in which a grant of exclusive, enforceable rights is possible only in a written instrument. The downside of this flexible German system, however, is that neither the creator nor the producer can adequately assess their ownership status in the absence of an explicit agreement.

While statutory or judicial presumptions may serve as a safety net for a producer if he should have failed to stipulate a written grant, they often give rise to uncertainty about their applicability, the scope of the presumed grant and the validity of the presumed grant in the event of conflicting grants to third parties. In the absence of unambiguous transitional provisions, presumptions may furthermore give rise to uncertainty if copyright law should be amended to incorporate new rights. These uncertainties will not induce producers to rely on the presumption as an alternative to a written grant and may even motivate them to use standard formulas specifying each possible mode of exploitation of the work in detail so as to ensure that the scope of the grant is not interpreted restrictively in the light of the statutory or judicial presumption.

The study has indicated that the Dutch and German presumptions of transfer in case of film works are relatively clear as far as the exclusivity and scope of rights are concerned, but do give rise to uncertainty about the validity of the presumption in the event of conflicting transfers and about the meaning of the presumption if the parties have regulated the ownership situation in a written agreement.

Attribution of authorship to the producer removes all the obstacles producers may encounter when they seek to acquire title from creators. As author, the producer is vested with all the attributes normally accorded to authors under copyright law, unless provided otherwise. This far-reaching consequence is acceptable only if it is unequivocally clear in which situations the rule applies and whether the parties have an opportunity to agree otherwise. This method must be preferred to the American rule for employment works, which does not allow the parties to designate the employee as author.

As a possible alternative to the allocation of rights in works of authorship to producers, I have also briefly discussed the role of neighbouring rights for producers in cases in which they incorporate works of authorship in their products. We have seen that neighbouring rights enable producers to sue for infringement independently, but that infringement only occurs if the producer's contribution has been copied. If only the copyrightable work has been copied, the producer must still obtain title from the author in order to bring an action for infringement. For this reason, neighbouring rights are probably more effective for producers of films and sound recordings than for publishers. In the case of the publication of literary works, a statutory provision conferring the right to sue on exclusive licensees may therefore be more effective than a publisher's right.

Perhaps even more important than the right to sue independently, however, is the scope of producers to obtain a share of the income from collectively-administered uses. If the neighbouring right is extended to these collectively-administered uses, the producer is ensured income from these uses, even if the author has entrusted his rights to the collecting society directly. In view of the ever-growing number of uses which are administered collectively, the allocation of income from the use of creative works will be increasingly determined in collective negotiations on the distribution of the fees collected, rather than in individual negotiations between creators and producers.

Chapter 7

The applicability of statutory provisions allocating rights to producers: the judicial interpretation

7.1 Introduction

In Chapter 4, I argued that the allocation of copyright ownership to producers is most obvious in those situations in which the creator shifts the major financial, organizational and associative moral risks involved in the work's creation and publication to the producer.[1] I also argued, however, that the allocation of ownership according to the distribution of risks between the creator and producer cannot in itself provide sufficient security, because the distribution of risks differs from case to case and is not always easy for the parties to assess correctly at the time of contracting. To ensure predictability of copyright ownership, the statute must therefore define the situations in which it allocates rights to producers, e.g. by defining the type of work, the type of producer or the type of relationship between the creator and the producer. If this definition is unclear or based on factors which can only be established after the work has been created, it may be difficult for creators and producers to evaluate the ownership situation correctly and, consequently, to substantiate their remuneration claims and to prove title in infringement suits against third parties.[2] In this situation, in which the parties have some security only if they agree on the allocation of copyright ownership in a written agreement, the special ownership provision fails to meet its objective of improving efficiency and security.

In Chapter 4, I analyzed to which extent the American, Dutch and German provisions allocating rights to producers reflect the distribution of financial, organizational and associative risks between creators and producers. In this Chapter, I will analyze whether the interpretation of these provisions by the various courts reflects the other basic precondition for allocating rights to producers, i.e. the predictability of copyright ownership. For reasons of economy, I will confine the discussion to those elements in the statutory provisions which have given rise to the greatest uncertainty:

7.2: the meaning of 'employee' in the definition of 'work made for hire' in § 101(1) USCA;

---

1. *See supra* 4.1.
2. *Cf.* Hamilton, at 1305: '[S]ince her rights in the artwork are not definitely hers, she is likely to receive less if she tries to alienate those rights than she would have received had she had absolute rights in the work.'

7.4: the meaning of 'specific works' in the Dutch provision on employment works (§ 7 DCA);

7.6: the meaning of 'film producer' in the presumptions of § 45d DCA and § 89 GCA.

In addition, I will discuss a number of American and Dutch cases in which producers have sought to prove title to works made on their commission by claiming co-authorship or sole authorship in their capacity as designer of the plan and/or supervisor of the creative process (7.3; 7.5).

7.2 The meaning of 'employee' in the definition of a 'work made for hire'

7.2.1 THE EMPLOYEE-INDEPENDENT CONTRACTOR DICHOTOMY

The definition of a 'work made for hire' in § 101 USCA distinguishes between works 'prepared by an employee within the scope of his or her employment' (§ 101(1)) and nine categories of 'specially ordered or commissioned' works (§ 101(2)).[3] The first are 'works made for hire' *per se*, while the second group of works may be deemed a 'work made for hire' in a written instrument (§ 101(2)).

Although this distinction seems to suggest that a work made by an independent contractor can only be a 'work made for hire' if it falls within one of the nine categories set forth in § 101(2) and if the parties have signed a work-for-hire agreement,[4] several courts have applied different criteria, arguing that a work is made by an 'employee' in the sense of § 101(1) if the hiring party has a right to control the product (right to control test),[5] or if the hiring party has actually controlled and supervised the work's preparation (actual control test).[6] As a result of these extensive interpretations of the term 'employee', courts were able to treat commissioning parties as 'authors', even if the work involved did not meet the requirements of § 101(2) USCA.[7]

---

3. *See supra* 2.14 for the full text of the 'work made for hire' definition in § 101 USCA.
4. *See* H.R. Rep. No. 94-1476, 94th Cong., 2nd Sess., 121 (1976): 'The definition now provided by the bill represents a compromise which, in effect, spells out those specific categories of commissioned works which can be considered "works made for hire" under certain circumstances.' *See also* Whelan Associates, Inc. v. Jaslow Dental Laboratory, Inc., 609 F.Supp. 1307 (D.C.Pa. 1985), *aff'd on other grounds*, 797 F.2d 1222 (3rd Cir. 1986), *cert. denied* 479 U.S. 1031 (1987); Easter Seal Society for Crippled Children and Adults of Louisiana, Inc., v. Playboy Enterprises, 815 F.2d 323 (1987); Dumas v. Gommerman, 865 F.2d 1093 (9th Cir. 1989).
5. Aitken, Hazen, Hofmann, Miller P.C. v. Empire Constr. Co., 542 F.Supp. 252 (D.Neb. 1982); Peregrine v. Lauren Corp., 601 F.Supp. 828 (D.Colo. 1985).
6. *See* Aldon Accessories Ltd. v. Spiegel, Inc., 738 F.2d 548, 552 (1984), *cert. denied* 105 S.Ct. 387 (1984); Gallery House, Inc. v. Yi, 582 F.Supp. 1294, 1297 (1984); Evans Newton, Inc. v. Chicago Systems Software, 793 F.2d 889, 894 (7th Cir.), *cert.denied*, 107 S.Ct. 434 (1986).
7. *See e.g. Aldon Accessories*, 738 F.2d 548, 552 (1984), in which the plaintiff sued the defendant for infringing on the copyrights in statuettes. The defendant argued that the plaintiff did not have the right to sue. By applying an 'actual control' test, the court was able to reject the defense, notwithstanding the fact that the statuettes had been made by independent contractors and did not fall within one of the nine categories of § 101(2) USCA. *But see Easter Seal*, 815 F.2d 323 (5th Cir.

Aside from the fact that the 'right to control' and the 'actual control' tests ignore the distinction made in the 'work made for hire' definition between employment works and works made on commission, both tests have been criticized for their lack of predictability.[8] By making the status of 'employee' dependent on the hiring party's supervision and control or on his right to supervise and control the creative process, the allocation of ownership is determined by the degree of control which the court requires. Case law indicates that this may very well differ from case to case.[9] And even if the courts were to apply the same criteria, the outcome of an 'actual control' test would still be difficult to predict, because it is only possible to establish the amount of control exercised by the hiring party after the work has been completed.[10]

The U.S. Supreme Court acknowledged this criticism in the 1989 case of *Community for Creative Non-Violence v. Reid*[11], stating that the 'right to control' and the 'actual control' tests are inconsistent with the language and structure of the work-for-hire provisions and that they impede 'Congress' paramount goal of revising the 1976 Act of enhancing predictability and certainty of copyright ownership'.[12] According to the court, a work can only be a 'work made for hire' if it meets the requirements of § 101(2) USCA or if it is made by an employee within the scope of his employment, 'employee' to be understood according to its normal meaning in the general common law of agency.[13]

1987), stating that the *Aldon* court might have achieved the same result by finding that the plaintiff was co-author of the statuettes.

8.   *See Easter Seal*, 815 F.2d 323, 331-334 (1987); Dumas v. Gommerman, 865 F.2d 1093, 1103 (9th Cir. 1989); Hamilton, at 1305.

9.   Compare Murray v. Gelderman, 566 F.2d 1307 (5th Cir. 1978), in which the court held that the defendant had a right to control, even though the plaintiff had stipulated absolute creative freedom. The court interpreted the creative freedom clause as the defendant's choice not to exercise his right to supervise and control. Aitken, Hazen, Hofmann, Miller P.C. v. Empire Constr. Co. 542 F.Supp. 252 (D.Neb. 1982): architectural plan is not a work made for hire. The architect's client had the right to control the product, but not the details and means with which the product was made. *Cf. also* Peregrine v. Lauren Corp., 601 F.Supp. 828 (D.Colo. 1985): pictures for an advertising brochure made by a freelance photographer are works made for hire, because the advertising agency could veto any ideas or change the course, scope or fact of the photographic activities. Hardy, at 204, has argued convincingly that these cases are more consistent if one analyzes which party was in the best position to exploit the work.

10.   *See Easter Seal*, 815 F.2d 323, 333 (5th Cir. 1987). Hamilton, at 1304: the 'actual control' test enables hiring parties to unilaterally obtain work-for-hire rights years after the work has been completed as long as they directed and supervised the work.

11.   109 S.Ct. 2166 (1989). For a note on this case, see Kernochan, 144 RIDA 148 (1990).

12.   109 S.Ct. 2166, at 2177, 2178 (1989).

13.   *Id.* at 2178. *See also Easter Seal*, 815 F2d 323 (1987); M.G.B. Homes, Inc. v. Ameron Homes, Inc., 903 F.2d 1486 (11th Cir. 1990); Kunycia v. Melville Realty Co., Inc., 755 F. Supp. 566 (S.D.N.Y. 1990); Effect Associates v. Cohen, 908 F.2d 555 (9th Cir. 1990); Dae Han Video Productions, Inc. v. Kuk Dong Oriental Food, Inc., 19 U.S.P.Q.2d (BNA) 1294 (D.Mar. 1990); Moore Pub., Inc. v. Big Sky Marketing, Inc., 756 F.Supp. 1371 (D. Idaho 1990); Marshburn v. U.S., 16 U.S.P.Q.2d 1809 (Ct.Cl. 1990); MacLean Assoc., Inc. v. Wm.M. Mercer-Meidinger Hansen, 952 F.2d 769 (3rd Cir. 1991); Aymes v. Bonelli, 980 F.2d 857 (2nd Cir. 1992); Johannsen v. Brown, 797 F.Supp. 835 (D.Ore. 1992); Schiller & Schmidt, Inc. v. Nordisco Corporation, 969 F.2d 410 (7th Cir. 1992); Marco v. Accent Publishing Co., 969 F.2d 1547 (3rd Cir. 1992); Forward v. Thorogood, 985 F.2d 604 (1st Cir. 1993); Respect Inc. v. Committee on the Status of Women, 815 F. Supp. 1112 (N.D.Ill. 1993).

7.2.2 An 'Employee' According to the General Common Law of Agency

Does the Supreme Court interpretation of 'employee' provide more predictability? According to the general common law of agency - the common denominator of the state laws of agency[14] - 'employee' is a reference to the conventional master and servant relationship. In order to determine whether such a relationship exists, one must look at the hiring party's right to control, but also at a large number of other factors: the skill required, the source of the instrumentalities and tools, the location of the work, the duration of the parties' relationship, whether the hiring party has the right to assign additional projects to the hired party, the extent of the hired party's discretion to decide when and how long to work, the method of payment, the hired party's role in hiring and paying assistants, whether the work is part of the hiring party's regular business, whether the hiring party is in business, the provision of employee benefits and the tax treatment of the hired party.[15] None of these factors is determinative in itself.[16]

> The Community for Creative Non-Violence hired the sculptor James Earl Reid to make a modern version of the Nativity scene to portray the plight of the homeless for the annual Christmas Pageant of Peace in Washington D.C. The sculpture was to consist of three life-size black figures positioned around a steam grate so as to give them the appearance of a homeless couple with a little baby. The steam grate was to be placed on top of a pedestal made by CCNV and was to be fitted with machinery to simulate steam. The work was to be entitled 'Third World America'. No written agreement was drawn up. At the instruction of CCNV members, and different from his own original drawings, Reid sculpted the parents bending over the steam grate and included a shopping cart holding their belongings. After the Pageant, CCNV decided to take the sculpture on a tour to raise money for the homeless. Reid objected and announced his own plans for a tour. He subsequently sued CCNV to establish the copyright ownership and to demand the return of the sculpture. The U.S. Supreme Court held that although the CCNV members had issued instructions on enough of Reid's work to ensure that it fitted their specifications, all the other factors indicated that Reid was not a CCNV employee. The work required skill, Reid used his own tools, he worked in his own studio, fixed his own working hours and hired his own assistants. Reid worked two months on the sculpture. CCNV paid Reid a lump sum to cover the costs of the material but did not pay income tax or social security contributions. CCNV was furthermore not in the position to commission other projects to Reid, and commissioning sculp-

---

14. In view of the Congressional objective of ensuring uniformity in the application of the copyright law, the Supreme Court chose to rely on the 'general common law of agency' instead of on the law of any particular state. CCNV v. Reid, 109 S.Ct. 2166, 2173 (1989).

15. *Id.* at 2178, referring to the Restatement of Agency § 220(2). The Restatement of Agency is a non-authoritative compilation of agency rules most states have in common.

16. *Id.* at 2179.

tures was not part of CCNV's regular activities. The court concluded that since Reid was not an 'employee' in the sense of § 101(1) USCA and since the work did not satisfy the conditions of § 101(2) USCA, CCNV was not the 'author' under the work-for-hire doctrine.[17]

By interpreting the term 'employee' according to its meaning in agency law, the *CCNV* test provides more predictability than the 'actual control' and 'right to control' tests. However, since the agency law test depends on a multitude of factors, some of which can only be established after the creative process has commenced, it may still be difficult, in borderline cases, to determine at the time of contracting whether the creator is an employee or an independent contractor and, consequently, who the work's author will be.[18] How should a work be assessed if some of the factors point to an 'employee' status and others to an 'independent contractor' status? How many factors must point to the employee status before it can be safely assumed that the creator is an employee?[19]

It it is interesting in this respect to note that the Supreme Court did not follow the Ninth Circuit's interpretation of 'employee' in § 101(1) USCA as a formal, salaried employee.[20] Although in applying this 'formal, salaried employee' test the Ninth Circuit only relied on factors which can be determined in advance,[21] the

---

17. *Id.* at 2179, 2180. After mediation, CCNV and Reid agreed to recognize Reid as sole author of the sculpture and CCNV as owner of the original copy. The parties also reached agreement on the conditions for exploiting the two-dimensional reproductions. *See* Latman/Gorman/Ginsburg, Appendix at 85.

18. In this sense also Kernochan, 144 RIDA 171 (1990); Nimmer, § 5.03[B] 5-24 (1989); Landau, at 137.

19. *See e.g.* Aymes v. Bonelli, 980 F.2d 857 (2nd Cir. 1992): the plaintiff designed software for the defendant. The relationship covered a substantial period of time and the work required skill. The plaintiff worked at home, but tested the software on the defendant's location. The defendant assigned additional projects to the plaintiff. Some work was performed at an hourly rate, some for a flat fee, and some of the payments were in cash without deduction of taxes and employee benefits. The defendant did not sell computer software, but modifying programs for its computers was part of its regular activities. The District Court held that the plaintiff was an 'employee'. 21 U.S.P.Q.2d 1716 (S.D.N.Y. 1991). The Second Circuit reversed this decision, emphasizing the fact that the defendant did not pay income tax and did not provide employee benefits. *See also* Dae Han Video Productions, Inc. v. Kuk Dong Oriental Food, Inc., 19 U.S.P.Q.2d (BNA) 1294 (D.Mar. 1990): scripts for films are works for hire. The writers worked for networks on a long-term basis, were represented by a union-type organization when negotiating with the networks, produced scripts for many episodes of a particular show, and received weekly or monthly pay from which taxes were deducted. At the most, all the factors in favour of and against the employee status are equally balanced, which is not sufficient reason to dismiss the permanent injunction given on the basis of an 'actual control' test before the *CCNV* decision.

20. CCNV v. Reid, 109 S.Ct. 2166, at 2174 nt. 8, referring to Dumas v. Gommerman, 865 F.2d 1093, 1104 (9th Cir. 1989). The 'formal, salaried employee' test was supported by: Brief of the Register of Copyrights as *Amicus Curiae* Supporting Respondent, CCNV v. Reid, 846 F.2d 1485 (D.C.Cir. 1988), *aff'd* 109 S.Ct. 2166; Brief of Volunteer Lawyers for the Arts *et al.* as *Amici Curiae* in support for the respondent, 13 Colum.VLA.J.L. & Arts 145, 147 (1988); Patry, at 119; Kernochan, 144 RIDA 172 (1990); Landau, at 130, 137.

21. Dumas v. Gommerman, 865 F.2d 1093, 1095 (9th Cir. 1989): whether the artist worked in his or her own studio or on the buyer's premises; whether the buyer was in the regular business of creating works of the type purchased; whether the artist worked for several buyers at a time, or exclusively for one; whether the buyer retained the authority to assign additional projects to the artist; the tax treatment of the parties' relationship; whether the artist was hired via the channels customarily used for hiring new employees; whether the artist received all the benefits which the buyer customarily granted to its regular employees. Restatement Second of Agency § 220(2)(b-j).

Supreme Court held the agency law test to be more consistent with the formulation of § 101(1) USCA.[22] By opting for the agency law test with its 'right to control' element, the Supreme Court thus accepts that courts still have a certain discretion to determine whether the creator is an 'employee'.

7.3 Commissioned works after *CCNV*: the joint authorship alternative

The *CCNV* decision underlines that the work-for-hire rule is only applicable to commissioned works if they fall within one of the nine categories listed in § 101(2) USCA and if the parties have entered into a work-for-hire agreement. Parties commissioning contributions to sound recordings, computer programs, works of visual art or musical works,[23] must therefore rely more heavily than before on express transfers of copyright ownership in order to secure title.

In the meantime, many commissioning parties who relied on the extensive interpretation of § 101(1) USCA in pre-*CCNV* case law and who therefore did not stipulate an express transfer or enter into a work-for-hire agreement, have encountered problems in proving title. In order to safeguard their alleged ownership interests, many have claimed to be joint author of the commissioned work.[24]

As co-owner of the copyright, a joint author has the right to sue for infringement. The use of the work by one co-owner does not infringe on the other owner's copyright interest, however.[25] The concept of joint authorship is therefore unreliable if the commissioning party wishes to exploit the work on an exclusive basis, but it may help him to prove title vis-à-vis third parties if he has failed to stipulate an express transfer and if the work does not meet the 'work-for-hire' criteria.[26]

Determining joint authorship in the case of commissioned works is not without pitfalls, however. If the parties collaborate during the creative process, it may be difficult to distinguish between their individual contributions. If they were assisted by others, the scope of their contributions can only be assessed after it has been

---

22. CCNV v. Reid, 109 S.Ct. 2166, at 2174, nt 8.

23. These works may nevertheless be 'works made for hire' if they are contributions to a collective or audiovisual work, or if they are used as a translation, compilation or supplementary work, and if the parties expressly agree that the work shall be deemed a work made for hire in a written instrument (§ 101(2) USCA). *See supra* 4.3 note 47.

24. Joint authorship was denied in: S.O.S. Inc. v. Payday, Inc., 886 F.2d 1081 (9th Cir. 1989); Ashton Tate Corp. v. Ross, 916 F.2d 516 (9th Cir. 1990); Andrien v. Southern Ocean County Chamber of Commerce, 927 F.2d 132 (3rd Cir. 1991); M.G.B. Homes, Inc. v. Ameron Homes, Inc., 903 F.2d 1486 (11th Cir. 1990); BancTraining Video Sys. v. First American Corp, 21 U.S.P.Q.2d 21014 (6th Cir. 1992); Forward v. Thorogood, 985 F.2d 604 (1st Cir. 1993). *Cf. also* Moore Pub., Inc. v. Big Sky Marketing, Inc., 756 F.Supp. 1371 (D. Idaho 1990): record insufficient for a summary judgment on joint authorship.

25. *See Easter Seal* 815 F2d 323, 337 (1987): use of work by joint author and his licensees does not infringe on other author's copyright interest. *See also* Strauss v. The Hearst Corp., 8 U.S.P.Q.2d 1832 (S.D.N.Y.1988); CCNV v. Reid, 846 F.2d 1485, 1498 (D.C.Cir. *aff'd* 109 S.Ct. 2166 (1989); Geshwind v. Garrick, 16 U.S.P.Q.2d 1707 (S.D.N.Y.1990); Words & Data, Inc. v. GTE Communications Services, 765 F.Supp. 570 (W.D.Mo. 1991).

26. *See* Katzman, at 896; Landau, at 150; Scher, at 67.

established whether the contributions of the assistants are 'works made for hire'.[27] There is furthermore no consensus when a contribution to a commissioned work qualifies for joint authorship. According to the Supreme Court in *CCNV*, the 'author' is the person who translates an idea into a fixed, tangible expression which qualifies for copyright protection.[28] Does this require the commissioning party to translate his ideas into a fixed, tangible expression personally, or is it sufficient that his ideas are translated into a fixed expression by the commissioned party according to his instructions? Several courts and commentators seem to have adopted the first view, arguing that each contribution should be eligible for copyright protection in its own right.[29] Others have argued, with reference to the text of the 1976 Act, that independently copyrightable contributions are not required.[30]

Either way, the fact that the commissioning party does not translate his ideas into a fixed, tangible expression personally, should not preclude joint authorship *per se*. It is generally acknowledged that a commissioning party may become the sole author if the execution of his instructions by the commissioned party does not require an intellectual modification in order for the product to be eligible for copyright protection.[31] Similarly, it may be argued that if part of the 'fixed, tangible expression entitled to copyright protection' originates from the commissioned party, while the other part is dictated to him by the commissioning party, the parties may have joint authorship if both parts of the expression meet the required standard of originality and the parties have the intention of merging the parts into a unitary whole. In determining whether the parties qualify as joint authors, several courts have indeed

---

27. CCNV v. Reid, 846 F.2d 1485, 1498 (D.C.Cir.), *aff'd* 109 S.Ct. 2166 (1989). *But see Easter Seal*, 815 F2d 323, 337 (1987), in which the court stated that the tapes made of a musical jam session had been jointly authored by the television station and the society which had commissioned the taping and whose volunteers had taken part in the jam session, without questioning whether the volunteers' contributions were 'works made for hire'.

28. CCNV v. Reid, 109 S.Ct. 2166, 2171 (1989).

29. *See* Ashton Tate Corp. v. Ross, 916 F.2d 516 (9th Cir. 1980); Childress v. Taylor, 945 F.2d 500 (2nd Cir. 1991); Johannsen v. Brown, 797 F.Supp. 835 (D.Ore. 1992). *See also* Statement of Ralph Oman, Register of Copyrights, before the Subcommittee on Patents, Trademarks and Copyrights of the Senate Committee on the Judiciary, 101st Cong., 1st Sess., 210-211 (1989); Goldstein, I, at 379; Fine, at 175. The contribution of ideas was held to be insufficient in Aitken, Hazen, Hoffman, Miller P.C. v. Empire Construction Co., 542 F.Supp. 252, 259 (D.Neb. 1982); Whelan Associates, Inc. v. Jaslow Dental Laboratory, Inc., 609 F.Supp. 1307 (D.C.Pa. 1985), *aff'd on other grounds*, 797 F.2d 1222 (3rd Cir. 1986), *cert.denied* 479 U.S. 301 (1987); M.G.B. Homes v. Ameron Homes, 903 F.2d 1486, 1493 (11th Cir. 1990); S.O.S. Inc. v. Payday, Inc., 886 F.2d 1081, 1087 (9th Cir. 1989).

30. Ginsburg, *Developments*, at 159; Katzman, at 888; Nimmer, § 6.07 at 18.2 (1990): a work may be considered to be a work of joint authorship if one party contributes ideas which the other party weaves into a completed literary expression, provided both contributions are more than *de minimis*. *See also* CCNV v. Reid, 846 F.2d 1485, 1496 (D.C.Cir.), *aff'd* 109 S.Ct. 2166 (1989), citing Nimmer. *Cf. also Easter Seal*, 815 F2d 323, 337 (1987): the field tapes of a musical jam session were joint works, because the jam session by the plaintiff's volunteers was a work of authorship which only needed fixation to be copyrightable, while the fixation by the television station was in itself sufficiently creative to qualify as a work of authorship.

31. *See* Andrien v. Southern Ocean County Chamber of Commerce, 927 F.2d 132 (3rd Cir. 1991); Lakedreams v. Taylor, 932 F.2d 1103 (5th Cir. 1991). *See also supra* 3.3.3.

examined whether the commissioning party contributed to the concept of the work and controlled and/or dictated the commissioned party in realizing the work.[32]

> Without giving a definite ruling on the issue, the appellate court argued in *CCNV v. Reid*[33] that 'Third World America' might qualify as a text-book example of a jointly authored work, considering Reid's original and creative contribution to the figures and CCNV's contribution to the pedestal, in addition to the initial conceptualization and ongoing direction of the realization of 'Third World America'. Following CCNV's original conception of the sculpture, the CCNV members monitored the work's progress, not only to approve Reid's embodiment of their idea, but to guide his expression and to coordinate CCNV's construction of the steam grate pedestal with his efforts.[34] The Supreme Court subsequently stated, with reference to the definition of 'joint work' in § 101 USCA, that CCNV could be considered to be a joint author if the District Court were to rule in appeal that CCNV and Reid had made the work 'with the intention that their contributions be merged into inseparable or interdependent parts of a unitary whole'.[35] The fact that the Supreme Court did not mention the element of originality may perhaps imply that it agreed with the appellate court's view that CCNV's and Reid's respective contributions were sufficiently creative to qualify for joint authorship.

It is clear that, where a commissioning party's contribution may vary from submitting general specifications to full conceptualization of the work and from minor supervision to dictating the expression, the courts have considerable discretion to determine whether the commissioning party is a joint author, especially in those situations in which the court does not require that each contribution is copyrightable in its own right. To improve predictability for the commissioned party in this respect, attempts have been made - unsuccessfully sofar - to amend the law so as to require that each contribution is original and that, in the case of a commissioned work, the parties must designate the work as a 'joint work' in a written instrument before the creative process commences.[36] In *Childress v. Taylor*,[37] the Second Circuit made a further attempt to improve predictability, stating that if one of the

---

32. *See* Strauss v. the Hearst Corp., 8 U.S.P.Q.2d 1832 (S.D.N.Y.1988): a photographer and a magazine publisher were considered to be the joint authors of pictures published in a magazine. The photographer had taken the photos so as to leave space for the text of the article, while the publishher's employees supplied and arranged the equipment for the shooting, supervised some of the shootings, retouched the pictures and superimposed captions and other copy. Fisher v. Klein, 16 U.S.P.Q.2d 1795, 1799 (S.D.N.Y 1990): notwithstanding the fact that the plaintiff was the main contributor, the defendant was joint author of the jewelry, because she had contributed to the idea and the manner of expression in small, but distinct ways through discussions which led to specific modifications. *Easter Seal*, 815 F.2d 323, 333 (1987): '[A]ny buyer satisfying a seriously enforced "actual control" test will ordinarily be a co-author of the work.' Compare also Katzman, at 891, favouring an 'actual control' test to establish joint authorship.

33. CCNV v. Reid, 846 F.2d 1484, 1497 (D.C.Cir.), *aff'd* 109 S.Ct. 2166 (1989).

34. *Id.* at 1497.

35. CCNV v. Reid, 109 S.Ct. 2166, 2180.

36. S. 1253, 101st Cong., 1st Sess. (1989). *See also supra* 6.3 notes 40-41.

37. 945 F.2d 500 (2nd Cir. 1991).

parties is the dominant contributor, the parties can only have joint authorship if the contributors regard each other as joint authors.[38]

Both the legislative proposal and the *Childress* court made joint authorship dependent on the expressed intention to acquire the legal status of joint author. While this may improve predictability, it is not a factor which is relevant for determining authorship in the creator doctrine *stricto sensu*.[39] One might perhaps argue that, since joint authorship already deviates from the creator doctrine in that it gives a person an ownership interest in the result of another person's creative labour, it is only one step further down the road to require that the parties provide evidence of their intention to become co-authors and, consequently, co-owners of each other's contribution. The need for predictability is not as pressing here as it is in the work-for-hire context, however. Whereas the work-for-hire doctrine deprives the commissioned party of copyright ownership altogether, joint authorship gives the parties an undivided ownership of the work. As co-owner, the commissioned party is entitled to a proportion of the profits generated by the commissioning party,[40] while he may license others to use the work.[41] In view of these consequences of joint authorship, the commissioning party's interest in acquiring (co-)ownership in the event his contribution to the work turns out to be substantially creative, should arguably prevail over the commissioned party's interest in knowing at the time of contracting whether it will become sole or joint author.

7.4 The Dutch provision on employment works (§ 7 DCA)

7.4.1 LABOUR PERFORMED IN THE SERVICE OF ANOTHER

Section 7 of the Dutch Copyright Act provides that if the labour performed in the service of another person consists of making specific literary, scientific or artistic works, the person in whose service these works are made is designated as its author,

---

38. *Id.* at 508. *See also* Respect Inc. and Coleen Mast v. Committee on the Status of Women, 815 F. Supp. 1112 (N.D.Ill. 1993), in which the court followed the *Childress* court in arguing that the fact that Mast was the only person mentioned as the book's author led to the presumption that Mast did not intend the Committee and herself to become joint authors of the book.

39. Compare Words & Data, Inc. v. GTE Communications Services, 765 F.Supp. 570, 579 (W.D.Mo. 1991): the absence of an express copyright claim by the hiring party does not mandate a finding of sole authorship of the hired party. For a critical note on *Childress*, see Ginsburg, *Developments*, at 159: the *Childress* court probably sought to rule out pretextual collaborations. However, since the court, in order to achieve this result, not only required intent but also that each co-author contributed independently copyrightable material, the court seems to exclude from co-authorship those collaborations in which one person furnishes the idea, and the other supplies the expression.

40. *See* H.R. Rep. No. 1476, 94th Cong., 2d Sess., 121 (1976); Oddo v. Ries, 743 F.2d 630, 631 (9th Cir. 1984); CCNV v. Reid, 846 F.2d 1485, 1498 (D.Cir. 1988) *aff'd* 109 S.Ct. 2166 (1989). The co-owner pursuing the right to an accounting must prove a direct connection between the use of the joint work by the other co-owner and any profits made by the latter. *See* Strauss v. The Hearst Corp., 8 U.S.P.Q.2d 1832 (S.D.N.Y.1988).

41. *See supra* 3.3.2.

unless the parties had agreed otherwise.[43] 'Labour performed in the service of another' is generally understood to refer to an employer-employee relationship in both the private and the public sector.[44]

According to the Netherlands Civil Code, an employment relationship is based on a contract in which the employee undertakes to perform labour in the service of the employer for a certain period of time, in return for payment of wages or salary.[45] The existence of an employment contract presupposes a state of subordination[46] and obliges the hired party to perform the labour in person.[47] Subordination does not require the hiring party to actually supervise and control the hired party.[48] Instead he must have a certain right to control the hired party's work and/or determine his employment conditions (time, place, attitude, restraint on competitive activities, etc.).[49] The hiring party's right to supervise and control the creative process may be relevant in this respect, but is not the only decisive factor.[50] Hence, the fact that someone undertakes to create a work according to the hiring party's instructions is not sufficient to conclude in favour of an employment relationship,[51] nor does the fact that the hired party has stipulated creative freedom necessarily imply that there *cannot* be an employment relationship.[52]

In practice, courts take account of all the circumstances of the case to determine whether there is an employment relationship. As is the case with the agency law test applied by the U.S. Supreme Court, this evaluation of the facts is a test which can adequately distinguish between true employees and true independent contractors, but

---

43. *Cf. also* § 6(1) Uniform Benelux Designs and Models Act of 1966, Trb. 1966, 292: if a model or design was made by an employee in the course of his duties, the employer is considered to be the designer, unless agreed otherwise.

44. *See* the Memorandum of Reply to § 7 DCA, Parl.Gesch. 7.4. *See also* Judgment of December 29, 1989, Ambt. Amsterdam, Netherlands, Computerrecht 141 (1990) (Kinders v. Gemeente Amsterdam): § 7 DCA was applicable to works made by civil servants in the course of their employment. *See also* Gerbrandy (1988), at 50; Van Lingen/Van Niftrik, at 51; Spoor/Verkade, at 36.

45. § 7A:1637a BW. *See also* Schuijt, at 177. *See also* Judgment of October 12, 1981, Pres.Rb. Utrecht, Netherlands, 51 BIE 79 (1983) (HWK v. Volmac): § 7 DCA not applicable to a slogan commissioned by an advertising agency and made by a freelancer. Judgment of July 18, 1984, Rb. Middelburg, Netherlands, NJ 1985, 882 ('flower box'): § 7 DCA not applicable to a work made by student pursuant to and during a practical course at a local government agency.

46. *See* Judgment of November 17, 1967, HR, Netherlands, NJ 1968, 163 note Hirsch Ballin (Den Hollander v. Luitingh). *See also* Bakels, 3.1.1; Schuijt, at 183.

47. § 7A:1639a(1) BW.

48. *See* Judgment of September 28, 1983, HR, Netherlands, NJ 1984, 92 ('employment'). *See also* Schuijt, at 183, 317.

49. *See e.g.* Judgment of June 24, 1966, HR, Netherlands, NJ 1966, 547. Schuijt, at 191, 219, 317: the right to control concerns both labour and the labour organization. The dominant factor in establishing whether there is question of subordination is not so much whether the hiring party has a right to control or can exercise control over the product, but whether the hired party is an integral part of the hiring party's labour organization.

50. *See* Judgment of November 17, 1967, HR, Netherlands, NJ 1968, 163, note Hirsch Ballin (Den Hollander v. Luitingh). *See also* Schuijt, at 191, 317.

51. *See* Judgment of November 17, 1967, HR, Netherlands, NJ 1968, 163 note Hirsch Ballin (Den Hollander v. Luitingh).

52. *See* Croon, 25 NJB 626 (1950); Schuijt, at 183. *But see* Hirsch Ballin, *Auteursrecht der hoogleraren*, at 552; NJ 1968, 163, at 580; Smit, at 1064, both arguing that § 7 DCA is not applicable to academic writings on account of the lack of subordination. In their view, subordination implies the right to control the fruits of the hired party's labour, which is not appropriate in the case of academic writings by university professors.

it may give rise to uncertainty in those cases in which the hired party works for a hiring party on a long-term basis in a relationship which does not have all the characteristics of a formal employment relationship.[53]

7.4.2 THE 'SPECIFIC WORKS' CLAUSE

Apart from the existence of an employment relationship, § 7 DCA requires that the employee's labour consists of 'making specific literary, scientific or artistic works'. It is generally understood that this 'specific works' requirement is met if the work is made by the employee in the course of fulfilling his employment duties.[54] Case law and doctrine are divided, however, on the question when a particular work can be said to fall within the employee's regular duties.

If the employee's duties are defined in the employment contract, both parties can assess which works will be subject to § 7 DCA and can negotiate accordingly. The job description however does not always provide a straightforward answer to the question whether a particular work falls within the employment duties. In particular uncertainty may arise if the employee accepts an incidental order to create a work above and beyond his regular duties or if he takes the initiative to create a work which was not referred to specifically in the employment contract.

In *Van der Laan v. Schoonderbeek*, the Hoge Raad affirmed the Court of Appeal's decision that an employee's acceptance of an incidental order to create a certain work above and beyond his normal duties may, under certain circumstances, constitute an implied, temporary modification of the employment contract.[55]

> Van der Laan, general secretary of a publishing company, wrote a book at his employer's request. The Court of Appeal decided that he had written the book in the course of his employment duties based on

---

53. *See e.g.* Judgment of May 7, 1987, Ktg. Zaandam, Netherlands, Prg. 1987, 2732 (Cohen v. Forbo): an employment contract, notwithstanding the fact that the hiring party did not pay social security contributions and income tax and that the hired party's fees included sales tax. The hired party worked for the hiring party for five years; she worked in the hiring party's studio almost daily; the hiring party issued instructions when, where and how to work; the hired party did not work for others during the period she worked for the hiring party; the hiring party exploited copyright to the works made by the hired party as if she were an employee. *Cf. also* Van Lingen/Van Niftrik, at 51; Schuijt, at 307, questioning whether there is an employment contract if a freelance journalist works for a particular periodical or newspaper on a regular basis. *See also* Van Esch, *Juridische aspecten*, at 246, discussing the situation in which an employee is seconded to a hiring party by a software house for a fixed period (body-shopping).

54. Judgment of January 19, 1951, HR, Netherlands, NJ 1952, 37, note Veegens (Van der Laan v. Schoonderbeek): the question of whether labour was performed in the service of an employer in the sense of § 7 DCA is the same question as whether the employee performed the labour in the course of his duties under the terms of the employment agreement. *See also* Memorandum to § 7 DCA, Parl.Gesch., at 7.3; Spoor/Verkade, at 37; Smit, at 1064. *But see* De Beer, at 399, concluding on the basis of Judgment of October 14, 1987, Ger. 's-Gravenhage, Netherlands, NJ 1989, 220 (Rooijakkers v. Rijksuniversiteit Leiden) that the 'specific works' clause and fulfilment of employment duties are two different, cumulative requirements. *See also* Quaedvlieg, 17 Informatierecht/AMI 95 (1993): the question whether the creation of a work falls within employment duties is not the same as the question whether a work is 'specific' in the sense of § 7 DCA.

55. Judgment of May 25, 1950, Ger. Amsterdam, Netherlands, NJ 1951, 213 *aff'd* Judgment of January 19, 1951, HR, Netherlands, NJ 1952, 37 note Veegens.

the following circumstances: he had more literary than commercial qualities and had already done some editing and translation work for the company, for which he had not been remunerated separately; he did some of the research for the book during office hours; he used the company's research material; the company paid him the research expenses and he had authorized his employer to print proof copies in preparation of publication.[56]

This decision indicates that § 7 DCA may be applicable to works made by an employee pursuant to an *ad hoc* order issued in the course of the employment relationship, if the work is not completely at variance with the employee's previous duties and if the employee has used the employer's facilities and financial resources to prepare the work and has not stipulated special conditions for the employer's use of the work. The same circumstances were considered relevant in a case in which an employee took the initiative to create certain works which had not been specifically agreed by the parties at the time of contracting. In *Van Gunsteren v. Lips*,[57] the Court of Appeal of 's-Hertogenbosch stated that § 7 DCA may be applicable in this situation if the employee has considerable discretion in the performance of his duties, if the work falls within the field of special expertise for which he has been hired, and if he permits the employer to use the works for its business purposes.[58]

In the course of his employment as scientist with the propeller manufacturer Lips, Van Gunsteren wrote several articles and computer programs and published a doctoral thesis consisting of a compilation of articles. The Court of Appeal held that the company was the author of the articles and computer programs made by Van Gunsteren in the course of his employment contract, while Van Gunsteren was the author of the thesis and the articles in the thesis written by him before he had entered into the employment contract. The relevant circumstances: Van Gunsteren had had considerable freedom in the execution of his duties; all the articles were in the field of special expertise for which he had been hired; some articles had been co-written with other employees; the company had paid some of the research expenses; one of the articles concerned programs for 'our' computer as well as company products which had been designed with these programs; the computer programs were useful for the company; Van Gunsteren had not objected to the company's use of the programs. In view of Van Gunsteren's scientific duties, the question whether or not the works had been made during office hours was not considered relevant, nor was it considered relevant that the parties

---

56. *Id.* at 104-105.
57. Judgment of May 24, 1978, Ger. 's-Hertogenbosch, Netherlands, 53 BIE 99, 100, 101 (1985).
58. *Id.* at 100, affirming the District Court judgment.

had not agreed specifically on the work's creation when they entered into the employment relationship.[59]

If interpreted in this way, the fact that the work was not referred to specifically in the job description does not preclude the applicability of § 7 DCA. The *Van Gunsteren* court, in fact, creates a strong presumption in favour of the employer in those cases in which the employee has a certain discretion in the way in which he performs his duties and the work falls within the field of special expertise for which he was hired. In this situation, it would seem to be up to the employee not to give rise to the impression that the creation of the work falls within his regular duties.[60] If he makes use of the employer's financial, technical and human resources to prepare the work and allows the employer to use the work without reserving authorship and without negotiating additional remuneration - in other words, if the employee transfers the production, organizational and associative risks to the employer[61] - there is little chance that he will be able to escape the fate of § 7 DCA.

The Court of Appeal of the Hague applied a more restrictive interpretation of the 'specific works' clause in a case on a scientific report written by a university researcher. In *Rooijakkers v. Rijksuniversiteit Leiden*,[62] the court argued that, although university professors and members of the academic staff are employed to undertake research and to make the results public, they are free to decide which research they will carry out and how they will publish the results. As such, they are not employed to deliver a specified, concrete scientific product, so that their labour cannot be said to consist of 'making specific scientific works' in the sense of § 7 DCA.[63]

---

59. *Id.* at 100, 101.
60. *See* Judgment of November 22, 1977, Pres.Rb. Breda, Netherlands, 46 BIE 84 (1978) ('Gorlaeus Laboratory'): the head of the glass laboratory at the University of Leyden must be considered to be the author of drawings of the lab's glassware stocks because he had made the drawings in his own time and has always reserved his rights when selling copies to third parties, while the university had never claimed any rights on the basis of the employment contract. *See also* Judgment of December 23, 1988, Pres.Rb. Amsterdam, Netherlands, Computerrecht 149 (1989) ('Navalconsult'): the plaintiffs initiated a plan to design computer program to be based on other program already made by them in the course of employment. According to the plan, the project would require three months. After they submitted the plan to the employer, the latter instructed them to design the program. It took almost a year to develop the program in practice. The court: under these circumstances, the fact that the plaintiffs did some of the designing in their own time was irrelevant. § 7 DCA applicable. *See also* Judgment of May 27, 1992, Rb. 's-Gravenhage, Netherlands, 17 Informatierecht/AMI 94 (1993) note Quaedvlieg (Gorter v. PTT), discussed *infra* note 70 and accompanying text.
61. *See supra* 4.1.
62. Judgment of October 14, 1987, Ger. 's-Gravenhage, Netherlands, NJ 1989, 220.
63. *Id.* at 708. *See also* Judgment of April 28, 1981, Pres.Rb. Zutphen, Netherlands, 6 Informatierecht/AMI 16, 17 (1982) (Huijgen v. Kluwer): the fact that the plaintiff was a university employee does not imply that he wrote the texts at the university's direct orders. Approval with *Rooijakkers* by Cohen Jehoram, 12 Informatierecht/AMI 18 (1988); Quaedvlieg, 17 Informatierecht/AMI 95 (1993). Woltring, *Wetenschapsbeoefening*, at 67, agrees with the test, but not with the outcome of the test in the *Rooijakkers* case. Gerbrandy (1988), at 52: § 7 DCA is only applicable to specific works which the employee is required to make, not to works which the employee creates at his own initiative with his employer's implicit approval.

In the case at hand, the court did find § 7 DCA applicable. The University of Leyden had hired Rooijakkers on a temporary basis to carry out a specific research project and to write a report on the basis of the results. This fact, combined with the fact that other employees had already started the project and that, as a result, the method and system of the research as well as the manner of reporting had already been largely determined when Rooijakkers commenced his duties, convinced the court that the report was a specific result of Rooijakker's temporary employment which had been envisaged upon his appointment. As such, Rooijakker's labour consisted of making a specific scientific work in the sense of § 7 DCA.[64]

The *Rooijakkers* court seems to require that both the work's subject matter and manner of expression be specified in considerable detail at the time of contracting, which obviously provides more predictability than the criteria applied by the *Van Gunsteren* court. The Hoge Raad's decision in *Van der Laan v. Schoonderbeek* however indicates that § 7 DCA may, under certain circumstances, also be applicable if the work has not been specifically agreed upon at the time of contracting, but made pursuant to incidental instructions issued by the employer at a later date.[65] The high degree of specificity required by the *Rooijakkers* court furthermore does not comply with the Hoge Raad's statement that § 7 DCA may designate a person as author who has nothing to do with the actual creation of the work.[66] The *Rooijakkers* criteria would at any rate exclude a large number of works which are generally considered to fall within the scope of § 7 DCA: works made by employees who have a duty to create works of a particular category, but who are more or less at liberty to choose the subject matter and manner of expression and are expected to do so, as is often the case with journalists.

At this point, it has been advocated that the employer should at least have the *right* to control the manner of expression.[67] Verkade has argued that employers generally have such a right with respect to articles written by journalists in employment, while such right to control is absent in the case of academic writings.[68] A 'right to control' test may indeed exclude academic writings from the scope of § 7 DCA, but it may also give rise to uncertainty in many other cases. What if an

---

64. *Id.* at 708, 709.

65. Judgment of January 19, 1951, HR, Netherlands, NJ 1952, 37 note Veegens.

66. *See* Judgment of June 28, 1940, HR, Netherlands, NJ 1941, 110, at 162, note Meijers ('Fire over England I'): '[S]ection 6 DCA does not in any way underlie the intention - as is the case with section 7 - to statutorily label someone as author of an artistic work who, himself, is foreign to the actual creation.' [translation JS] *See also* de Beer, at 400. *But see* Woltring, *Wetenschapsbeoefening*, at 69, arguing that § 7 DCA can only be applicable if the employee's contribution is non-original or of an almost non-original nature, as is the case with the assembly of a technical object on the basis of detailed technical drawings. In *Rooijakkers*, the court explicitly stated that the department for which the plaintiff had worked was not foreign to the actual creation, because the head of department had been closely involved in the preparation of the report and was responsible for its final editing. NJ 1989, 220.

67. *See* Spoor/Verkade, at 38; Verkade, *Een nog net niet verboden artikel*, at 1237; Verkade, *Het beste artikel 7*, at 13.

68. *Id.*

employee enjoys considerable creative freedom, but the publication of his works is subject to the employer's veto rights? What if the publisher has a contractual obligation not to unduly interfere with the work of his editorial staff?[69] Can an employee secure authorship by stipulating creative freedom? Etc., etc.

Case law indicates that the existence of a right to control, although not decisive, may be a relevant factor for determining whether the creation of the work fell within the employee's regular duties. In *Gorter v. PTT*,[70] the District Court of the Hague adhered to the *Van Gunsteren* approach in examining whether the work fell within the field of special expertise for which the employees had been hired, whether the employees had had a certain discretion in the performance of their duties, and whether they had made the works at the employer's expense. On the basis of this evaluation, the court concluded that the employees had made the works in the course of fulfilling their employment duties and added that this conclusion was reinforced by the fact that the employees had acknowledged that they were accountable to their superiors at the time of creation.[71]

The following pattern, if any, may be found in Dutch case law on the applicability of § 7 DCA. If the employer has to some extent specified the work's subject matter and the mode of expression at the time of contracting, § 7 DCA will be applicable. If the work has not been specified at the time of contracting, applicability of § 7 DCA may however be evidenced by the following circumstances:

- the work is made pursuant to specific instructions issued by the employer in the course of the employment relationship;
- the employee has a certain discretion in the performance of his duties;
- the creation of the work falls within the field of special expertise for which the employee has been hired;
- the employee has performed similar activities for the employer before, without stipulating additional remuneration;
- the employee has made use of the employer's financial, organizational and/or human resources to create the work (transfer of production and organizational risks to the employer);
- the employee had acknowledged before or during the creative process that the work would be subject to the employer's control;
- the work is tailor-made for use in the employer's business;

---

69. Verkade, *Een nog net niet verboden artikel*, at 1237, n. 13, does not interpret the publisher's contractual duty as an obligation not to exercise control, but as the executive's delegation of the right to control to the editorial staff, without any repercussions for the copyright ownership.

70. Judgment of May 27, 1992, Rb. 's-Gravenhage, Netherlands, 17 Informatierecht/AMI 94 (1993) note Quaedvlieg.

71. *Id.* at 94. The relevant circumstances: the plaintiffs had been trained as system designers at the employer's expense in the first 18 months of their employment, after which they were employed by the Support and Computerization Department. As members of this new department, they where expected to undertake the department's tasks, which had been circumscribed in general terms, in accordance with the PTT's general organization and information policy; during this initial period, the department would remain under the responsibility of the department for information system development; in the preparatory definition study the plaintiffs wrote that they were accountable to their superiors, which indicates that they considered the creation of the system to fall within their regular duties.

- the employee submitted the completed work to the employer's use for business purposes;[72]
- the employee's name is not identified on the work, and the employee has not made reservations as to authorship otherwise (transfer of associative risk to the employer);
- the employee did not negotiate for additional remuneration;
- the employer did not state that he considered the creation of the work to be beyond the scope of the employee's duties.[73]

While none of these circumstances are in itself determinative, their accumulation may convince a court that § 7 DCA was applicable. Only in the case of computer programs will a specific instruction issued by the employer during the employment relationship suffice in order for § 7 DCA to be applicable. Article 2(3) of the EC Software Directive provides that '[w]here a computer program is created by an employee in the execution of his duties *or following the instructions given by his employer*, the employer exclusively shall be entitled to exercise all economic rights in the program so created, unless otherwise provided by contract.' The Dutch government has taken the position that this provision is sufficiently covered by the present wording of § 7 DCA.[74]

7.5 Authorship of commissioned works in Dutch copyright law

Aside from § 7 DCA, which only applies to works made in the course of an employment relationship, the Dutch Copyright Act provides three other avenues via which hiring parties can become the author:

- co-authorship;[75]
- the hiring party's sole authorship if the work was made according to his plan and under his direction and supervision (§ 6 DCA);[76]

---

72. Compare in this respect Judgment of September 27, 1990, BGH, Germany, 93 GRUR 523, 525 (1991): unlike the research undertaken by the employees of a commercial enterprise, the results of the research undertaken by university professors are in general not intended for submission to the university for commercial or scientific purposes. *See also* Latman/Gorman/Ginsburg, Appendix, at 88: while academic writings may have been written by an employee within the scope of his employment, they may not have been prepared at the university's behest for its own use.

73. *See* Judgment of December 20, 1989, Ambt. Amsterdam, Netherlands, Computerrecht 141 (1990) (Kinders v. Gemeente Amsterdam): the head of the accounts department was relieved of all his other duties in order to concentrate on the introduction of a computerized bookkeeping system, consisting of a ledger system and a budgetary control system. When he announced a year later that he would be leaving the department, he suggested using the remaining two month-period to develop a computerized budgetary control system, but was ordered to give complete priority to the introduction of the computerized ledger system. He finally managed to make the ledger system operational as well as designing software for a budgetary control and account control system. The design of the budgetary control and account control systems was not held to be a part of his employment duties.

74. Statement of Minister of Justice, TK 1991-1992, 22531, no. 3, at 5.

75. *See also supra* 3.3.3.

76. *See also supra* 3.3.3.

- the hiring party's sole authorship on the basis of the first, lawful publication of the work without identification of the actual creator (§ 8 DCA).[77]

These three concepts of authorship are mostly invoked by hiring parties to prove title in cases in which they have failed to reach express agreement on copyright ownership and cannot obtain title on the basis of § 7 DCA. As a result of the Hoge Raad's restrictive interpretation, co-authorship claims and claims based on § 6 DCA are however rarely successful. In a judgment rendered in 1940, the Hoge Raad held that the originator of a work's basic concept may only be its author under the terms of § 6 DCA if he supervises the execution of his concept in such a way that the executor's contribution, although more or less creative and therefore not purely mechanical, cannot be described as constituting an individual creation.[78] On the basis of this restrictive interpretation of § 6 DCA, the courts have denied authorship to:

- a film producer who commissioned and supervised the composition of film music;[79]
- a translator who sub-contracted another to translate a novel according to his instructions and who subsequently modified the completed translation on minor points;[80]
- a professor who hired a researcher to carry out a specific research project and who supervised the writing of the report and modified and edited the end product;[81]
- a foundation which hired an audiovisual production company to produce an educational film on drug abuse;[82]
- a carnival society which organized a parade and fixed the route and the sequence of the participating floats and groups;[83]

The restrictive interpretation of the co-authorship concept has resulted in a similar string of negative decisions. In 1949, the Hoge Raad held that co-authorship can only occur if the degree of collaboration is such that the individual contributions can no longer be seen in isolation from the whole, so that they can not be the object of

---

77. *See* also *supra* 4.4, 6.3.
78. Judgment of June 28, 1940, HR, Netherlands, NJ 1941, 110, at 162-163, note Meijers ('Fire over England I'). *See also supra* 3.3.3 note 39 and accompanying text.
79. *Id. See also* Judgment of March 25, 1949, HR, Netherlands, NJ 1950, 643 note Veegens ('La Belle et la Bête').
80. Judgment of January 5, 1967, Ger. Amsterdam, Netherlands, *aff'd on other grounds* Judgment of November 17, 1967, HR, Netherlands, NJ 1968, 163 (Luitingh v. den Hollander).
81. Judgment of July 7, 1986, Pres.Rb. 's-Gravenhage, Netherlands, *rev'd on other grounds* Judgment of Judgment of October 14, 1987, Ger. 's-Gravenhage, Netherlands, NJ 1989, 220 (Rooijakkers v. Rijksuniversiteit Leiden).
82. Judgment of February 10, 1992, Pres.Rb. 's-Gravenhage, Netherlands, 17 Informatierecht/AMI 109 (1993) note Kabel ('Geen weg terug voor Jolanda').
83. Judgment of February 28, 1992, Pres.Rb. 's-Hertogenbosch, Netherlands, 16 Informatierecht/AMI 115 (1992) note Schuijt (Stichting Carnavalsviering Oss v. Stichting Lokale Televisie en Radio Omroep Oss).

separate artistic assessment in isolation from the whole.[84] This requirement of inseparability implies that contributions of a different kind could not constitute a work of co-authorship, even if they had been made in collaboration and merged into a unitary whole.[85] Hence, co-authorship was denied to the combination of film music and other contributions to a film work,[86] and to the lyrics and music of a song.[87]

More recent developments point to a more favourable attitude of the Dutch legislator and courts towards co-authorship of multi-professional collaborative works. In 1985, the Dutch Copyright Act was amended so as to specifically recognize the co-authorship of film works, thereby disqualifying the requirement of inseparability with respect to creative contributions to film works.[88] The diminished predictability resulting from the abolishment of the inseparability requirement has been mitigated by defining the 'authors of a film work' as the natural persons who made a contribution of a creative nature to and aimed at realizing the film work (§ 45a DCA).

Case law now also seems to be moving slowly towards the recognition of co-authorship of multi-disciplinary combinations. While the Hoge Raad, in a 1987 decision, was still reluctant to recognize co-authorship of contributions which were eligible for separate artistic assessment (a postage stamp with a portrait and typeface designed by different artists),[89] it specifically suggested the possibility of co-authorship in a 1990 case concerning a work, at least one of the contributions of which was eligible for separate, artistic assessment in isolation from the whole.[90]

> The Dutch publisher Kluwer commissioned the freelance photographer Lamoth to make photographs of needlework for publication in its needlework magazine 'Ariadne'. The magazine's editorial staff and stylist, who were employed by Kluwer, selected the objects and location and arranged the objects. The photographs were developed by Lamoth. Both Kluwer and Lamoth claimed authorship, Kluwer arguing that the photographs had been made according to the plan

---

84. Judgment of March 25, 1949, HR, Netherlands, NJ 1950, 643, note Veegens, at 1095 (La belle et la bête).

85. Critical about this consequence, Vermeijden, at 93; Verkade/Spoor, at 378; Attorney General Asser, NJ 1991, 377; Cohen Jehoram, 40 AA 75 (1991).

86. Judgment of March 25, 1949, HR, Netherlands, NJ 1950, 643 note Veegens ('La Belle et la bête').

87. Judgment of March 4, 1969, Pres.Rb. Amsterdam, Netherlands, NJ 1972, 319.

88. Act of May 30, 1985, S. 307. See supra 3.2. Attorney-General Asser, NJ 1991, 377, and Cohen Jehoram, 40 AA 75, 76 (1991), have both argued that this amendment abolished the inseparability requirement for all categories of works. But see Gerbrandy (1988), at 391, who continues to distinguish between co-authorship and authorship of film works.

89. Judgment of May 29, 1987, HR, Netherlands, NJ 1987, 1003 note Wichers Hoeth ('Beatrixpostzegel'): the Court of Appeal's decision that the publication of an enlarged version of a postage stamp with a modified, less subtle typeface had destroyed the artistic unity of the portrait and typeface and therefore infringed on the moral rights of both artists, was not, as the plaintiff alleged, based on a finding of co-authorship. The Court of Appeal did no more than decide that a mutilation of the artistic unity constitutes an infringement of both artists' moral rights. With this decision, the Hoge Raad ignored the conclusion of Attorney-General Franx, that the appellate court considered the postage stamp to be a work of co-authorship of which the contributions were not eligible for separate artistic assessment. NJ 1987, 1003, at 3496.

90. Judgment of June 1, 1990, HR, Netherlands, NJ 1990, 377 note Verkade (Kluwer v. Lamoth).

and under the direction and supervision of its employees (§§ 6 and 7 DCA). The District Court of Amsterdam held that Kluwer and Lamoth were co-authors.[91] The Amsterdam Court of Appeal reversed this decision and qualified Lamoth as the photographs' sole author.[92] The Hoge Raad, in its turn, reversed the decision in appeal, stating that the view that the creative labour involved in the arrangement of the objects is insufficient to constitute authorship or co-authorship, is generally incorrect. According to the Hoge Raad, the Copyright Act serves to protect the intellectual creation, as is also apparent from § 6 DCA, so that it is not merely decisive who made the tangible object in which this creation is expressed. As such, the authorship of a photograph may, under certain circumstances, be based completely or in part on the selection and arrangement of the objects.[93] In this decision, the Hoge Raad paved the way for the recognition, on remand, of Kluwer's sole authorship on the basis of § 6 DCA or Kluwer's and Lamoth's co-authorship. The case never got to this stage, however, because it was settled out-of-court after the Hoge Raad's decision.[94]

Several commentators have argued that *Kluwer v. Lamoth* marked the Hoge Raad's departure from its inseparability requirement, which it replaced by the requirement that the co-authors must have the intention of merging their contributions into a unitary whole.[95] The arrangement of the objects was indeed eligible for separate artistic assessment, but the development of the photographs was not. It therefore remains to be seen whether the courts are willing to recognize co-authorship in those situations in which each individual contribution to the work is eligible for separate artistic assessment, as is the case with the text and photographs of a magazine article. The fact that the Hoge Raad suggested that co-authorship might be possible in the *Kluwer v. Lamoth* case however seems to indicate that the individual contributions need not be eligible for copyright protection in isolation from the whole in order to qualify for co-authorship.[96]

---

91. Judgment of November 27, 1985, Rb. Amsterdam, Netherlands, 15 Informatierecht/AMI 7 (1991) note Spoor.

92. Judgment of April 7, 1988, Ger. Amsterdam, Netherlands, NJ 1991, 377.

93. NJ 1991, 377, at 1614, 1615. Spoor, 15 Informatierecht/AMI 12 (1991), suggests that this statement could constitute a basis for recognizing authorship of performances.

94. *See* NJ 1991, 377, at 1618.

95. Cohen Jehoram, 40 AA 75 (1991); Thole, at 119. Verkade, NJ 1991, 377, at 1617, argues that, without departing from the old inseparability requirement, Kluwer's arrangement of the objects might be considered to be an independent work of authorship and Lamoth's photographic development of the objects a reproduction which, if found to be sufficiently creative, might qualify as a derivative work. Verkade apparently disregards the element of collaboration between Lamoth and Kluwer's employees. I would argue that, if his contribution is sufficiently creative, Lamoth deserves to have an ownership interest in the contribution made by Kluwer's employees (and Kluwer in his).

96. Compare Gerbrandy (1992), at 37, 38, questioning whether a person with a lively imagination who hires another person to write an exciting novel on the basis of his fantasies, should not become co-author. Co-authorship was denied in Judgment of October 25, 1989, Ger. 's-Hertogenbosch, Netherlands, 58 BIE 223 (1990) (Verhoeven v. Van den Broek): a production company hired to

All in all, *Kluwer v. Lamoth* seems to have expanded the opportunities for commissioning parties to claim co-authorship of works made by independent contractors, thereby overthrowing the certainty which independent contractors have had for years that Dutch courts do not recognize co-authorship easily. Since a work of joint authorship can only be exploited by the collective co-owners,[97] co-authorship implies that an independent contractor is risking an action on account of infringement if he decides to exploit a co-authored work himself. It also means, however, that a commissioning party cannot address an infringement action brought by an independent contractor simply by claiming co-authorship.[98] This, combined with the fact that co-authorship is still not very predictable, means that an express agreement regulating copyright ownership is still the safest way for both commissioning parties and independent contractors to control the exploitation of the work.

More than through their own creative contribution to the work, commissioning parties have been considered to be the author on the basis of the fact that they published the work legitimately as a legal entity without mentioning the name of the actual creator as author (§ 8 DCA). This authorship rule may lead to unpleasant surprises for independent contractors, especially in the case of works which do not by nature give the name of the actual creator, such as advertisements, business cards, corporate designs, designs for packaging, etc.[99] If an advertising agency or design studio creates such a work, commercial practice will imply that the party commissioning the work is authorized to disclose it, even if there are no explicit stipulations to this effect.[100] The commissioning party's disclosure of such a work is therefore lawful in the sense of § 8 DCA.[101] More in general, the nature of the relationship between an independent contractor and a commissioning party may

---

make an industrial film sub-contracted other producer who made the film, not on the basis of the production company's script, but on a script written by an independent contractor. The production company was not co-author of the film. For a more detailed discussion of this case, see *infra* 7.6.

97. Van Lingen, at 28.

98. *But see* the District Court's decision in *Kluwer v. Lamoth*, Judgment of November 27, 1985, 15 Informatierecht/AMI 7 (1991) note Spoor, *rev'd on other grounds* Judgment of April 7, 1988, Ger. Amsterdam, NJ 1991, 377, *rev'd* Judgment of June 1, 1990, HR, Netherlands, NJ 1991, 377: the relationship between co-authors is governed by the principles of good faith and reason. Under the circumstances, Lamoth's refusal to authorize the additional exploitation was unreasonable, because he would probably not have been able to exploit the photographs individually without Kluwer's descriptions of the needlework, and because a refusal would have unreasonably restricted Kluwer's commercial activities. Kluwer nevertheless acted 'tortiously' under Dutch law by going ahead with the exploitation without compensating Lamoth. The damages were based on the compensation which Lamoth could have negotiated. *See also supra* 3.3.2 note 32 and accompanying text.

99. *See also supra* 4.4.

100. Judgment of June 4, 1980, Ger. Amsterdam, Netherlands, 49 BIE 239 (1981) (Van den Biggelaar v. Katholieke Universiteit Nijmegen); Judgment of February 21, 1992, Pres.Rb. 's-Gravenhage, Netherlands, 60 BIE 393 (1992) ('brochures'). *Cf. also* Judgment of October 12, 1981, Pres.Rb. Utrecht, Netherlands, 51 BIE 79 (1983) (HWK v. Volmac): the question whether an advertiser is the author of advertising material made by advertising agency *ex* § 8 DCA need not be answered, because the agreement between the advertiser and the agency already implied that the advertiser had the right to use the material, even after the termination of their relationship.

101. *See* Judgment of June 4, 1980, Ger. Amsterdam, Netherlands, 49 BIE 239 (1981) (Van den Biggelaar v. Katholieke Universiteit Nijmegen).

imply that the latter has a right to use the work.[102] To therefore prevent the commissioning party being deemed the work's author under § 8 DCA, the independent contractor must ensure that he is referred to as the author on or in relation to the work,[103] or that he claims authorship in another explicit manner.

Industrial designs may lead to a similar unpleasant surprise for independent contractors. The Benelux Designs and Models Act provides that, unless agreed otherwise, the party who commissions a design for commercial purposes is considered its 'designer' and, as such, holds the copyright to the design.[104] If an independent contractor wishes to retain his rights, he must therefore claim 'designership' or reserve copyright ownership in his agreement with the commissioning party.

Although theoretically creators should be aware, from § 8 DCA and the Benelux Models and Designs Act, that they must claim authorship credit or reserve copyright ownership when they work on commission, the sanction for not doing so - the forfeiture of all the rights to the work - would seem to be unnecessarily onerous in those cases in which the commissioning party has not assumed responsibility for the organizational and associative risks involved in the work's creation and publication.[105]

7.6 The allocation of rights in audiovisual works

According to American copyright law, the rights to audiovisual works are allocated on the basis of the 'creator' doctrine, unless the 'work made for hire' rule is applicable. If an employee makes a creative contribution to an audiovisual work within the scope of his employment, the employer is considered to be the author of that contribution (§§ 101(1), 201(b) USCA). If the contribution is commissioned for use as part of an audiovisual work, and the parties have agreed in a written instrument that the work shall be deemed a 'work made for hire', the commissioning party is considered to be the author of that contribution (§§ 101(2), 201(b) USCA). If the contribution to an audiovisual work does not qualify as a 'work made for hire',

---

102. *See* Gerbrandy (1988), at 56; Spoor/Verkade, at 41. *See also* Judgment of September 12, 1984, Rb. Breda, Netherlands, KG 1984, 312: as managing partner of a company during its establishment and later as its manager, the plaintiff must have cooperated in publishing the logo which he created. The company's publication without reference to his name as author was lawful in the sense of § 8 DCA. *Cf. also* Judgment of June 12, 1985, Ger. 's-Gravenhage, Netherlands, 53 BIE 15 (1985) ('Onderzoek binnenvaart'): the plaintiff was the (co)author of scientific models, but since he developed some of the models during his employment contract with the defendant and some after the termination of that employment relationship in return for a sizeable fee from the defendant, and since he was aware that the parties who hired the defendant to conduct research on their behalf usually acquired the rights in the results, he could not invoke his copyright against the defendant's use of the models for other research projects.

103. *See e.g.* Judgment of July 18, 1984, Rb. Middelburg, Netherlands, NJ 1985, 882 (1985): the defendant, the local government of Goes commissioned the plaintiff to design a flower box. The plaintiff submitted newspaper articles about the flower boxes, in which he was referred to as the designer, as evidence of his authorship. Even if these articles were not based on the defendant's press release, the defendant must have informed the press in some other way that the plaintiff had designed the flower boxes. § 8 DCA not applicable.

104. §§ 6, 23 Benelux Designs and Models Act. *See also supra* 4.2 note 7.

105. *See also supra* 4.2.

either because there is no work-for-hire agreement[106] or because the contribution was made at the creator's own initiative, the contributor is considered to be the author and the first owner of the copyright to his contribution.

The above implies that the creative contributors to a film can assess their ownership situation by categorizing their relationship with their contractual partner. If it is an employment relationship, they can only secure ownership by making an express stipulation to that effect (§ 201(b) USCA) but if it is a commissioning party-independent contractor relationship, they must ensure that they do not sign any work-for-hire or transfer agreement if they wish to retain ownership.[107]

Dutch and German copyright legislation adopt a different approach when allocating rights in audiovisual works. All special ownership provisions relating to audiovisual works allocate rights to the 'film producer' (in Dutch: the 'producent van het filmwerk'[108] and in German: the 'Filmhersteller').[109] This applies not only to the statutory presumption of transfer (§ 45d DCA; § 89 GCA) but also to the neighbouring right to the first fixation of a film (§ 94; 95 GCA).[110]

It is important to know who this 'producer' is, not only for the creative contributors but also for those involved in the financial, organizational or technical side of the film production. However, in the case of more or less complex contractor-subcontractor situations (e.g. A hires B, B hires C, C hires D and C and D make the film), it may not be easy to identify the 'producer' (or co-producers). For anyone with high stakes in the production of a film, it may therefore be quite hazardous to rely on the statutory presumption of transfer of § 89 GCA and § 45d DCA.

In case of contractor-subcontractor situations, the concentration of rights in the 'producer' has another repercussion. Under Dutch copyright law, the authors of a film work can only rebut the presumption of transfer by entering into a written

---

106. *See* Effects Associates v. Cohen, 908 F.2d 555 (9th Cir. 1990), *cert. denied* 111 S.Ct. 1003 (1991).

107. Compare in this respect, Schiller & Schmidt v. Nordisco Corporation, 908 F.2d 555 (9th Cir. 1990), discussed *supra* 6.3, in which the court required that the work-for-hire agreement be signed prior to the creation of the work. This decision seems to undercut the practice in the American film industry to purchase scripts on 'spec', i.e. finished scripts written at the writer's initiative. Under U.S. law, both producers and screenwriters have an interest in treating these scripts as 'works made for hire', because the producer will be considered the 'author' and the writer, as an 'employee', may invoke the terms of the collective bargaining agreement for screenwriters. In view of the *CCNV* and *Schiller* decisions, it is however doubtful whether these scripts can still be considered works made for hire. Compare in this respect Nimmer, § 5.03[B]: a work is 'specially ordered or commissioned' if the impetus for the creation came from someone other than the creator.

108. § 45a DCA. It is however possible to allocate rights to the employer or legal entity under Dutch law. The Copyright Act designates as authors of a filmwork, *without prejudice to § 7 and § 8 DCA*, the natural persons who made a creative contribution to and aimed at the realization of the film work (§ 45a DCA). *See also supra* 3.2.2.

109. §§ 89, 94 GCA.

110. § 94 GCA: 'Filmhersteller'. Section § 95 GCA provides that § 94 GCA is also applicable to non-copyrightable films. *See also* the Memorandum of Reply to the Dutch bill implementing the EC Rental Directive, TK 1993-1994, 23 246, no. 5, at 27.

agreement to this effect with the 'producer' (§ 45d DCA).[111] In order to retain their rights, the authors must therefore contract with the 'producer'. In a complex contractor-subcontractor relationship, this may very well be someone other than the person who actually hired them.[112]

The legislative history of both the Dutch and German Copyright Acts indicate that the status of 'film producer' does not require a creative contribution.[113] The Dutch Copyright Act defines the 'producer of the film work' as the natural person or legal entity who or which is responsible for the realization of the film work with a view to its exploitation (§ 45a DCA). According to legislative history, the film producer's essential task is to provide capital, run financial risks and hire the creative contributors to the film.[117] The German Copyright Act does not define the term 'producer', but it is clear from the Memorandum to the Act that the film producer qualifies for neighbouring rights because of his financial risks and his organizational activities.[118] The EC Rental Directive refers to organization, economic risk and financial and contractual responsibility as indicators for the capacity of film producer.[119] While there is therefore general agreement that the capacity of film producer presupposes financial, organizational and contractual responsibilities, it is not entirely clear who the producer is if these responsibilities are distributed amongst different parties.

In a 1969 decision concerning the Nazi propaganda film 'Triumph des Willens', the German Bundesgerichtshof described the task of the 'film producer' as providing capital, selecting and acquiring rights to underlying material, hiring creative and technical contributors, providing other facilities, supervising the production until the exploitable film is completed, and contracting in his own name and at his own expense.[120] According to the court, the 'film producer' is the person who makes

---

111. The remuneration for every mode of exploitation guaranteed to film authors under § 45d DCA must also be agreed with the 'producer' in a written instrument (§ 45d DCA). It is unclear what happens if the authors do not agree on the remuneration in a written instrument with the 'producer'. See supra 2.15 notes 335-336 and accompanying text.

112. See Judgment of December 24, 1993, Pres.Rb. Amsterdam, Netherlands, KG 1994, 42 ('Hoffman's Honger'): agreements between film actors and the casting company hired by the film producer cannot rebut the presumption of § 45d DCA (applicable to film actors pursuant to § 4 WNR). See also supra 6.2.2. note 18.

113. See Memorandum to § 85, 89, 94 GCA, 45 UFITA 265 (1965); Memorandum to § 45a DCA, TK 1980-1981, 16740, no. 3-4, at 12; TK 1988-1989, 21244, no. 3, at 4. See also Judgment of October 22, 1992, BGH, Germany, 95 GRUR 472, 473 (1993) ('film producer').

117. TK 1980-1981, 16740, no. 3-4, at 12.

118. 45 UFITA 265 (1965). See Judgment of October 22, 1992, BGH, Germany, 95 GRUR 472 (1993) ('film producer'), referring to the assumption of the economic responsibility and organizational activities necessary for realizing the completed, exploitable film.

119. COM(90) 586 final - SYN 319, at 40.

120. Judgment of January 10, 1969, BGH, Germany, 55 UFITA 313, 320 (1970). Leni Riefenstahl made the film 'Triumph des Willens' in 1934 at the request of Adolph Hitler. She licensed UfA to distribute the film on behalf of Hitler's party NSDAP, in return for 50% of the gross receipts and a DM 300,000 guarantee to cover the production costs. The film was confiscated by the Russians in 1945, and later transferred to the government of the former German Democratic Republic. The defendant used parts of the film for a documentary he made in 1960. His German distributor acquired a license from Riefenstahl for West Germany and for Austria. For several other countries, the defendant acquired a license from the East German government. The plaintiff, to whom Riefenstahl had transferred her alleged rights for these other countries, claimed damages

a film as a result of these activities, and who needs rights to exploit it.[121] It is irrelevant whether this exploitation consists of distributing copies or of granting distribution rights to a distribution company.[122] In a decision rendered in 1992, the Bundesgerichtshof re-affirmed this interpretation of 'film producer', adding that the 'film producer' is not the natural person who actually performs these activities, but the natural person or legal entity (employer/enterprise) to whom these activities can be attributed.[123]

The Bundesgerichtshof does not require the producer to bear the financial risk personally, but merely that he provides capital through contracts with third party investors.[124] Dutch case law also seems to indicate that the fact that a commissioning party undertakes to pay a fee covering the production costs upon delivery of the work, does not preclude the commissioned party from being qualified as the 'producer'.[125] In the relation between the commissioned party and a subcontractor, however, the allocation of financial risks may be considered relevant in determining which one of them qualifies as 'producer'.

> A foundation had hired the advertising agency Reclameteam Verhoeven B.V. to make a video. After having done some preparatory work and after the foundation had rejected the initial script, the agency sub-contracted video producer Van den Broek to make the film on the basis of a new script. Van den Broek found a script writer and shot the film. The agency subsequently brought injunction proceedings to order Van den Broek to make the original tapes available for copying and to prevent Van den Broek from publishing or reproducing the film. The Court of Appeal qualified the agency as producer on the basis of the following circumstances: it had undertaken the obligation to make the film; it had reached agreement with the foundation that it would recoup some of the production costs from the sale of distribution copies; the agency maintained responsibility for realizing the film with a view to its

---

for the screening of the documentary in these other countries. The defendant argued that not Riefenstahl, but the NSDAP was the producer. The Bundesgerichtshof did not consider it necessary to decide on the question whether Riefenstahl qualified as 'producer', because in either case the rights to the film had been implicitly transferred to the NSDAP as commissioning party.

121. Id. at 320.

122. Id.

123. Judgment of October 22, 1992, BGH, Germany, 95 GRUR 472, 472 (1993) ('film producer'): the provision that the enterprise in which the phonogram is made must be considered the 'phonogram producer' (§ 85(1) GCA), is of analogous application to the meaning of 'film producer' in § 94 GCA. See also Nordemann/Hertin, at 376; Schricker/Katzenberger, at 1007.

124. Id. at 473.

125. See Judgment of February 10, 1992, Pres.Rb. 's-Gravenhage, Netherlands, 17 Informatierecht/ AMI 109 (1993) note Kabel ('Geen weg terug voor Jolanda'): a foundation paid an audiovisual production company NLG 210,000 to produce an educational film on drug abuse. Oral agreement. In the absence of any evidence to the contrary, the production company must be considered to be the 'producer' in the sense of § 45d DCA. See also Spoor/Verkade, at 468. But see Kabel, 17 Informatierecht/AMI 110 (1993): the party who is commissioned to produce a film about a certain topic should not be considered the 'producer' if the commissioning party pays for all the produc-ti-on costs with the apparent aim of reproducing and distributing the film.

exploitation, because it paid both Van den Broek and the script writer, so that the writer must be considered to have been hired by the agency at Van den Broek's recommendation; the agency submitted locations which might be suitable for filming. The fact that the agency was not involved in the actual shooting was not considered to be relevant.[126]

The court emphasized that the agency did and Van den Broek did not run financial risk. This fact, combined with the fact that it was not the agency but the foundation which assumed the major financial risks, seems to suggest that assuming the financial risk is not sufficient in itself, but may result in 'producership' if combined with organizational and contractual activities. The dividing line between mere contractorship, co-producership and producership remains blurred in this system, however.

It is clear that the American 'work for hire' rule provides more predictability in this respect. Contrary to the Dutch and German systems however, the 'work for hire' rule does not necessarily concentrate all rights in one person. Imagine that A commissions B to produce a film, that B subcontracts C and D, that C writes the script and that D's employees E and F direct, shoot and edit the film. The contributions made by E and F are works made for hire. The contributions by C and D are works made for hire if both C and D sign a work-for-hire agreement with B. Only in that case will all rights be statutorily allocated to B.

In the 'concentration of rights' approach of the Dutch and German copyright laws, maximum predictability may arguably be achieved by allocating ownership to the person responsible for hiring the creative and technical contributors, contracting with the holders of rights to existing works and hiring the suppliers of technical facilities, *and* who is the first person in line who needs to acquire title to the completed, exploitable film in order to recoup his own investments or to comply with his contractual obligations vis-à-vis third parties (bank, distribution company, commissioning party, etc). In the above-mentioned example, this person would be B.

7.7 Conclusions

Rules which allocate rights to producers can only meet their objectives of improving security and efficiency if it is clear when they are applicable and, consequently, when they provide a safe alternative to a written transfer. It is also necessary for special ownership rules to be predictable in order for creators to know what they must do in order to retain rights to their works. I have discussed case law on the provisions in American, Dutch and German copyright legislation which allocate rights to producers from this perspective: the predictability of copyright ownership. I have in particular examined the judicial interpretation of the terms 'employee' in

---

126. Judgment of October 25, 1989, Ger. 's-Hertogenbosch, Netherlands, 58 BIE 223 (1990) (Verhoeven v. Van den Broek').

§ 101(1) USCA, 'specific works' in § 7 DCA and 'producer' in § 45a DCA and § 89 GCA.

Creators and producers can maximize security by regulating ownership in a written agreement before commencing the creative process. However, aside from § 101(2) USCA, which allows the parties to vest authorship in the producer in certain cases by signing a work-for-hire agreement, all special allocation rules in the American, Dutch and German copyright systems are designed to allocate rights to producers *in the absence* of a written agreement, which means that their applicability is dependent on criteria other than the existence of a written agreement.

These criteria are most predictable if they depend on circumstances which can be established before the creative process commences: is the producer in the regular business of creating works of the type purchased; does the creator only work for this particular producer; is the work created pursuant to a specific order issued by the producer, etc., etc. The analysis of the case law has however demonstrated that most judicial decisions on the applicability of special allocation rules are based on an overall evaluation of the circumstances of the case before, during and after the creative process.

There would however seem to be a consensus that this evaluation should not involve the producer's *creative* input. Although one might perhaps argue that it is more acceptable to allocate rights to a producer if he has exercised a certain creative control, the consequences of special ownership rules (e.g. employer is 'author') are too far-reaching for the parties to wait until after the work has been created to find out whether the producer has exercised sufficient creative control in order for such a rule to be applicable.

The producer's creative involvement, on the other hand, must be taken into account if he claims co-authorship or sole authorship on the basis of his plan for the work and his direction of the creative process (cf. § 6 DCA). As elaborations of the creator doctrine, these concepts of authorship are based on creative input and, strictly speaking, should be applied irrespective of the parties' views on the legal status of their contributions. In order to protect independent contractors against unexpected co-authorship claims by commissioning parties, American courts and politicians have tried to introduce the requirement that the parties must have expressed their intention to treat the merger of their contributions as a work of co-authorship. So far this departure from the creator doctrine has not met with general approval in case law and Congress, however.

In Dutch copyright law, the scope for producers to claim co-authorship (directly or indirectly via their employees' contributions) would seem to have expanded. Although co-authorship of multi-disciplinary collaborative projects has been statutorily recognized with respect to contributions to film works only, case law would seem to be moving away from the old 'inseparability test' towards the general recognition of co-authorship of multi-disciplinary combinations. The definition of 'author of a film work' in § 45a DCA may perhaps serve as a guideline for developing this new co-authorship concept. Under this provision, the contributors to a film can only become the author of that film if their contributions have been specifically made for that film.

In the final paragraph of this Chapter, I have discussed the allocation of rights in audiovisual works. According to American law, the allocation of rights in audiovisual works depends on the applicability of the 'work for hire' rule and, consequently, on the nature of the relationship between the contributor and the party who contracts with him to acquire rights to his contribution (employment, commission, purchase of rights to pre-existing work). This system differs from the Dutch and German copyright systems, which both allocate rights to the 'film producer', being the person who hires the creative contributors to the film and who is financially and organizationally responsible for the realization of the film work.

Although these two systems will in many cases lead to the same results, the Dutch and German systems concentrate ownership in the completed film, which is not necessarily the case under the American system. The American system, however, may be more predictable in cases in which the financial, organizational and contractual responsibilities are distributed amongst different parties and, consequently, in which it is difficult to identify the 'film producer'.

Chapter 8

Conclusions

8.1 Brief conclusions

THE CREATOR DOCTRINE

In the first chapter of this study, I introduced the *creator doctrine* as the basic rule for allocating copyright ownership: copyright initially vests in the creator of a work. In order to facilitate a comparative study of the American, Dutch and German copyright systems, I defined the term 'creator' as the originator of a work eligible for copyright protection under the applicable law, and the 'author' ('Urheber' or 'maker') as the natural or legal person who or which is considered the initial copyright owner under the applicable law. According to the creator doctrine, the terms 'creator' and 'author' are synonymous.

If copyright vests in the creator, the title to exploit a work must be derived from the creator. By granting exclusive or non-exclusive rights, creators are thus able to lay down terms for the use of their works by others. Most copyright systems however provide rules which depart from this basic mechanism of copyright law by directly allocating rights to the person who seeks to exploit a work. In this study, I have examined the motives behind these special allocation rules and discussed the various methods which the American, Dutch and German copyright systems have for allocating rights to persons other than the creator of the work.

Proceeding on the assumption that legislatures generally only allocate exclusive rights to the creator or to someone who has a certain relationship with the creator, I have focused primarily on the allocation of rights between the creator and the natural or legal person who or which enters into a contractual relationship with the creator in order to acquire title to the work. For the purposes of this study, I have referred to this person as the 'producer'.

THE HISTORICAL DEVELOPMENT OF THE CREATOR DOCTRINE

In order to explain the creator doctrine in its continental-European and Anglo-American manifestations, I have devoted the second chapter of the study to a discussion of the origins of the creator doctrine and the way it has been elaborated in the present American, Dutch and German copyright laws. We have seen how the protection against the reprinting of books gradually evolved from printing privileges granted to publishers into a statutorily-recognized exclusive right of the author to his literary work. In this transition period, in which the protection against copying became institutionalized and more dependent on the author's cooperation, hybrid forms of protection occurred, such as privileges granted to authors and statutory protection of publishers.

In 1710, Queen Anne of England enacted a statute which recognized an exclusive right of the author or his assignee to print a book for a certain period of time. This recognition of the author as the beneficiary of protection did not fundamentally change the relationship between authors and publishers, because an author was still considered to have assigned his copyright upon handing over the manuscript. The major shift in focus from publisher to author, however, occurred when, in the footsteps of *John Locke*, theorists proclaimed that every man has a natural right to the fruits of his intellectual labour. While, in continental Europe, this idea gradually developed into a statutorily-recognized author's right upon creation with economic and moral aspects, any attempt to gain statutory recognition for such a concept was long doomed to failure in Anglo-American countries.

English and American courts had decided at an early stage that, although authors may have a right to prevent the disclosure of their works in common law, the statute is the only source of protection once a work has been made public. In the United States of America, this view was inspired by the constitutional mandate given to Congress to 'promote the Progress of Science and useful Arts, by securing for limited Times to Authors and Inventors the exclusive Right to their respective Writings and Discoveries'. Because of this incentive rationale, copyright legislation focused on making the work available to the public rather than on creation. Protection could be secured by any person who, with the creator's authorization, published a work for the first time in compliance with statutory formalities. It was not until the adoption of the Copyright Act of 1976 and the ratification of the Berne Convention in 1989, that the United States fully abandoned this system and embraced the creator doctrine as the general rule for the allocation of copyright ownership. Copyright now automatically vests in the 'author' upon creation, and the 'author' is the natural person who created the work. There is one major exception to this rule, however, which covers a considerable proportion of all the works created: in the case of works made by employees within the scope of employment as well as in the case of nine specified categories of commissioned works which have been designated as a 'work made for hire' in a written instrument signed by the parties, the employer or commissioning party is considered author and initial copyright owner (the 'work made for hire' doctrine).

Under the influence of the idea that the fruits of intellectual labour belong to their originator and are indissolubly linked with their originator as expressions of his personality, continental European copyright legislation is generally more loyal to the creator doctrine than Anglo-American copyright legislation. The unbreakable bond between creator and work has been recognized most explicitly in the German Act of 1965 on Author's Right and Related Rights. Under the terms of this Act, the author's right vests in the author ('Urheber'), defined as the person who created the work. On the basis of the idea that the creator's intellectual and economic interests in the work are inter-related, both the moral and economic rights are considered inalienable as long as the creator is alive. A work can be exploited on the basis of a constitutive grant of a 'right to use' which the grantee may invoke vis-à-vis third parties if it is exclusive.

Adopted as it was at a time when the debate on the theoretical basis of moral rights and their relation to the author's economic rights was still in full swing, the Dutch Act of 1912 on Author's Right reflects a more pragmatic approach. Aside from certain specified moral rights, a copyright can be assigned in full. Ownership vests in the 'author' (in Dutch: the 'maker'), the work's actual creator. If the work was however made by an employee within the scope of employment or if it was lawfully published by or under the auspices of a legal entity without mentioning a natural person as its author, the employer or legal entity is considered to be the 'author'.

ALLOCATION OF RIGHTS IN WORKS OF AUTHORSHIP IN THE LIGHT OF THE ALLOCATION OF RISKS BETWEEN CREATORS AND PRODUCERS

In order to benefit from his work, a creator must ensure that his work is marketable, that it is being distributed and that he controls the distribution. In most cases, the creator is dependent on a producer to organize these activities. In his relationship with the producer, a creator may bring in his legal position as first copyright owner to stipulate adequate compensation and creative control during and after the creative process. Producers, in their turn, are dependent on creators to create new works and to acquire title in order to be able to control the distribution of these works. While copyright is thus an important means for creators to benefit from the fruits of their works, it is also traditionally the basis on which producers found their business.

It follows that it is in the interests of both parties that the production and distribution are organized as adequately as possible. At best, the person responsible for the production and distribution should have exclusive, transferable and enforceable rights to the work. As we have seen in Chapter 3, however, the creator doctrine poses many obstacles to the acquisition of such exclusive, transferable and enforceable rights. Problems may occur if there is uncertainty about the identity of the author(s), the nationality and term of protection, the possibility of conflicting transfers, the scope, exclusivity and duration of the transfer, the author's right to exercise inalienable rights and, in Dutch copyright law in particular, about the effects of exclusive licences on third parties.

These uncertainties are likely to increase if the product involves multiple creative contributions, if the work does not yet exist at the time of contracting, if it is distributed internationally, if it requires regular updating, and if the nature of the business requires the producer to repeat the process of acquiring title with great frequency. As modern techniques facilitate the combining of creative contributions (multimedia) and seem to take away any barrier to wide-scale distribution that may still exist (electronic highway), these factors will increasingly characterize the production and distribution of creative works.

The more uncertainties there are, the higher the costs will be for producers to establish title vis-à-vis financiers, buyers and infringers. Where possible, these

163

costs should be cut by measures which do not directly affect the creator's ability to dictate terms in his agreement with the producer, e.g. by making the nationality of collaborative works dependent on the producer's country of domicile. The more radical measure of statutorily allocating rights to a producer is appropriate only in those cases in which the creator's chances of negotiating separately on each of these rights are limited *de facto*, while the producer is running considerable risks in the case of defective title. This will in particular be the case if, before commencing the creative process, the producer has undertaken to pay for the costs of creation (*production risk*), if the marketability of the work is largely a result of his organizational efforts (*organizational risk*) and if the work is presented or by its nature perceived by the public as originating in the producer rather than the actual creator (*associative risk*).

In chapter 4, I have examined to which extent the allocation of these risks between creator and producer is reflected in the American, Dutch and German provisions on ownership. All three copyright systems allocate rights to an employer in the case of works made by an employee within the scope of employment. In other cases, rights are allocated to producers if they are likely to assume responsibility not only for the production but also for the organizational risks, i.e. if the work is made at the producer's expense and the value of the work is dependent on the producer's organizational investments to transform the work into a marketable product. All three copyright systems thus allocate exclusive rights to producers in the case of commissioned contributions to film works. The American and German copyright systems also allocate rights to publishers in the case of certain commissioned contributions to larger publishing projects, such as supplementary works and contributions to periodicals, compilations and educational works. The absence of similar provisions in the Dutch Copyright Act may explain why Dutch publishers are seeking statutory neighbouring rights for their own financial and organizational contributions.

None of the three copyright systems differentiate between the various categories of works on the basis of originality only. The fact that a certain category reflects little authorship tends to influence the legislature's decision to allocate rights to the producer, but only in those cases in which the producer assumes responsibility for the production and organizational risks.

THE ALLOCATION OF RIGHTS TO PRODUCERS UNDER THE AMERICAN, DUTCH AND GERMAN COPYRIGHT SYSTEMS

Most modern copyright systems are based on a combination of the incentive rationale and 'felt justice'. Aside from the economic importance of the copyright industries, these two rationales form the strongest possible justification for copyright protection. Differences between the copyright systems may still exist however where the various legislators commit themselves to one of these rationales. Of the three countries covered by this study, the incentive rationale is still most visible in American copyright law, while, more than the American and Dutch systems, the German copyright system is based on the idea that author's rights are a matter of justice rather than the outcome of a political weighing up of interests.

These differences between the American, Dutch and German copyright systems are not so much reflected in the situations in which they allocate rights to producers, but more in the methods with which and the extent to which they do this. In Chapters 5 and 6, I have discussed the theoretical and practical ramifications of these various methods for allocating rights to producers. German copyright law rejects the attribution of copyright ownership to producers on the basis of the view that statutory copyright protection is a confirmation of a creator's natural right to his work and therefore automatically vests in the creator. Instead, German law allocates rights to producers via statutory and judicial presumptions on the scope and exclusivity of grants of rights to use in case of doubt. Producers' interests are granted further protection via an extensive package of neighbouring rights.

In the United States, the statutory regulation of the scope of transfers runs counter to a deep-rooted commitment to contractual freedom. Rather than regulating the scope of transfers, therefore, the 1976 Copyright Act reflects an all-or-nothing approach to balancing the interests of creators and producers. The interests of producers are accommodated by treating them as authors in the case of 'works made for hire', while in the case of works other than 'works made for hire' creators' interests are accommodated by allowing them to terminate transfers of copyright ownership 35 years after the right was granted. As long as the constitutional objective of promoting the progress of science and the arts remains the primary objective of copyright protection, the U.S. Congress will have more discretion to define authorship than it would have if copyright were primarily seen as a natural reward for creators.

The allocation of rights to producers under Dutch copyright law is traditionally based on attribution of authorship, although less drastic methods, such as statutory presumptions of assignment and neighbouring rights have been introduced more recently. In spite of an ongoing discussion in legal doctrine on the question of who should be entitled to moral rights protection in the event that the employer is considered to be the 'author', the Dutch legislature has so far not considered it necessary to amend the provision which attributes authorship to employers, nor has it excluded those works of which an employer is considered author from moral rights protection. In Chapter 5, I discussed this issue of authorship and moral rights protection as part of a larger discussion on the imperativeness of the 'creator' doctrine and, consequently, on the admissibility of attributing initial copyright ownership to producers.

THE IMPERATIVENESS OF THE CREATOR DOCTRINE

Although the creator doctrine is generally accepted as the basic principle for attributing copyright ownership, its application is not equally imperative in every situation. Creators need initial copyright ownership in order to negotiate their share of the economic fruits of their works and to stipulate conditions for the use of their works by others. The more a creator transfers the production, organizational and associative risks to a producer, however, the less effective his ownership status will become when negotiating remuneration and other conditions for the use of his work. The benefits which creators may derive from initial copyright ownership therefore differ from case to case.

Aside from the practical argument that creators need initial copyright owner-ship in order to negotiate terms for the use of their works, it is often argued that the creator doctrine is imperative because of the personal bond between the creator and his work. According to the monistic concept of author's rights, the bond between the creator and his work requires that the author's right as a whole is vested in the creator and that it remains vested in the creator during his life. In Chapter 5, I have argued that it is possible to distinguish between ownership of exploitation rights and the entitlement to the moral rights of attribution and integrity.

An author's right to object to the mutilation of his work or any other deroga-tory action in relation to his work which would be prejudicial to his honour or reputation (the right of integrity), is in my view a recognition of every person's interest in respect for his personal integrity in the specific situation in which he has expressed his *persona* in a work of authorship. Although this interest may be protected by exercising ownership of the exclusive right of adaptation, it may also find protection under other theories such as contracts or torts law or constitutional provisions guaranteeing the right of privacy and freedom of expression. The nature of the protection implies that a creator's ability to invoke this protection should not depend on whether he is considered 'author' and first owner for the purposes of the copyright law, but on whether the work reflects on his person. Similarly, a producer (natural person *or* legal entity) should be able to invoke this protection, not because he is deemed the 'author' under the copyright law, but because his identity, corporate or otherwise, is expressed in the work as a result of which the use of the work reflects on his reputation.

Although the right to claim authorship (the right of attribution) may be considered to be an exclusive right to the work, the ownership of this right does not necessarily need to be reserved for the person who is vested with the exploitation rights to the work. It should be possible to vest exploitation rights in the producer, while the creator is granted the right of attribution. In that case the producer could be qualified as the 'first owner of the exclusive rights of exploitation' and the creator as the 'author'. By designating employers and legal entities as 'authors', however, the Dutch legislator has apparently chosen to allocate the exploitation rights and the right of attribution to one entity.

THE PRACTICAL IMPLICATIONS OF ATTRIBUTION OF AUTHORSHIP AND PRESUMPTIONS OF TRANSFER

In Chapter 6, I discussed the practical consequences of the two most important methods for allocating rights to producers in the United States, Germany and the Netherlands: attributing authorship and the presumption of transfer. The first, most radical method removes all the obstacles producers may encounter when they seek to acquire title from creators. As author, the producer is vested with all the attributes normally accorded to authors under copyright law, unless the parties have provided otherwise. This far-reaching consequence is acceptable only if it is unambiguously clear in which situations the rule applies and if the parties have the opportunity to agree otherwise. This method is to be preferred over the American provision on employment works, which does not allow the parties to designate the employee as author.

According to the second method, rights are allocated to producers via a statutory or judge-made presumption on the rights which a producer acquires in the absence of a written transfer or in the case of doubt about the scope of the transfer. Under German copyright law, the grant of exclusive, enforceable rights of use may be implied in the circumstances, which allows courts to allocate rights on a case-by-case basis. The downside of this flexibility is however that neither the creator nor the producer can adequately predict their ownership status in the absence of an explicit agreement.

The extent to which presumptions of transfer facilitate proof of title depends on the moment at which the transfer is presumed to have taken place and on the scope, exclusivity and duration of the rights which are presumed to have been transferred. Only if the relevant statute provides unequivocal provisions on these issues, will producers know which rights will be theirs if they do not make express agreements. If not, such presumptions merely provide a minimum security safety net for producers who fail to make express agreements. The study has shown that, while the Dutch and German presumptions of transfer to film producers are relatively clear as far as the scope of the rights is concerned, they do not fully clarify the status of the presumption in the case of conflicting transfers and in the event the parties have regulated the ownership situation in a written agreement.

At the end of Chapter 6, I briefly discussed the role of neighbouring rights for producers who incorporate works of authorship in their products. Neighbouring rights enable producers to sue for infringement in their own right. An infringement of the neighbouring right only takes place however if the producer's contribution has been copied. If only the work of authorship incorporated in the product has been copied, the producer still has to obtain title from the author in order to bring an infringement action. For this reason, neighbouring rights are probably more effective for producers of films and sound recordings than for publishers. In this respect, a statutory provision granting exclusive licensees the right to sue may be more effective than a publisher's right.

Perhaps even more important than the right to sue, however, is the chance for producers to participate in the income from collectively-administered uses. If the neighbouring right is extended to these collectively-administered uses, the producer is guaranteed income from these uses, even if the author has entrusted his rights to the collecting society directly. In view of the ever-growing number of uses which are administered collectively, the allocation of income from the use of creative works is increasingly determined in collective negotiations about the distribution of collected fees, rather than in individual negotiations between creators and producers. In the light of this development, the recognition of exclusive or remuneration rights for producers and publishers in their own right seems to be inevitable.

167

PREDICTABILITY OF COPYRIGHT OWNERSHIP AND THE ALLOCATION OF RIGHTS TO PRODUCERS

If the relevant statute allocates rights to producers, it must be clear from the statutory definition when this special allocation rule is applicable. Creators must know what to do in order to retain rights to their works, and producers must know whether or not they must stipulate an express transfer in order to acquire title. From this perspective of predictability of copyright ownership, I have analyzed case law on the meaning of 'employee' in the American 'work for hire' rule (§ 101(1) USCA), on the meaning of 'specific works' in the Dutch provisions on employment works (§ 7 DCA), and on the meaning of 'producer' in the Dutch and German provisions on film works (§ 45a DCA; § 89 GCA).

Allocation rules are most predictable if they are based on circumstances which can be established before the creative process commences. The analysis of the relevant case law has however indicated that courts prefer to decide on the applicability of special allocation rules on the basis of an overall evaluation of the circumstances before as well as during the creative process.

In the final paragraph of Chapter 7, I have discussed the allocation of rights to audiovisual works. Under American law, the allocation of rights to audiovisual works depends on the applicability of the 'work for hire' rule and, consequently, on the nature of the relationship between the contributor and the party who contracts with him to acquire rights to his contribution (employment, a commission contract, the purchase of rights to an existing work). This system differs from the Dutch and German copyright systems which allocate rights to the 'film producer', being the person who hires the persons making creative contributions to the film and who is financially and organizationally responsible for the realization of the film work.

Although the two systems will lead to the same results in most cases, the Dutch and German systems concentrate ownership of the completed film in one person, which is not necessarily the case under the American system. The American system may provide more predictability however in cases in which the financial, organizational and contractual responsibilities are distributed amongst different parties and, consequently, in which it is difficult to identify the 'film producer'.

8.2 Outlook

I hope that this study will have made one thing clear: there is no uniform approach to the allocation of rights between creators and producers. When allocating rights to producers, the American, Dutch and German copyright systems all differentiate between categories of works and the type of relationship between the creator and the producer. Differentiation is the name of the game, and it should be in a field of law which covers so many diverse situations.

In most cases, creators are dependent on others to finance the creative process and to put their works on the market as consumable products. The discussion on the allocation of copyright ownership is therefore appropriate, however much one would like to keep alive the image of copyright as a right of the independent creator. There are still many creators who work in financial and creative freedom and, especially for those who obtain their primary source of income from the exploitation of their works, copyright ownership is indeed crucial. It would be denying reality, however, to model our copyright laws solely on this type of creator. If the 'creator' doctrine remains the basic rule from which we differentiate according to the work's specific characteristics and the allocation of risks between creator and producer, it will be possible to improve the security and efficiency of the production and distribution of creative works where this is needed most and where it will damage creators least.

Maximum security can only be achieved, however, if the same allocation rules are applied worldwide. Harmonization of copyright ownership is necessary, not in the last place because of the international confusion on the meaning of the term 'author'. Harmonization of copyright ownership is furthermore necessary to complement projects harmonizing other issues of copyright law, because these other issues can only be really successfully harmonized if they are combined with explicit rules on authorship and copyright ownership.

Harmonization remains difficult, however, despite the fact that most national copyright laws provide rules which allocate rights to producers in certain areas such as audiovisual works and works made in the course of employment. If, in order to reach international consensus about the allocation of rights in a certain type of creator-producer relationship it would be necessary to settle for the more generally accepted presumption of transfer method, this solution should include explicit provisions on the moment of transfer as well as on the consequences of the transfer in terms of scope, duration, territory, exclusivity and transferability. The presumption would furthermore have to be complemented by unambiguous provisions of transitional law. If it should prove to be impossible to achieve international agreement on authorship and copyright ownership, efforts should be made to harmonize the provisions of international private law determining the law applicable to authorship, copyright ownership and copyright transactions.

Bibliography

Abrams
Abrams, H.B., 'The Historic Foundation of American Copyright Law: Exploding the Myth of Common Law Copyright', 29 *Wayne Law Review* 1119 (1983)

Ad Hoc Working Group
Ad Hoc Working Group on U.S. Adherence to the Berne Convention, 'Final Report of the Ad Hoc Working Group on U.S. Adherence to the Berne Convention', 10 *Columbia-VLA Journal of Law & the Arts* 513 (1986)

Alberdingk Thijm
Alberdingk Thijm, Y.J., *Uitgeversrecht opnieuw in wording*, Deventer (1988)

Angel/Tannenbaum
Angel, D., Tannenbaum. S.W., 'Works Made For Hire Under S. 22', 22 *New York Law School Law Review*, 211 (1976)

Asscher, *Viewpoint from the Netherlands*
Asscher, M., 'Viewpoint from the Netherlands', in: *Copyright, Economic and Cultural Challenge*, report of the Conference of the International Publishers Association, Paris, 11-13 April 1990, 307 (1991)

Asscher, *What Publishers Need*
Asscher, M., 'What Publishers Need in National Copyright Laws', 5 *Rights* 10 (1991)

Auf der Maur
Auf der Maur, R., *Das Urheberrecht des Produzenten*, Basel/Frankfurt am Main (1991)

Bakels
Bakels, H.L., *Schets van het Nederlandse arbeidsrecht*, Deventer (1992)

Bappert
Bappert, W., *Wege zum Urheberrecht*, Frankfurt am Main (1962)

Barta
Barta, J., 'Copyright and employee creativity', 121 *Revue internationale du droit d'auteur* 68 (1984)

Baumgarten/Meyer
Baumgarten, J.A., Meyer, Chr. A., 'Effects of U.S. adherence to the Berne Convention', 56 *Bijblad Industriële Eigendom* 115 (1988)

De Beaufort (1909)
de Beaufort, H.L., *Het auteursrecht in het Nederlandsche en internationale auteursrecht*, Utrecht (1909)
De Beaufort (1932)
de Beaufort, H.L., *Auteursrecht*, Zwolle (1932)
De Beer
de Beer, A.C.G., 'Auteursrecht van universitaire auteurs', in: D. Kokkini-Iatridou, F.W. Grosheide (eds.), *Eenvormig en vergelijkend privaatrecht 1989*, 385, Lelystad (1989)
De Boer, *Aanknoping*
de Boer, Th.M., 'Aanknoping in het internationale auteursrecht', 108 *Weekblad voor Privaatrecht, Notariaat en Registratie* 673 (1977)
De Boer, *Filmauteursrecht*
de Boer, Th.M., 'Filmauteursrecht en internationaal privaatrecht', 17 *Informatierecht/AMI* 3 (1993)
Du Bois, *Enkele aspecten*
du Bois, R.L., 'Over enkele aspecten van het morele recht van de auteur', 8 *Auteursrecht* 56 (1984)
Du Bois, *Het contractenrecht*
du Bois, R.L., 'Het contractenrecht in het Europese auteursrecht', 8 *Auteursrecht* 23-25, 99-103 (1984)
Bowker
Bowker, R.R., *Copyright; Its History and its Law*, London/New York (1912)
Boytha, *Some Private International Law Aspects*
Boytha, G., 'Some Private International Law Aspects of the Protection of Author's Rights', 24 *Copyright* 399 (1988)
Boytha, *National Legislation on Author's Contracts*
Boytha, G., 'National Legislation on Author's Contracts in Countries Following Continental European Legal Traditions', 27 *Copyright* 198 (1991)
Breyer
Breyer, S., 'The Uneasy Case For Copyright: A Study Of Copyright In Books, Photocopies, And Computer Programs', 84 *Harvard Law Review* 218 (1970)
CLR
Omnibus Copyright Revision Legislative History, Buffalo, N.Y. (1961-1966)
De Cock Buning
de Cock Buning, M., '"Computer generated works", een test voor de grondslagen van het auteursrecht?', *Computerrecht* 10 (1993)
Cohen Jehoram, *Grenzen*
Cohen Jehoram, H., 'Grenzen aan de contractsvrijheid in het auteursrecht', 51 *Nederlands Juristenblad* 521 (1976)
Cohen Jehoram, *The Author's Place*
Cohen Jehoram, H., 'The Author's Place in Society and Legal Relations between Authors and those Responsible for Distributing their Works', 14 *Copyright* 385 (1978)

Cohen Jehoram, *Het filmrecht*
  Cohen Jehoram, H., 'Het filmrecht in Nederland, de bestaande situatie', 2 *Auteursrecht* 17 (1978)
Cohen Jehoram, *Uitgaveovereenkomst revisited*
  Cohen Jehoram, H., 'Het Nederlandse ontwerp voor een uitgaveovereenkomst revisited', 6 *Auteursrecht* 48 (1982)
Cohen Jehoram, *Actuele hoofdlijnen*
  Cohen Jehoram, H., 'Actuele hoofdlijnen in het auteurs- en mediarecht en het recht van de industriële eigendom', 58 *Nederlands Juristenblad* 329 (1983)
Cohen Jehoram/Asscher
  Cohen Jehoram, H., Asscher, M. (eds.), *Uitgeefovereenkomsten,* Zwolle (1988)
Cohen Jehoram, *Netherlands*
  Cohen Jehoram, H., 'Netherlands', in: M. Nimmer, P.E. Geller, *International Copyright Law and Practice,* New York (1988...)
Cohen Jehoram, *Critical Reflections*
  Cohen Jehoram, H., 'Critical Reflections on the Economic Importance of Copyright', 20 *International Review of Industrial Property and Copyright Law* 485 (1989)
Cohen Jehoram, *The Nature*
  Cohen Jehoram, H., 'The Nature of Neighbouring Rights of Performing Artists, Phonogram Producers and Broadcasting Organizations', 15 *Columbia-VLA Journal of Law & the Arts* 75 (1990)
Cohen Jehoram, *Bescherming van de auteur*
  Cohen Jehoram, H., 'Bescherming van de auteur tegen zijn exploitant: art. 3 Ontwerp-Richtlijn verhuurrecht', 15 *Informatierecht/AMI* 110 (1991)
Cohen Jehoram, *Opportuniteit*
  Cohen Jehoram, H., 'Auteursrecht: Opportuniteit of recht?', 16 *Informatie-recht/AMI* 63 (1992)
Cohen Jehoram, *Schrap één onzalig woordje*
  Cohen Jehoram, H., 'Schrap één onzalig woordje uit de Auteurswet 1912', 67 *Nederlands Juristenblad* 1542 (1992)
Corbet
  Corbet, J., 'Does Technological Development Imply a Change in the Nation of Author?, 148 *Revue internationale du droit d'auteur* 58 (1991)
Croon
  Croon, C., *De rechtspositie van de ontwerper, de maker en de uitvinder in dienstbetrekking,* Zwolle (1964)
Curtis
  Curtis, F.R., 'Protecting Authors in Copyright Transfers: Revision Bill § 203 and the Alternatives', 72 *Columbia Law Review* 799 (1972)
Darnton
  Darnton, R., *The Literary Underground of the Old Regime,* Cambridge, Mass./ London (1982)

Davies/von Rauscher auf Weeg
Davies, G., von Rauscher auf Weeg, H.H., *Challenges to Copyright and Related Rights in the European Community*, Oxford (1983)
Desbois
Desbois, H., *Le droit d'auteur en France*, Paris (1978)
Dessemontet
Dessemontet, F., 'Letter from Switzerland: The New Copyright Act', 17 *Informatierecht/AMI* 183 (1993)
Dietz (1968)
Dietz, A., *Das Droit Moral des Urhebers im neuen französischen und deutschschen Urheberrecht, eine rechtsvergleichende Untersuchung*, Munich (1968)
Dietz (1978)
Dietz, A., *Copyright Law in the European Community: a Comparative Investigation*, Alphen aan den Rijn (1978)
Dietz (1984)
Dietz, A., *Das primäre Urhebervertragsrecht in der Bundesrepublik Deutschland und in den anderen Mitgliedstaaten der Europäischen Gemeinschaft*, Munich (1984)
Dietz, *Entwickelt*
Dietz, A., 'Entwickelt sich das Urheberrecht zu einem gewerblichen Schutzrecht?', in: W. Barfuss, H. Torggler, Ch. Hauer, L. Wiltschek, G. Kucsko (eds.), *Wirtschaftsrecht im Theorie und Praxis, Gedenkschrift für Frits Schönherr*, 111, Vienna (1986)
Dietz, *Transformation of authors rights*
Dietz, A., 'Transformation of authors rights change of paradigm', 138 *Revue internationale du droit d'auteur* 23 (1988)
Dietz (1989)
Dietz, A., *Das Urheberrecht in Spanien und Portugal*, Munich (1989)
Dietz, *The United States*
Dietz, A., 'The United States and Moral Rights: Idiosyncracy or Approximation', 142 *Revue internationale du droit d'auteur* 222 (1989)
Dietz, *Thesen*
Dietz, A., 'Thesen zum Thema: Werke angestellter Urheber und Auftragswerke in rechtsvergleichender Sicht', in: *The Reform of Copyright Law: Experiences Abroad*, report of the conference in Lausanne on 3 November 1989, 11, Zurich (1990)
Dietz, *The Relation Employer - Employee*
Dietz, A., 'The Relation Employer - Employee under the Copyright Act in Germany', in: *Werkgeversauteursrecht*, at 35
Dietz, *The concept of author*
Dietz, A., 'The concept of author under the Berne Convention', 155 *Revue internationale du droit d'auteur* 2 (1993)
Dittrich
Dittrich, R., *Arbeitnehmer und Urheberrecht*, Vienna (1978)

Dock

Dock, M.C., 'The Origin and Development of the Literary Property Concept', 79 *Revue internationale du droit d'auteur* 126 (1974)

Dommering

Dommering, E.J., *De informatiedriehoek. Enige beschouwingen over de regulering van informatiestromen*, Deventer (1989)

Dommering, *De sportprestatie*

Dommering, E.J., 'De sportprestatie: bescherming en vrije berichtgeving', in: W.F. Korthals Altes, G.A.I. Schuijt (eds.), *Sport en informatiemonopolies*, 9, Amsterdam (1991)

Dommering, *Introduction*

Dommering, E.J., 'An Introduction to Information Law. Protecting Works of Fact at the Crossroads of Freedom and Protection', in: E.J. Dommering, P.B. Hugenholtz (eds.), *Protecting Works of Fact, Copyright Freedom of Expression and Information Law*, 1, Deventer/Boston (1991)

Dommering, *De software richtlijn*

Dommering, E.J., 'De software richtlijn uit Brussel en de Nederlandse Auteurswet', 16 *Informatierecht/AMI* 83 (1992)

Dreier/von Lewinsky

Dreier, Th., von Lewinsky, S., 'Kolorierung von Filmen, Laufzeitänderung und Formatanpassung: Urheberrecht als Bollwerk?', *Gewerblicher Rechtsschutz und Urheberrecht - Internationaler Teil* 635 (1989)

Dworkin

Dworkin, G., 'Authorship of Films and the European Commission Proposals for Harmonizing the Term of Copyright', 15 EIPR 155 (1993)

Van Engelen, *Uitvoerende kunstenaars*

van Engelen, Th.C.J.A., 'Uitvoerende kunstenaars en vertolkers, naburige rechten en auteursrechten', 9 *Auteursrecht* 83 (1985)

Van Engelen, *Geschriften-bescherming*

van Engelen, Th.C.J.A., 'De geschriften-bescherming in de Auteurswet en de bescherming van daarmee op één lijn te stellen prestaties', 55 *Bijblad Industriële Eigendom* 243 (1987)

Van Engelen, *Overdracht*

van Engelen, Th.C.J.A., 'Overdracht van toekomstig auteursrecht naar Nieuw BW', 16 *Informatierecht/AMI* 49 (1992)

Van Engelen

van Engelen, Th.C.J.A., *Prestatiebescherming en ongeschreven intellectuele eigendomsrechten*, Zwolle (1994)

Van Esch, *Zekerheidsrechten*

van Esch, R.E., 'Zekerheidsrechten op auteursrecht op software in ontwikkeling', 15 *Informatierecht/AMI* 63 (1991)

Van Esch, *Juridische aspecten*

van Esch, R.E., 'Juridische aspecten van body-shopping en turn-key projecten', in: F. de Graaf, J.M.A. Berkvens (eds.), *Hoofdstukken Informatierecht*, third edition, 243, Alphen aan den Rijn (1992)

Feather
Feather, J.P., 'Authors, Publishers and Politicians: The History of Copyright and the Book Trade', 12 *European Intellectual Property Review* 377 (1988)

Fidlow
Fidlow, B.J., 'The "Works Made for Hire" Doctrine and the Employee/Independent Contractor Dichotomy: the Need for Congressional Clarification', 10 *Hastings Communications & Entertainment Law Journal* 591 (1988)

Fine
Fine, S.I., 'The Fate of Joint Authorship After *Community for Creative Non-Violence v. Reid*', 9 *Cardozo Arts & Entertainment Law Journal* 151 (1990)

Françon
Françon, A., 'Authors' Rights beyond Frontiers: A Comparison of Civil Law and Common Law Conceptions', 149 *Revue internationale du droit d'auteur* 2 (1991)

De Freitas
de Freitas, D., 'Copyright Contracts, A Study of the Terms of Contracts for the Use of Works Protected by Copyright under the Legal System in Common Law Countries', 27 *Copyright* 222 (1991)

Frequin/Grosheide
Frequin, M.J., Grosheide, F.W., 'Uitgeversrecht. Een studie naar de noodzaak tot een versterking van de rechtspositie van de uitgever', 14 *Informatierecht/ AMI* 43 (1990)

Frey
Frey, M.A., 'Die internationale Vereinheitlichung des Urheberrechts und das Schöpferprinzip', 98 *Archiv für Urheber-, Film-, Funk- und Theaterrecht* 53 (1984)

Gallay
Gallay, P., 'Authorship and Copyright of 'Works Made for Hire': Bugs in the Statutory System', 8 *Columbia Journal of Law & the Arts* 573 (1984)

Von Gamm
von Gamm, O.F., 'Zur Lehre vom geistigen Eigentum', 94 *Archiv für Urheber-, Film-, Funk- und Theaterrecht* 73 (1982)

Geller, *Harmonizing Copyright-Contract Conflicts Analyses*
Geller, P.E., 'Harmonizing Copyright-Contract Conflicts Analyses', 25 *Copyright* 49 (1989)

Geller, *Worldwide 'Chain of Title'*
Geller, P.E., 'Worldwide "Chain of Title" to Copyright', *Copyright World* 49 (1990)

Gerbrandy (1988)
Gerbrandy, S., *Kort commentaar op de Auteurswet 1912*, Arnhem (1988)

Gerbrandy (1992)
Gerbrandy, S., *Auteursrecht in de steigers*, Arnhem (1992)

Von Gierke
von Gierke, O., *Deutsches Privatrecht*, Vol. 1, Leipzig (1895)

Ginsburg, *Colors in Conflicts*
Ginsburg, J.C., 'Colors in Conflicts: Moral Rights and the Foreign Exploitation of Colorized U.S. Motion Pictures', 35 *Journal of the Copyright Society of the USA* 81 (1988)

Ginsburg/Kernochan
Ginsburg, J.C., Kernochan, J.M., 'One Hundred and Two Years Later: The U.S. Joins the Berne Convention', 13 *Columbia-VLA Journal of Law & the Arts* 1 (1988)

Ginsburg, *Federalism*
Ginsburg, J.C., 'Federalism and Intellectual Property', 139 *Revue internationale du droit d'auteur* 19 (1989)

Ginsburg, *Moral Rights*
Ginsburg, J.C., 'Moral Rights in a Common Law System', 1 *Entertainment Law Review* 121 (1990)

Ginsburg, *Copyright in the 101st Congress*
Ginsburg, J.C., 'Copyright in the 101st Congress, Commentary on the Visual Artists Rights Act and the Architectural Works Copyright Protection Act of 1990', 14 *Columbia-VLA Journal of Law & the Arts* 477 (1990)

Ginsburg, *A Tale of Two Copyrights*
Ginsburg, 'A Tale of Two Copyrights: Literary Property in Revolutionary France and America', 47 *Revue internationale du droit d'auteur* 124 (1991)

Ginsburg/Sirinelli
Ginsburg, J.C., Sirinelli, P., 'Authors and Exploitations in International Private Law: The French Supreme Court and the Huston Film Colorization Controversy', 15 *Columbia-VLA Journal of Law & the Arts* 135 (1992)

Ginsburg, *No "Sweat"?*
Ginsburg, J.C., 'No "Sweat"? Copyright and Other Protection of Works of Information after Feist v. Rural Telephone', 92 *Columbia Law Review* 339 (1992)

Ginsburg, *Developments*
Ginsburg, J.C., 'Developments in U.S. Copyright Law since 1990', *Revue internationale du droit d'auteur* 133 (1994)

Goldstein
Goldstein, P., *Copyright, Principles, Law and Practice*, Vol. I-II, Boston/Toronto/London (1989)

Gordon
Gordon, W.J., 'An Inquiry into the Merits of Copyright: The Challenges of Consistency, Consent, and Encouragement Theory', 41 *Stanford Law Review* 1343 (1989)

Grosheide
Grosheide, F.W., *Auteursrecht op maat*, Deventer (1986)

Grosheide, *Juridische typologie*
Grosheide, F.W., 'Opmerkingen over de juridische typologie van internationale licentiecontracten', in: D. Kokkini-Iatridou, F.J.A van der Velden (eds.), *Eenvormig en vergelijkend privaatrecht 1989*, 149, Lelystad (1989)

Grosheide, *Auteurswet*
Grosheide, F.W., 'Auteurswet 1912 - wet 1985 - bescherming van filmproducenten en andere exploitanten - oecumenische kanttekeningen', 14 *Informatierecht/AMI* 121 (1990)
Grosheide/Hartkamp
Grosheide, F.W., Hartkamp A.S., 'Auteursrecht en Nieuw Burgerlijk Wetboek - een inleiding', 15 *Informatierecht/AMI* 211 (1991)
Grosheide, *Publishers' Rights*
Grosheide, F.W., 'Copyright and Publishers' Rights: Exploitation of Information by a Proprietary Right', in: W.F. Korthals Altes, E.J. Dommering, P.B. Hugenholtz, J.J.C. Kabel (eds.), *Information Law Towards the 21st century*, 295, Deventer/Boston (1992)
Grosheide, *Contractuele exploitatie*
Grosheide, F.W., 'Contractuele exploitatie van intellectuele eigendomsrechten in internationaal verband' in: F.W. Grosheide (ed.), *Eenvormig en vergelijkend privaatrecht 1992*, 401, Lelystad (1992)
Grosheide/Obertop
Grosheide, F.W., Obertop, F.W., 'Proeve van een Wet op het Uitgeversrecht', 16 *Informatierecht/AMI* 163 (1992)
Grosheide, *Paradigms*
Grosheide, F.W., 'Paradigms in Copyright Law', in: B. Sherman, A. Strowel (eds.), *Of Authors and Origins*, Oxford (1994)
Hamilton
Hamilton, M., 'Commissioned Works as Works Made for Hire under the 1976 Copyright Act: Misinterpretation and Injustice', 135 *University of Pennsylvania Law Review* 1281 (1987)
Hardy
Hardy, I.T., 'An Economic Understanding of Copyright Law's Work-Made-for-Hire Doctrine', 12 *Columbia-VLA Journal of Law & the Arts* 181 (1988)
Heevel, *Leistungsschutz*
Heevel, G.J., 'Leistungsschutz für ausübende Künstler und Tonträgerhersteller in den Niederlanden', 92 *Gewerblicher Rechtsschutz und Urheberrecht - Internationaler Teil* 204 (1990)
Heevel, *Wet 1991?*
Heevel, G.J., 'Wet 1991? Uitvoerend kunstenaars, naburig recht, auteursrecht of art. 1401 BW?', 14 *Informatierecht/AMI* 133 (1990)
Hesse
Hesse, C., 'Enlightenment Epistemology and the Laws of Authorship in Revolutionary France, 1771-1793', in: R. Post (ed.), *Law and the Order of Culture*, 109 (1990)
Hilty
Hilty, R.M., 'Gedanken zum Schutz der nachbarrechtlichen Leistung - einst, heute und morgen', 116 *Archiv für Urheber-, Film-, Funk- und Theaterrecht* 31 (1991)

Hirsch,

Hirsch, E.E., 'Urheberrecht und verwandte Rechte', in: *Aktuelles Filmrecht* 18, Baden-Baden (1958)

Hirsch Ballin, *Auteursrecht der hoogleraren*

Hirsch Ballin, E.D., 'Auteursrecht der hoogleraren', 25 *Nederlands Juristenblad* 550, 730, 893 (1950)

Hirsch Ballin

Hirsch Ballin, E.D., *Auteursrechtelijke opstellen*, Deventer (1970)

Holtzer

Holtzer, M., 'Onpersoonlijke geschriftenbescherming en informatievrijheid', 17 *Informatierecht/AMI* 63 (1993)

Holzhauer/Teijl

Holzhauer, R.W., Teijl, R., *De toenemende complexiteit van het intellectuele eigendomsrecht, een economische analyse*, Arnhem (1991)

Hösly

Hösly, B., *Das urheberrechtlich schützbare Rechtssubjekt*, Berne (1987)

Hubmann

Hubmann, H., *Urheber- und Verlagsrecht*, fifth edition, Munich (1987)

Hugenholtz/Spoor

Hugenholtz, P.B., Spoor, J.H., *Auteursrecht op software*, Amsterdam (1987)

Hugenholtz

Hugenholtz, P.B., *Auteursrecht op informatie*, Deventer (1989)

Hunziker, *Monismus*

Hunziker, M., 'Monismus oder Dualismus im schweizerischen Urheberrecht?', 97 *Archiv für Urheber-, Film-, Funk- und Theaterrecht* 127 (1984)

Hunziker, *Urheberrecht*

Hunziker, M., 'Urheberrecht nach beendetem Arbeitsverhältnis', 101 *Archiv für Urheber-, Film-, Funk- und Theaterrecht* 49 (1985)

Huydecoper

Huydecoper, J.L.R.A., 'De overgang van ondernemingen en de overgang van rechten uit licentieovereenkomsten', 16 *Informatierecht/AMI* 66 (1992)

Kabel

Kabel, J.J.C., 'Beeldende kunst en auteursrecht', in: J.J.C. Kabel et al., *Kunst en beleid in Nederland 5*, 65, Amsterdam (1991)

Karlen

Karlen, P.H., 'Joint ownership of moral rights', *Journal of the Copyright Society of the USA* 242 (1991)

Karnell

Karnell, G., 'Employment for Hire - A Nonlegislative Approach', 33 *Journal of the Copyright Society of the USA* 100 (1986)

Kastenmaier

Kastenmaier, R.W., 'The 1989 Horace C. Manges Lecture - Copyright in an Era of Technological Change: A Political Perspective', 14 *Columbia-VLA Journal of Law & the Arts* 1 (1989)

Katzenberger
Katzenberger, P., 'Beteiligung des Urhebers an Ertrag und Ausmaß der Werkverwertung, Altverträge, Drittwirkung und Reform des § 36 UrhG', 85 *Gewerblicher Rechtsschutz und Urheberrecht - Internationaler Teil* 410 (1983)

Katzman
Katzman, J., 'Joint authorship of commissioned works', 89 *Columbia Law Review* 867 (1989)

Kerever
Kerever, A., 'Copyright, The Achievements and Future Development of European Legal Culture', 26 *Copyright* 130 (1990)

Kernochan, *Imperatives*
Kernochan, J.M., 'Imperatives For Enforcing Author's Rights', 11 *Columbia-VLA Journal of Law & the Arts* 587 (1987)

Kernochan, *Moral Rights*
Kernochan J.M., et al., 'Moral Rights - Practical Perspectives', 14 *Columbia-VLA Journal of Law & the Arts* 25 (1989)

Kernochan, II/IV
Kernochan, J.M., *Cases and Materials on Intellectual Property*, vol. II and IV, 9th ed., New York (1990)

Kernochan, *Works-Made-For-Hire*
Kernochan, J.M., et al., 'Works-Made-For-Hire - Practical Perspectives: A Roundtable Discussion', 14 *Columbia-VLA Journal of Law & the Arts* 507 (1990)

Kernochan, *After U.S. Adherence*
Kernochan, J.M., 'After U.S. Adherence to Berne: Problems and Prospects - Comments', in: *Copyright 1990*, ALAI Study Session Helsinki, 28-30 May 1990, 169, Paris/Stockholm (1991)

Klaver
Klaver, F., 'Het auteursrecht is ook een mensenrecht', 6 *Auteursrecht* 125 (1982)

Kohler
Kohler, J., *Das Autorrecht, eine zivilistische Abhandlung*, Jena (1880)

Komen/Verkade
Komen, A., Verkade, D.W.F., *Compendium van het auteursrecht*, Deventer (1970)

Kummer
Kummer, M., *Das urheberrechtlich schützbare Werk*, Berne (1968)

Kuypers
Kuypers, C.W., 'Droit moral: grondslag en uitwerking', 12 *Informatierecht/AMI* 9 (1988)

Ladd
Ladd, D., 'Securing the future of copyright: a humanist endeavour', 10 *Informatierecht/AMI* 91 (1986)

Landau
Landau, M.B., '"Works Made For Hire" After *Community v. Creative Non-Violence v. Reid*, The Need for Statutory Reform and the Importance of Contract', 9 *Cardozo Arts & Entertainment Law Review* 107 (1990)

Landes/Posner
Landes, W.M., Posner, R.A., 'An Economic Analysis of Copyright Law', 18 *The Journal of Legal Studies* 325 (1989)

Larese
Larese, W., *Urheberrecht in einem sich wandelnden Kulturbetrieb*, Berne (1979)

Larese, *Fragen*
Larese, W., 'Fragen zum Urheberrechtserwerb im beruflichen Abhängigkeitsverhältnis', 28 *Zeitschrift für Urheber- und Medienrecht* 191 (1984)

Latman/Gorman/Ginsburg
Latman, A., Gorman, R.A., Ginsburg, J.C., *Copyright for the Nineties, Cases and Materials*, third edition, Charlottesville (1989)

Lehmann, *Property*
Lehmann, M., 'Property and Intellectual Property - Property Rights as Restrictions on Competition in Furtherance of Competition', 20 *International Review of Industrial Property and Copyright Law* 1 (1989)

Letterkundig Eigendomsrecht
Het letterkundig eigendomsrecht in Nederland (1865)

Limperg
Limperg, Th., 'Werknemer en auteursrecht', *Rechtsgeleerd Magazijn Themis* 507 (1980)

Van Lingen
van Lingen, N., *Auteursrecht in hoofdlijnen*, third edition, Alphen aan den Rijn (1990)

Van Lingen/Van Niftrik
van Lingen, N., van Niftrik, H.M., 'Auteursrecht van journalisten', 7 *Auteursrecht* 50 (1983)

Van Lingen, *Morele rechten*
van Lingen, N., 'Morele rechten van fictieve makers', in: G.J. Bijleveld c.s. (eds.), *Qui bene distinguit bene docet. Auteursrechtelijke opstellen aangeboden aan S. Gerbrandy*, 191, Arnhem (1991)

Linnemann, *Omroep en auteursrecht*
Linnemann, M.J.T., 'Omroep en auteursrecht', 14 *Informatierecht/AMI* 35 (1990)

Linnemann, *Tegen het viertje*
Linnemann, M.J.T., 'Tegen het viertje in "Twin Peaks"', 15 *Informatierecht/ AMI* 115 (1991)

Litman
Litman, J.D., 'Copyright, Compromise and Legislative History', 72 *Cornell Law Review* 857 (1987)

Locke
Locke, J., *Two Treatises of Government* (1690), ed. P. Laslett, New York (1965)

Maeijer
Maeijer, J.M.M., 'Rechtspersoonlijkheid, persoonlijkheidsrechten en vatbaarheid voor beslag van het auteursrecht', 58 *Bijblad Industriële Eigendom* 352 (1990)

Mak

Mak, W., 'Phonogrammen en droits voisins', 31 *Nederlands Juristenblad* 119 (1956)

Meijers

Meijers, E.M., *Ontwerp voor een nieuw Burgerlijk Wetboek, Boek 7*, the Hague (1972)

Melville

Melville, L., 'A Law of Activities - the choice of words and their limiting effect', 4 *European Intellectual Property Review* 63 (1982)

Möller

Möller, M., 'Author's Right or Copyright?', 34 *Zeitschrift für Urheber- und Medienrecht* 65 (1990)

Mom

Mom, G.J.H.M., *Kabeltelevisie en auteursrecht*, Lelystad (1990)

Nieuwenhuis

Nieuwenhuis, A.J., *Persvrijheid en persbeleid*, Amsterdam (1990)

Nimmer

Nimmer, M.B., *Nimmer on Copyright: a Treatise on the Law of Literary, Musical and Artistic Property, and the Protection of Ideas*, New York (1963...)

Van Nispen

van Nispen, C.J.J.C., 'Verbod en bevel in het auteursrecht onder het Nieuw BW', 16 *Informatierecht/AMI* 90 (1992)

Nordemann/Vinck/Hertin/Meyer

Nordemann, W., Vinck, K., Hertin, P., Meyer, G., *International Copyright and Neighbouring Rights Law: Commentary with Special Emphasis on the European Community*, New York (1990)

Nordemann/..

Nordemann, W., Vinck, K., Hertin, P., *Urheberrecht: Kommentar zum Urheberrechtsgesetz und zum Urheberrechtswahrnehmungsgesetz*, Stuttgart/Berlin/Koeln/Mainz (1988)

Nordemann, Vorschlag

Nordemann, W., 'Vorschlag für ein Urhebervertragsgesetz', 93 *Gewerblicher Rechtsschutz und Urheberrecht* 1 (1991)

Nordemann, Mängel der Staatsaufsicht

Nordemann, W., 'Mängel der Staatsaufsicht über die deutschen Verwertungsgesellschaften?', 94 *Gewerblicher Rechtsschutz und Urheberrecht* 584 (1992)

Van Oven

van Oven, J.C., 'Overdracht van auteursrecht', 15 *Nederlands Juristenblad* 1 (1940)

Patterson

Patterson, L.R., *Copyright in Historical Perspective*, Nashville (1968)

Parl.Gesch.

de Vries, L. (ed.), *Parlementaire geschiedenis van de Auteurswet 1912, zoals sedertdien gewijzigd*, the Hague (1991...)

Ploman/Clark Hamilton
Ploman, E.W., Clark Hamilton, L., *Copyright - Intellectual Property in the Information Age*, London/Boston/Henley-on-Thames (1980)

Pohlmann
Pohlmann, H., 'Zur Überwindung der "Eigentums"-vorstellungen im Urheberrecht', 36 *Archiv für Urheber-, Film-, Funk- und Theaterrecht* 61 (1962)

Pollaud-Dulian
Pollaud-Dulian, F., 'Moral Rights in France, through recent case law', 145 *Revue internationale du droit d'auteur* 126 (1990)

Prescott
Prescott, P., 'The Origins of Copyright: A Debunking View', 12 *European Intellectual Law Review* 453 (1989)

Quaedvlieg (1987)
Quaedvlieg, A.A., *Auteursrecht op techniek*, Zwolle (1987)

Quaedvlieg, *Overdraagbaarheid*
Quaedvlieg, A.A., 'Overdraagbaarheid van licenties naar Nieuw BW: hetzelfde en toch iets anders', in: *Onderneming en nieuw burgerlijk recht*, 485, Zwolle (1991)

Quaedvlieg (1992)
Quaedvlieg, A.A., *Auteur en aantasting, werk en waardigheid*, Zwolle (1992)

Quaedvlieg, *The economic analysis*
Quaedvlieg, A.A., 'The Economic Analysis of Intellectual Property Law', in: W.F. Korthals Altes, E.J. Dommering, P.B. Hugenholtz, J.J.C. Kabel (eds.), *Information Law towards the 21st Century*, 379, Deventer/Boston (1992)

Quaedvlieg, *Het belang*
Quaedvlieg, A.A., 'Het belang van de werkgever', 17 *Informatierecht/AMI* 83 (1993)

Ransom
Ransom, H., *The First Copyright Statute*, Austin (1956)

Recher
Recher, B., *Der Arbeitnehmer als Urheber und das Recht des Arbeitgebers am urheberrechtsschutzfähigen Arbeitsergebnis*, Zurich (1975)

Rehbinder, *Recht am Arbeitsergebnis*
Rehbinder, M., 'Recht am Arbeitsergebnis', 91 *Zeitschrift für schweizerisches Recht* 1 (1972)

Rehbinder, *Recht am Arbeitsergebnis und Urheberrecht*
Rehbinder, M., 'Recht am Arbeitsergebnis und Urheberrecht', in: W. Herschel, F. Klein, M. Rehbinder (eds.), *Festschrift für Georg Roeber*, 481, Berlin (1973)

Rehbinder, *Das Namennennungsrecht*
Rehbinder, M., 'Das Namennennungsrecht des Urhebers', 35 *Zeitschrift für Urheber- und Medienrecht* 220 (1991)

Resius
Resius, F.J., 'Uitgeversbescherming', 14 *Informatierecht/AMI* 67 (1990)

Ricketson

Ricketson, S., *The Berne Convention for the Protection of Literary and Artistic Works: 1886-1986*, London (1987)

Ricketson, People or Machines

Ricketson, S., 'The 1992 Horace S. Manges Lecture - People or Machines: The Berne Convention and the Changing Concept of Authorship', 16 *Columbia VLA Journal of Law & the Arts* 1 (1992)

Roos/Seignette

Roos, W.A., Seignette, J.M.B., 'Bootlegs in the Netherlands: the Final Blow?' 4 *Entertainment Law Review* 178 (1993)

Rossbach

Rossbach, C., *Die Vergütungsansprüche im Deutschen Urheberrecht*, Baden-Baden (1990)

Saunders

Saunders, D., *Authorship and Copyright*, London/New York (1992)

Savatier

Savatier, R., 'La distinction, en droit français, de l'oeuvre collective et de l'oeuvre de collaboration', 64 *Archiv für Urheber-, Film-, Funk- und Theaterrecht* 1 (1972)

Schack, Der Vergütungsanspruch

Schack, H., 'Der Vergütungsanspruch der in- und ausländischen Filmhersteller aus § 54 I UrhG', 33 *Zeitschrift für Urheber- und Medienrecht* 267 (1989)

Schack, Wem gebührt das Urheberrecht

Schack, H., 'Wem gebührt das Urheberrecht, dem Schöpfer oder dem Produzenten?', 34 *Zeitschrift für Urheber- und Medienrecht* 59 (1990)

Schricker/..

Schricker, G. (ed.), *Urheberrecht: Kommentar*, first edition, Munich (1987)

Schuijt

Schuijt, G.A.I., *Werkers van het woord. Media en arbeidsverhoudingen in de journalistiek*, Deventer (1987)

Schuijt, Schrap artikel 7

Schuijt, G.A.I., 'Schrap artikel 7 Auteurswet!', in: *Werkgeversauteursrecht*, 21-28.

Schwarz

Schwarz, M., 'Schutzmöglichkeiten audiovisueller Werke von der Idee bis zum fertigen Werk - aus der Sicht der anwaltlicher Beratung', 34 *Zeitschrift für Urheber- und Medienrecht* 317 (1990)

Seignette, Het wetsontwerp

Seignette, J.M.B., 'Het wetsontwerp naburige rechten', 6 *Intellectuele Eigendom en Reclamerecht* 1 (1990)

Seignette, Inkleuring

Seignette, J.M.B., 'Inkleuring van speelfilms: commerciële vondst, artistieke gruwel', 65 *Nederlands Juristenblad* 1623 (1991)

Seignette, Subjectbepaling

Seignette, J.M.B., 'Subjectbepaling in het internationale auteursrecht', 14 *Informatierecht/AMI* 195 (1990)

Sher
Sher, J., 'Community For Creative Non-violence v. Reid and the Work Made for Hire Doctrine Under the Copyright Act of 1976: A Progression Towards Regression', 4 *Software Law Journal* 51 (1990)

Smit
Smit, H.J., 'De auteur in dienstbetrekking', 49 *Nederlands Juristenblad* 1063 (1974)

Sobel
Sobel, L.S., 'Copyright Renewal after the 1992 Amendments: The Strategic Choices to be Made between Automatic Renewal and Applied-For Renewals', 14 *Entertainment Law Reporter* 3 (1992)

Soetenhorst
Soetenhorst, W.J., *De bescherming van de uitgeefprestatie*, Zwolle (1993)

Spautz
Spautz, W., 'Wann kommt das Urhebervertragsgesetz?', 36 *Zeitschrift für Urheber- und Medienrecht* 186 (1992)

Spector
Spector, H.M., 'An Outline of a Theory Justifying Intellectual and Industrial Property Rights', 11 *European Intellectual Property Review* 270 (1989)

Spoor
Spoor, J.H., *Scripta manent, de reproduktie in het auteursrecht*, Groningen (1976)

Spoor, *De filmkwestie*
Spoor, J.H., 'De VvA en de filmkwestie', 2 *Auteursrecht* 19 (1978)

Spoor, *De auteursrechtelijke positie*
Spoor, J.H., 'De auteursrechtelijke positie van de uitvoerende kunstenaar', *Rechtsgeleerd Magazijn Themis* 324 (1973)

Spoor, *Onzekere zekerheid*
Spoor, J.H., 'Onzekere zekerheid en lastig beslag', 58 *Bijblad Industriële Eigendom* 358 (1990)

Spoor/Verkade
Spoor, J.H., Verkade, D.W.F., *Auteursrecht*, second edition, Deventer (1993)

Stewart
Stewart, S.M., *International Copyright and Neighbouring Rights*, London (1983)

Strömholm
Strömholm, S., *Le droit moral de l'auteur en droit allemand, français et scandinave* Vol. I-III, Stockholm (1966-1973)

Strowel
Strowel, A., *Droit d'auteur et copyright*, Brussels/Paris (1993)

Thole
Thole, E.P.M., 'De persoonlijkheidsrechten op software; In het bijzonder de rol van het persoonlijkheidsrecht ex art. 2 lid 3 Aw in het faillissement van een softwarebedrijf', *Computerrecht* 69 (1988)

Troller, *Bedenken*
Troller, A., 'Bedenken zum Urheberpersönlichkeitsrecht', 36 *Archiv für Urheber-Film-, Funk- und Theaterrecht* 257 (1962)

Troller

Troller, A., *Immaterialgüterrecht*, Vol. I-II, Basel (1983-1985)

Ullmann

Ullmann, E., 'Das urheberrechtlich geschützte Arbeitsergebnis - Verwertungsrecht und Vergütungspflicht', 89 *Gewerblicher Rechtsschutz und Urheberrecht* 6 (1987)

Ulmer

Ulmer, E., *Urheber- und Verlagsrecht*, Berlin/Heidelberg/New York (1980)

Ulmer (1978)

Ulmer, E., *Intellectual Property Rights and the Conflict of Laws*, Deventer (1978)

Varmer

Varmer, B., *Works Made For Hire And On Commission*, CLR Part 1, 123 (1958)

Verkade/Spoor

Verkade, D.W.F., Spoor, J.H., *Auteursrecht*, first edition, Deventer (1985)

Verkade, *Een nog net niet verboden artikel*

Verkade, D.W.F., 'Een nog net niet verboden artikel', 61 *Nederlands Juristenblad* 1235 (1986)

Verkade, *Gegevensbescherming*

Verkade, D.W.F., 'Gegevensbescherming en privaatrecht', in: *Gegevensbescherming; Handelingen 1988 der NJV, deel 1*, 35 (1988)

Verkade (1990)

Verkade, D.W.F., *Intellectuele eigendom, mededinging en informatievrijheid*, Deventer (1990)

Verkade, *Rechtsbeginselen*

Verkade, D.W.F., 'De rol van rechtsbeginselen in het recht van de intellectuele eigendom en de ongeoorloofde mededinging', 40 *Ars Aequi* 143 (1991)

Verkade, *Het beste artikel 7*

Verkade, D.W.F., 'Het beste artikel 7 Auteurswet', in: *Werkgeversauteursrecht*, at 9.

Vermeijden

Vermeijden, J., *Auteursrecht en het kinematografisch werk*, Zwolle (1953)

Vinck

Vinck, K., *Die Rechtsstellung des Urhebers im Arbeits- und Dienstverhältnis*, Berlin (1972)

Wandtke

Wandtke, A., 'Zum Vergütungsanspruch des Urhebers im Arbeitsverhältnis', 94 *Gewerblicher Rechtsschutz und Urheberrecht* 139 (1992)

Werkgeversauteursrecht

Mom, G.J.H.M., Keuchenius, P.J. (eds.), *Het werkgeversauteursrecht. Kan de werkgever het maken?*, Deventer (1992)

Woltring, *Mens-machine*

Woltring, H.J., 'Mens-machine communicatie: programmatuur in de scheppingsfase', 56 *Bijblad Industriële Eigendom* 178 (1988)

Woltring, *Wetenschapsbeoefening*
Woltring, H.J., 'Wetenschapsbeoefening: Bepaald of Onbepaald?', 4 *Intellectuele eigendom en reclamerecht* 67 (1988)
WIPO Guide
Masouyé, C., *WIPO Guide to the Berne Convention*, Geneva (1978)

Table of Cases

Dutch case law

English case law

French case law

German case law

U.S. case law

Index

Academic writings 34, 142, 145-146
Actual control 134, 137
Adaptation
  see derivative work
Advertisment work 90, 91, 93
Agreement
  see Contract
Anonymous work 38, 59
Assignment
  see Transfer
Assistantship 64
Associative risk   83-93, 94, 114, 115, 153
Audiovisual work
- author
  see Author
- allocation of rights 76, 89, 94, 117, 119, 153-157, 159
- nationality 68
- term of protection 68
Author 1, 6
- audiovisual work 39, 47, 60-61, 117, 150
- Berne Convention 2, 76
- director 60, 61, 78
- identification 57-58, 66, 80, 100
- maker 1, 5, 47
- persona 90, 109
- social position 10
- United States 38, 41
- Urheber 1, 5, 31
Authorship 1
- statutory attribution 97-114, 124-127
- credit 110-114
- degree 42, 93
- false attribution 111

- intellectual concept 1, 40, 42, 64
- presumption 59, 81
- right to claim 101, 110
Author's right 4, 53
- dualistic concept 28, 30
- human right 22, 102
- natural right 22-23, 26, 54, 102
- monistic concept 28-30, 97
Berne Convention 29, 40, 69, 77, 102
Bond between creator and work 24, 29, 101 103, 114
Book trade 7-8, 14
Broadcast 35, 49, 50
Censorship 9-10, 13, 18
Cessio legis 99, 124
Cinematographic work
  See Audiovisual work
Civil law 24, 27
Co-authorship 55, 65, 158
- Germany 60, 63
- Netherlands 60, 63, 148-152
- United States 61, 62, 138-141
Collective administration 5, 35, 67-68, 71, 127, 130
Collective work 46, 47, 65, 73, 78, 88, 89, 118
Collecting society
  See collective administration
Commissioned Work 4, 27, 37-42, 85-95
- Germany 86, 88-89
- Netherlands 148-153
- United States 39, 88, 134-141
Common law 15, 17, 21, 27
Common law copyright 20-21, 36, 38
Computer program 2, 42, 58, 93, 138, 148
Constitution 102
- Germany 25
- United States 1, 16, 36, 41
Contract
- regulation of 33, 44, 51-52, 54
- standard 53, 58
- waiver 81, 106, 110

About the author

Jacqueline Marie Bertine Seignette was born on 14 May 1964 in Lichtenvoorde, the Netherlands. She graduated from the University of Utrecht Faculty of Law in 1987 and was subsequently appointed assistant researcher at the Institute for Information Law of the University of Amsterdam, in which capacity she wrote this book. As visiting scholar, Ms Seignette gathered most of the material for her comparative study at the Columbia University School of Law, New York and the Max Planck Institute for Foreign and International Patent, Copyright and Competition Law in Munich. At present, Ms Seignette is an attorney at the Amsterdam law firm of Goudsmit & Branbergen. Ms Seignette has published several articles on copyright and neighbouring rights law.

This study was defended as a doctoral thesis at the University of Amsterdam on 23 September 1994.